THE MORAL NATURE
OF MAN

A Critical Evaluation of Ethical
Principles

By

A. CAMPBELL GARNETT

PROFESSOR OF PHILOSOPHY
THE UNIVERSITY OF WISCONSIN

THE RONALD PRESS COMPANY · NEW YORK

Library of Congress Catalog Card Number: 52-9467

PRINTED IN THE UNITED STATES OF AMERICA

To Jeanne and Gordon Garnett

PREFACE

For the past fifteen years it has been my privilege to teach courses in ethics at the University of Wisconsin, including both graduate seminars and elementary and intermediate courses for undergraduates. This experience, in a period when both our social institutions and the assumptions of philosophical theory have been shaken to the foundations, has forced upon me a constant re-examination of my own views and a critical evaluation of new work in the field.

In this volume I attempt to give, in terms which I believe will be readily intelligible to the average thinking person, a brief but systematic exposition of the major problems of ethics as I have now come to understand them, together with what seems necessary in the way of critical comparison with other points of view. This has been done, I believe, in such fashion that the book may be read by students in elementary courses, for at no point is any previous philosophical training assumed. My major purpose in writing, however, has been the hope that this book's criticisms of contemporary theories, and its solutions of ethical problems, will stimulate advanced students to fresh thinking and will meet with the approval of other philosophers who are working in this important and difficult field.

Yet another purpose of the book is indicated by its title. I have found the analysis of ethical problems inseparable from questions concerning the theory of human nature. I started out to write a book chiefly concerned with setting straight certain semantic confusions in ethical thought, and

I have ended with a work on the moral nature of man. In this development the book has become concerned with the problem that lies at the root of both the deep religious controversy and the violent political conflict of our day. For the convictions of religious thinkers as to the function of the church, and those of political thinkers as to the function of the state, rest basically upon their theories of the nature of man. It is the contention of this book that the moral consciousness of man plays a deeper and more decisive part in his life than that with which it is credited in the currently popular views of either naturalistic philosophers or political and religious thinkers. For this reason the book has something of importance to say to workers in the fields of religion and the social sciences as well as to students of philosophy.

In conclusion, I wish to thank the University of Wisconsin for a semester's leave of absence for research during which the first draft of this book was written, and the editors of *The Review of Metaphysics* and *Philosophy and Phenomenological Research* for permission to reprint portions of articles which have appeared in their columns.

A. Campbell Garnett

The University of Wisconsin
July, 1952

CONTENTS

THE MORAL NATURE OF MAN

INTRODUCTION

Opposing Philosophies of Human Nature

The revival of barbarism in two world wars has made us bitterly conscious of man's inhumanity to man. With the memory of its variously motivated horrors, from Hiroshima to Buchenwald, fresh in our minds, it may seem a cynical complacency to speak of the moral nature of man. Some have seen in this dark history evidence that his alleged moral nature is an illusion. Man, they say, is only an intelligent beast. His motivations are little more than hunger, lust, and fear. His civilization is merely a cunning way of satisfying his animal wants and pleasantly stimulating his mind. And when it fails him he goes back to the ways of the beast and the barbarian, rendered only more terrible by the knowledge and skill he has acquired. Others, holding a conviction that the Author of man and nature is supremely powerful and good, see in man's sinfulness a depravity worse than the blind passion of the beast. To them it is a lapse from perfection that has in it something demonic. It betrays a canker in man's soul that must ultimately defeat his every effort at genuine improvement of the social order. Sensitively sharing in the sense of collective guilt involved in the sins of all, they abase themselves and mankind before the Creator, feeling, paradoxically (for their minds rejoice in paradox), that they honor God by emphasizing the baseness of the creature He has made in His image. Heroically but hopelessly they turn from their

3

devotions to the duties of the daily task, to overcome evil and better the lot of their fellows, saddened and hampered, if not dispirited, by the conviction that, since Paradise was lost, man is condemned to the labors of Sisyphus, to roll the stone of progress up the hill, knowing that it will surely roll down again—or roll down another valley, requiring to be rolled up an equally difficult hill.

It is the thesis of this book that both these philosophies of human nature are untrue. In turning from such pessimism, however, we need not rush to the extreme of a foolish optimism, asserting that the course of evolution must involve an inevitable and continuous ascent of man, or that, since God is in His heaven, all must really be right with the world, whatever the appearances to the contrary. There is evil in the world, stark and real, including both those terrible, unforseeable, and unavoidable catastrophies of nature which a blasphemous theology has taught us to describe legally as "acts of God," and also the criminal deeds of responsible human beings. But there is also good in the world, a beneficence of nature and good will among men. It is the contention of this book that the moral nature of man, if adequately understood, gives grounds not for incautious optimism or for pessimistic despair, but for rational faith and hope.

To the Greeks the most remarkable thing about man was his intelligence. He alone is a rational animal. To one who views man in the light of modern science, the most remarkable thing about him is not his reason but his morality. For it is comparatively easy to understand how his intelligence has been developed as an instrument in the struggle for existence. But it is not so easy to see how the struggle for existence has developed a creature who believes it his duty sometimes to sacrifice his own welfare, or even his own existence, for that of others. To traditional theism, however, which views man as a direct product of the creative act of God, neither his rationality nor his morality appears remarkable, but rather his fall from pristine perfection, his sinfulness.

In these days in which the machine has so greatly magnified all man's activities, that sinfulness has attained such colossal proportions in its collective manifestations that it has rightly received new emphasis in every philosophy of human nature and theory of the social order. But there is no good reason why a theism which has accepted the evolutionary interpretation of nature should be more impressed with man's sin and decadence than with his virtue and progress. Both are facts of life and history, and it is only the latter that makes the former possible. Without virtue there could be no knowledge of sin, and without progress there could be no decadence. And it is the primary fact that is the most significant. That an intelligent individual should take the easiest and surest way to realization of his desires, even if he thereby ignores or violates the desires of others, is not illogical, and should not be surprising. What is remarkable is that he tends to be ashamed of it and to pronounce it in a peculiar way to be wrong. Man is a creature in whom reason functions, as David Hume pointed out, in the service of desire, and has no motive power of its own. But he has developed an inner conviction that he has a duty sometimes to sacrifice the pursuit of his own desires to the welfare of others. And, still more remarkable, he sometimes does it.

The typical naturalistic explanations of this are, as we shall see, superficial and unsatisfactory. Just as the old-fashioned, absolutistic theology has, to the minds of most contemporary American philosophers, been wrecked on the rock of the facts of physical evil in nature, so it may well turn out that the atheistic or agnostic naturalism, now widespread among them, becomes wrecked on the facts of the moral consciousness of man. Our concern here, however, is not with religious skepticism, but with an ethical skepticism which, though usually honest and well intentioned, is even more corrosive. Our problem is to disclose the roots of the moral life in human nature so that we may have some confidence in that ethical structure of human rights and duties with which we gird up our social order. If this can be done, we shall have achieved much; and the solution of this problem is of very real significance for other problems concerning social philosophy and the philosophy of religion. Its relevance to religion will be discussed in our concluding chapter, but the reason why it is of such fundamental importance for social theory may be briefly pointed out here.

THEORIES OF MAN AND THE INSTITUTIONS OF FREEDOM

Institutions which give a large measure of freedom to the individual, and institutions in which a large number of persons cooperate for the common good, are possible only in communities in which there prevails a considerable measure of confidence that, in general, people will not seriously abuse their freedom and will cooperate in the common task with a reasonable measure of good sense and good will. Cooperation is possible only in an atmosphere of mutual confidence. Freedom is conceded willingly only when there is confidence that it will not be abused. Where there is no such confidence, those who are capable of seizing power and holding it will do so, setting up institutions under their own authoritarian control.

Free institutions, therefore, tend to grow best in small, homogeneous communities wherein individuals can, to a considerable extent, know and understand one another.

Distance, diversity, and numbers promote misunderstanding and mistrust. Where free institutions have expanded over large areas and large populations, as in the United States and Great Britain, they have been in part an inheritance from institutions developed in small, homogeneous communities, and in part maintained by a traditional philosophy inculcating ideals of brotherhood and holding a relatively high view of human nature. Where these conditions do not hold, or hold in considerably less degree, democracy, if introduced or developed at all, has proved relatively unstable.

This reveals an important relationship between the prevailing philosophy of human nature and the expansion of institutions that enlarge freedom. Freedom flourishes in an atmosphere of faith in the general good will of human beings. Authoritarianism flourishes where that faith is denied or betrayed. It is possible, however, for faith in man to be too high and to encourage a removal of restrictions needed for the maintenance of social order. If this happens, then the disorders that result create a reaction to an attitude of hardness and distrust, and order is restored, if at all, by a reimposition of authoritarian controls. More often, however, faith in human nature is unnecessarily low. Man's fear and distrust of his fellows, especially of those beyond his immediate circle, hold back the development of institutions of social cooperation and impose unnecessary restrictions on freedom. It is only on comparatively rare occasions that the reverse happens—that an overoptimistic faith in human nature encourages an expansion of freedom and is betrayed by its abuse.

There is a prevailing view of human nature which might be called common-sense realism. It has dominated man's thought of his fellows in most communities through most of the centuries. In this view, man looks upon his fellows as creatures predominantly moved by appetite, fear, and pride, their reason being merely an instrument of long-range self-interest, their selfishness modified only by certain narrow loyalties to community, class, and clan, their moral conscience consisting merely of a fear of divine sanctions guarding the customary moral law. The institutions suggested by such a view are almost entirely those designed to protect individuals from one another, restricting, by threats of force, the freedom to injure another, and appealing to unselfish motives only within the narrow range of local community and kinship groups. Relations to other groups are, for the most part, dominated by distrust and fear. This is the outlook everywhere among the tribes of primitive man and it is rarely more than slightly modified even in the best thought of civilized peoples.

The most important modification of this view arises in the great ethical religions, struggling with varying success to modify the harshness of the institutions of the society concerned. It is the doctrine of immanence which declares that a divine influence is somehow operative in the moral conscience of man, guiding his insight into what is truly right and instilling into him a desire and a sense of obligation to be true to the moral law. This doctrine is found in the Confucian classics and the Indian Upanishads dating from the fifth century B.C. or somewhat earlier. Its first known expression goes back, however, to the "Memphite Drama" which Breasted dates as coming from the sun worshipers of Heliopolis about 5000 B.C.[1] To this philosophy the great Egyptologist attributes all that was best in the ancient civilization on the Nile, and the eventual decadence of that culture he blames upon the blighting of its moral philosophy by the growth of magic within the religion that took it

[1] J. H. Breasted, *The Dawn of Conscience* (New York: Charles Scribner's Sons, 1933).

over. Something of this same doctrine of immanence re-
appears in the wisdom literature of the Hebrews, such as
the Psalms and Proverbs. It also appears in the Platonic
and Stoic philosophies, and from both these sources it came
to be incorporated into Christianity. Its principal expression in the New Testament is in the prolegomena to the
Gospel of John. "In the beginning was the Word, and the
Word was with God, and the Word was God . . . in him
was life, and the life was the light of men . . . the true
Light, which lighteth every man . . ."

The social significance of this type of philosophy arises
from the fact that it gives to thinkers in ethics both a confidence in the validity of their own critical, rational thought
in ethical matters, as against mere tradition and authority,
and also a conviction that other persons cannot be entirely
uninfluenced by similar insights and feelings. It thus tends
to create both personal commitment to ethical ideals and a
faith that, with the progress of enlightenment, those ideals
can be given concrete form in better social institutions that
men in general will recognize and respect. The faith thus
generated, however, is subjected to rude shocks by the persistence of moral evil in society and the ethical obtuseness
of the majority. Sometimes it has issued in institutions
which have placed too great confidence in mere enlightenment. Sometimes the failure of such institutions has
brought on a reaction to still severer forms of authoritarianism.

In China the doctrine of immanence, with its high view
of human nature, was plainly enunciated by the Emperor
T'ang in 1766 B.C. "The great God has conferred even on
the inferior people a moral sense, compliance with which
would show their nature invariably right." [2] After the establishment of Confucianism, every schoolboy learned to recite

[2] *Shu Ching*, Part IV, Book III, ii.

from the opening page of the *Three-Character Classic:*
"Men at their birth are naturally good. Their natures are
much the same; their habits become widely different."
This meant that human beings can be trusted to develop
right habits of action so long as they are properly taught.
So China put her faith in learning and discipline, and allowed herself to be ruled for nearly two millenniums by a
selectively self-perpetuating company of Confucian scholars.
The result was the most impressive example of social stability in all human history. But the Achilles' heel of the
system lay in the fact that when scholarship became a
means to power, the community of scholars acquired a narrow vested interest in their own type of scholarship and
their own close community of scholars. Thus the Confucian system became a barrier to progress and proved unable
to adapt itself to the impact of ideas from the West.

In India the significance of the doctrine of immanence
became lost in the Pantheism which sees all things as
equally divine—good and evil alike.

In Christianity it has had a checkered history. In early
Christian society it survived the periods of persecution and
the disappointment of hopes for a speedy return of Christ.
Many of the Greek theologians held high hopes for the
transformation of society by the moral influence of Christianity, especially after the triumph of the religion in its
adoption by Constantine. The inherent decadence of Roman society and the hammering of the barbarians, however,
rendered abortive all attempts at reform, and in the despair
induced by the collapse of the ancient civilization the doctrine of man, as held by the Christian church, underwent a
drastic change. St. Augustine presented an interpretation
of the Pauline doctrines of predestination and original sin
which discouraged all hope for human society through human institutions, and placed man's only hope in divine

intervention mediated by the church. This low view of man led to a centralization of authority in the church and a growth of its power which eventually corrupted it—as undue power corrupts every human institution. The Protestant Reformation revolted against the power of the church, but in its earlier phases it only re-emphasized the gloomy Augustinian view of man. The early effect of Protestantism on secular institutions was therefore a tendency to tighten, rather than loosen, authoritarian control.

Modern Times: The Rise and Fall of Faith in Man

It was secular philosophy in the eighteenth century that reintroduced faith in man. This new faith was a response to the impressive achievements of human reason in science and discovery. It turned the ancient doctrine of a God-given moral reason into one of self-evident rights of man. It proclaimed the sufficiency of enlightened self-interest as a guide to moral conduct. It attributed human troubles almost entirely to ignorance and superstition, and looked forward to perpetual progress through the extension of human knowledge. The same factors that influenced the development of the optimistic secular philosophy also affected religious thought. Augustinianism was softened or rejected. The immanence of God in the moral reason of man was re-emphasized. A revised theology cooperated with secular philosophy in urging universal education and extension of freedom in political and economic institutions. Democracy and free enterprise flourished. The democratic states and the captains of commerce and industry increased in power. But once again history provided the lesson that, while freedom opens the road to progress and is not incompatible with order, the growth of power corrupts even those who rejoice in their freedom. The democracies developed rival imperialisms, and unrestricted free enterprise brought on the evils of the Industrial Revolution.

In those countries which have had little or no experience of democratic freedoms, these evils have led to a reaction to a low view of man and a surrender of the attempt to develop democratic freedoms. The reaction has taken the alternative forms of fascism and communism. Both are secular philosophies, and in them the low view of man is therefore unaffected by those conceptions of justice and charity which have softened the rigors of authoritarianisms induced by a low view of man in a religious philosophy. In the fascist view, man is a creature of unmitigated selfishness and fear-driven lust for power. Enlightenment makes him not more kindly, but merely more cunning. Power must therefore be placed in the hands of those who are able and willing to use it to build up the strength of the state for the inevitable crisis of war. In the communist view, man is a creature driven by economic motives, seeking to possess the material means of satisfying his desires. But his case is not hopeless. Though he is at present, with rare exceptions, conditioned to seek his goals by ruthless competition, he may be reconditioned to seek them by cooperation. By an appropriate process of education, under new institutions, the profit motive may be replaced by that of production for use. But, in the transition period of reconditioning, power must be held and ruthlessly directed by those few with the understanding and skill to maintain the necessary new institutions and direct the educational process.

Both fascism and communism, therefore, have placed power in the hands of the few. And never has the corrupting influence of power been more fearfully proved. In the case of communism, this outcome has a peculiar significance, for it undermines the theory of human nature on which communism is built. The economic interpretation of human motivation is seen to ignore the fact that power, whether political or economic, is sought not merely as a means to other satisfactions but as an end desired for its own sake. And the appetite grows as it is fed. Thus those who are given power to recondition society tend to condition it in ways that add to their own power. And they are not likely to surrender it voluntarily.

In those countries which have had experience of democracy, the reaction to the evils of imperialism and the Industrial Revolution has taken a different form. There has been some loss of the faith in man characteristic of eighteenth- and nineteenth-century liberalism. There has grown a skepticism about man's capacity for rational moral insight which has rejected the doctrine of self-evident rights and cast doubt on the doctrine of immanence. There has also been a growing conviction of the insufficiency of enlightened self-interest. As yet, however, these doubts and fears and loss of faith have resulted only in the determination to curb the power of those to whom our economic and political institutions have given too much. In particular, the method of checks and balances with which we have long been familiar in political affairs is being increasingly introduced to remedy inequities and anomalies in the economic sphere. In these adjustments we are responding experimentally to what seem to be the effects of established institutions in changing conditions. It is wise that our responses should be empirical, tentative, and experimental. But we cannot help but be influenced by our general theory of human nature. Too low a view may lead to a despair of the democratic process and the joining of some group that seeks power to impose its own program on the majority, or it may lead us to impose unnecessary and hampering restrictions on political or economic life. Too high a view may lead to the release of wholesome checks and balances which may set loose destructive social forces. No specific problem of social adjustment can be safely resolved by consideration of a general theory alone. Every decision must take account of a wide range of special circumstances. But our evaluation of the significance of the circumstances is inevitably affected by our fundamental theory of human nature. And that is the reason for a critical inquiry into the basic problems concerning the moral nature of man.

To understand man's moral nature is essentially a psychological problem. But it requires exploration of a great mass of data which is outside the ordinary sphere of the psychologist, as such, in an area which his investigations of conscience ordinarily neglect, namely, the history of moral ideas. And this study must pay attention not only, and not chiefly, to the history of ethical theory, but to the development of the moral tradition in the great religions, and to its roots in the moral conceptions of primitive man. The great obstacle to this investigation is the semantic confusion in which moral ideas are involved, both in popular thought and in philosophical criticism; for none of the languages of mankind has developed a set of terms adequate to distinguish the nuances of meaning involved in moral judgment. An important part of our discussion, therefore, has to be devoted to unraveling this verbal entanglement and developing a clear set of moral concepts.

The plan of this book is therefore first to trace the growth of man's moral convictions, both to discover the factors involved in that development and to note the distinctive conclusions at which they have arrived. Next we must give attention to the development of doubts in order to understand the grounds and extent of ethical skepticism, and the failure of naturalistic ethics, hitherto, to remove it. In Chapter 4 we shall see that we can secure a partial resolution of these doubts through the elimination of semantic confusion. We shall then seek, in an examination and interpretation of human nature, to disclose the factual referents of our fundamental ethical concepts and the basis for those moral convictions which commend themselves most clearly to the conscience of mankind. This will occupy us in Chapters 5, 6, and 7. In the last chapter we undertake an analysis of the relation of the moral life to the religious, and explore some of the implications for the philosophy of religion, and for theology, of the theory of human nature thus developed.

Chapter 1

THE HISTORY OF CONSCIENCE

THE CONSCIENCE OF THE PRIMITIVE

The records of early civilizations show many survivals from the primitive era which preceded them, and these disclose striking parallels in custom, life, and thought with the primitive peoples of today. The likenesses are so close and typical that there can be no doubt that the cultures of contemporary primitive tribes preserve ways of thought, feeling, and social organization which were once characteristic of all mankind. They are fossilized remains in which civilized man can study the thought forms once characteristic of his own ancestors. Our study of the development of conscience can therefore begin with a prehistory of civilized morality, based on examination of surviving primitive cultures of today.

Before the era of modern anthropology, it used to be assumed that primitive peoples must be practically devoid of moral laws—that every man would follow his desires without regard for the rights of his neighbors, limited only by his physical powers and fear of retaliation. Thus Thomas Hobbes could envisage the life of "savages" as a war of all against all, and few doubted that an age of promiscuity and lawlessness must have preceded the organization of the family and the state. Actual study of primitive tribes, however, soon led to a reversal of this view. They were found to have elaborate and rigid customs supported by belief in powerful and fearsome tabus. Their moral rules, such as they were,

were strictly kept. So the climate of anthropological opinion changed. The primitive was regarded as a creature of customs, never thinking to criticize and rarely daring to disobey the traditional rules by which his life was bound. But still he was not credited with a conscience. It was thought that he kept the rules from the sheer inertia of custom, or superstitious fear, and that was all.

In the last fifty years, however, these assumptions have given way before a mass of evidence accumulated in intimate studies of primitive peoples. These have disclosed wide differences in *views* as to *what* is right and wrong, especially in matters concerning sex. But in his *attitude* to what is *thought* right and wrong, man appears to be everywhere much the same. He feels guilt and shame and he expresses moral approval. He has a sense of honor and a conscience; and he hides his guilt and acts the hypocrite. Different tribes have different conceptions of the rights and duties of individuals, but none is without conceptions of right and duty.

One of the best studies bringing out the genuinely moral feeling of primitive man is that of B. Malinowski in the Trobriand Islands.[1] The operation of a sense of honor and fair dealing is especially manifest in his description of economic exchange between the fishing villages of the coast and the farming villages inland. They have no money and not even a system of barter, but every man in the coastal villages has a partner in an inland village to whom he makes a "gift" of fish when his canoe comes in with its catch, and from whom he expects a return gift of vegetables within a short time. There is no bartering of so much fish for so many vegetables, but the gifts bear proportion to the catch and the crops and to each other. They are made publicly

---

[1] See especially *Crime and Custom in Savage Society* (New York: Charles Scribner's Sons, 1933).

and with elaborate ceremonial so that all the neighbors know the size of the gifts made; and the sanction of public opinion as well as tit for tat operates to secure equity and even generosity. Often there are complaints of neglect or stinginess, and there are open arguments between the partners, in which appeal is made to the bystanders for judgment on fair dealing, but there are no laws other than a tradition of equitable exchange and no sanctions other than the reciprocal reaction of the partner and the esteem of their fellows. There is self-interest in the maintenance of the partnership, but the system does not rest on that alone. It could not work successfully were it not that generosity and fair dealing are publicly admired, and stinginess, neglect, and unfairness publicly condemned by each man's neighbors in his own village. And it is to secure the operation of this sanction that tradition requires the element of public ceremonial in the making of the gifts.

The operation of the same sanction of moral praise and blame is to be seen in other economic arrangements of these islanders, such as the organization of the crew of a canoe and the duties of the maternal uncle as guardian of his sister's children. Fishing is done in large canoes, of which one man is the owner and others the crew. Each crew member has a right to his place and to a share of the catch, and he has an obligation to go along or provide a substitute when the canoe goes out. The owner is also under obligation to take out his canoe or lend it to the crew at the appropriate times for fishing. Disputes are settled by open argument and appeal to public opinion. The system involves recognition of a rigid system of mutual obligations and duty, and sensitivity to moral approval and disapproval of the community.

This is also shown in the publicity and ceremonial involved in the performance of his duties by the maternal uncle. These people live under a matriarchal system in which a woman's brother, rather than her husband, is the legal guardian of her children; but matriarchy has been so far modified that she goes to live with her husband, often in another village. Her brother, however, is still under certain obligations to provide food for her and her children. This he does with great ceremony in order to show that he is performing his duty well. When yams are dug, the pick of the crop is put in one heap, the rest in another. The better and larger heap is for the sister. It is displayed to the neighbors and duly admired by them. It is set aside by ritual and transported with ceremony and a fanfare of trumpets to the sister's village, where it is handed over to her with similar ritual and publicity. Thus, once again, the social order is upheld by regard for praise and blame and the existence of a public opinion which holds in high esteem the proper performance of family and other social obligations.

Everywhere among primitive peoples the social rules, however they may differ, are upheld by public opinion. Honor and shame are motives often more powerful than hunger and the fear of death. Often they drive an individual exposed as a violator of the code to suicide. Always the rules create one or more social groupings within which there is mutual help and social solidarity. Often they operate to maintain conditions of hostility between groups, and they make virtues of brutality, deceit, and treachery directed toward the enemy. This is bad enough when the hostile groups are neighboring tribes. It is worse when such rules of honor maintain feuds between families in the same tribe, but it is worst of all when it creates hostility within the family, as it does in the Dobu Islands.[2] These islands are close

---

[2] Cf. R. F. Fortune, *The Sorcerers of Dobu* (London: George Routledge & Sons, Ltd., 1932); and Ruth Benedict, *Patterns of Culture* (Boston: Houghton Mifflin Co., 1932), chap. v.

neighbors of the Trobriands and are also peopled by Melanesians. But they have little fertile land and poor fishing. Population presses on the means of subsistence, and the hard struggle for existence has created a bitter internal strife. This has been enhanced by an excessive use of black magic which is probably a result of the same difficult economic conditions, and these conditions have been exacerbated by the existence of an awkward variant of the matriarchal system which maintains great social solidity of those connected by kinship through the female line while stipulating that husband and wife shall live together in alternate years in each other's family villages.

The result of this arrangement has been to make the rival groups, within which there is a code of social solidarity and mutual aid, cut across the family and divide every village. Custom requires fulfilment of a rigid set of obligations to maternal relatives, but the difficulties of life have created a keen struggle for existence with members of a person's own family and village outside this circle. Husband and wife, brothers and sisters, and neighbors in the same village are divided by the strife, and everyone believes his rivals are constantly using black magic against him. The fear and hostility thus generated have made lying, treachery, theft, adultery, incest, and even murder into honorable achievements in relations with rival groups, though within the maternal clan a very different code is maintained. It is no wonder that these people are described as dour, treacherous, and suspicious by white visitors and neighboring natives. But it cannot be said that they are devoid of concepts of obligation and honor. Their moral code is limited and, from the standpoint of broad social utility, it is perverse, but they have a code, and a conscience, and a sensitivity to social praise and blame in connection with the keeping of recognized obligations, and these moral convictions are apparently no less binding upon them than are those of their neighbors in the Trobriands. Their code, such as it is, is probably better kept than the very different code of the white people who read books about them.

In general, the moral codes of primitive peoples direct their activities into socially useful channels. Where this is not the case it will usually be found either that the custom is a survival from some stage of development when it was socially useful, or that, because of scientific ignorance, confusion, or superstition, it is incorrectly believed to be socially useful. The blood feud, for example, is an institution that originates as man's earliest attempt to set up a deterrent to crimes of violence before any system of public justice has been developed. It simply demands that a man's kinsmen shall support his right to security of life and limb, and thus faces the prospective murderer with the knowledge that murder will put his own life in continued jeopardy. It becomes a feud because of a failure to recognize the distinction between justified retribution and unjustified homicide; and it survives into the era when public justice has been developed to replace it because the maintenance of it has become a matter of honor. Orgiastic sex practices in fertility cults are due to the belief that imitative magical ceremonies are necessary for the fertilization of crops and domestic animals. Head-hunting is also usually associated with magical belief in the value or necessity of ritual utilizing blood and other symbols of life to secure the growth of food supplies or the multiplication of the tribe. Thus for all his "wicked" ways the heathen usually has what to him are good reasons, and what, even to us, must be recognized as commendable motives.

Further, his usually strict obedience to tribal law is not motivated merely by fear of punishment. Probably the motives of pure regard for human welfare and respect for moral values are no commoner with him than with us, or they may be less common; but his concern to avoid the condemnation of public opinion is not merely due to fear of physical retribution. Much more than that, it involves the sense of honor and shame as affected by public judgments of moral worth. The primitive lives in very close relationships with his fellow tribesmen and kinsmen, and what they think of him affects him deeply. And it is clear that he not only prizes their opinion of his physical appearance, cleverness, and skill, but also, and more deeply, their opinion of his moral worth, his courage, loyalty, fair dealing, generosity, and uprightness, as these are defined in the moral conceptions of the community.

Confusions in Primitive Ethical Thinking

The *spirit* of primitive morality is therefore not essentially different from that of civilized man, but great and important differences appear when we turn to examine the particular practical details of their codes. There are, of course, differences in the codes of primitive peoples, but these are relatively minor compared to certain differences in the codes of primitives as over against those of civilized peoples. In particular, there are four typical defects in the ethical ideas of primitive man which are gradually overcome as, with advancing civilization, more and more attention and thought are given to moral problems. And it is not merely by our own arbitrary standards that we call these defects, for they rest upon errors that are logical rather than axiological.

Three of these defects are due to failure to make distinctions in thought where there are real and relevant differences in the psychological and social facts referred to. They are examples of mental confusion which only gradually become clearly recognized in ethical thinking. The fourth is due to the making of an arbitrary distinction which is not really relevant to moral questions. But its irrelevance is only very gradually discerned and reluctantly admitted, and can be demonstrated only by a very thorough analysis of the nature of moral obligation. At this point moral progress has been achieved because the insight of the seers has been more penetrating than the argument of the philosophers; it will be a large part of the task of this book to show by careful analysis that in this case the seers have been right and those philosophers who have opposed them wrong. The way in which agreement on these points has grown as a result of more careful thinking is an indication of the reality of something basic and common in the moral nature of man—which is the main thesis of this book. And although agreement on the fourth is not yet complete, this thesis will be further confirmed if more thorough elucidation can reduce the extent of difference upon it.

The first and most obvious of these four typical material fallacies in the ethical thinking of primitive man is the failure to distinguish between intentional and unintentional injury. Commonly, among primitive peoples, blood calls for blood whether spilt accidentally or by design. If a man kills another by pure mischance, then it becomes the duty of the next of kin to avenge the manslaughter as though it were first degree murder. Primitive thought usually makes no such distinctions as those of our modern law. Or again, if a child be the accidental victim, then the father is apt to claim in return the life of a child of the man responsible for the mishap. In the early codes of civilization it is interesting to see a still halfhearted recognition of the distinction that to us now seems so obvious. Thus, in Deuteronomy, cities of refuge are assigned to which the unintentional homicide may flee for safety. And for "the slayer . . . which should kill his neighbour unawares, and hated him not in times past," [3] this sanctuary must be respected. But it is also implied that if the avenger of blood should pursue him "while his heart is hot, and overtake him, because the way is long," then mortal vengeance is still legitimate.[4] In other cases, as in early Germanic law, it is provided that payment of the wergild, or price of blood, should be arranged in cases of unintentional homicide and the blood feud should not be waged. In the traditional codes of China there is punishment for involuntary offenses, but on a reduced scale. And in Japan, accidental injury to one's parents carries heavy penalties in a code as late as that of 1871.[5]

The reason for this apparent obtuseness thus manifested is not difficult to see. Anger is aroused by the serious consequences of the act, and angry people do not think clearly or look for mitigating circumstances. Suffering and loss have been inflicted, and the injured parties cry out for satisfaction. The sympathy of the group is naturally with them rather than with the person who has caused the accident. So the demand for retribution is justified and allowed to take its course. Only after considerable reflection on the grounds for resentment and the social purpose of punishment does it become clear that both are irrelevant to accidental injuries, except so far as carelessness is involved. And even when this has been recognized, the distinction tends to be ignored when actual situations arise and passions are stirred; but the fact that calm thinking on the distinction has led to an almost unquestioned acceptance of the view that intentional and unintentional injury should not both be punished alike indicates that such thinking leads to the

[3] Deut. 4:42.
[4] Deut. 19:6.
[5] L. T. Hobhouse, *Morals in Evolution* (5th ed.; New York: Henry Holt & Co., 1923), p. 86.

discovery of factors of the moral life that are common to the nature of man.

The second of these typical defects in primitive ethical thinking is the assumption of collective responsibility, the holding of all the members of a tribe, clan, family, or other group responsible for a crime committed by any one of them. Thus a party of Australian aborigines, having decided by magical divination that a certain man in a neighboring camp is responsible for the death of one of their number, set out on a punitive expedition. After scouting the suspect's camp and finding him not in residence, they lie in wait for and kill his father. And justice has been duly done! In the blood feud it is usual to regard the principle of retribution as satisfied by the slaying of any kinsman or fellow tribesman of the offender when he is of a different tribe or kindred. And in cases where a man has killed another man's wife or child or slave, the law of retaliation commonly requires that the debt shall be paid, not by the death of the guilty man himself, but by that of one of his wives, children, or slaves, as the case may be.

In cases where exemplary punishment seems to be required, this principle of collective responsibility, even among comparatively civilized people, is often regarded as justifying the taking of several lives for one. Thus, for the breaking of a tabu which was believed to have brought defeat in battle upon his people, not only was the guilty Achan stoned to death, but his whole family as well.[6] And every distress that fell upon Israel, whether plague, or drought, or defeat, taking the lives of just and unjust, was interpreted as a punishment for someone's sin by a God who visited the sins of the fathers upon the children to the third and the fourth generation. It was not until the days of Jeremiah and Ezekiel that prophetic insight declared

[6] Josh. 7:24.

that Israel must repudiate the proverb "The fathers have eaten a sour grape, and the children's teeth are set on edge." [7] And collective responsibility was expressly repudiated in the Deuteronomic code which belongs to this same period.[8]

That the passion for vengeance should be thus undiscriminating is as natural as it is illogical. No people is yet so highly civilized and logically moral as not to be affected by impulses toward collective vengeance in time of war, or to be free from the stupid tendency to condemn and discriminate against a whole alien group because of the real or fancied objectionable behavior of some of its members. Living as we do in the glass house of race prejudice, we are not in a position to throw stones at peoples of a less enlightened age for the practice of collective retribution. Nevertheless we can clearly see that these are cases where emotion obscures judgment. We may still be considerably confused as to the morally legitimate grounds of punishment, but at least it is clear that they are not such as to justify its extension to innocent kindred. In civilized countries this is generally recognized as a clear piece of moral *knowledge*, acquired with assurance by civilized humanity even though still all too frequently forgotten. It is a phase of the moral life where civilized man has made some real *progress* beyond the primitive. And if knowledge and progress are recognized in this matter, and in that of the distinction between intentional and unintentional, it is not absurd to hope that they may be found in other matters too.

[7] Jer. 31:29; Ezek. 18:2.
[8] Deut. 24:16.

A Third Confusion: Custom and the Higher Law

The third of these typical defects of primitive ethics is the failure to distinguish between the law as it is and the law as it ought to be. Custom functions as a moral law, defining duties to which are attached the senses of honor and shame and judgments of praise and blame. It also functions as the explicit law of the community, to which each person is required to conform. There are magical influences, which work automatically in support of custom. The gods uphold it as required of men, even though, like men, they may occasionally violate it in practice. It is generally assumed that there is always good reason for the requirements of custom, and magical reasons are invented to justify customs for which no practical reason is discernible— customs which have drifted from their original basis in practical need or magical theory, or have outlived their usefulness, their origin being forgotten. Customs change gradually, almost unconsciously, and thus adapt themselves imperceptibly to changing conditions, but this process is often inept and much too slow. Yet, however wasteful, painful, injurious, or unfair a custom may be, it is hardly possible for the primitive to criticize it as morally wrong.

One reason for this is that his language does not provide him with terms in which to make the distinction clear. Ethical terms in most languages go back to roots referring to custom, as do our words "moral" and "ethical," from the Latin *mores* and the Greek *ethos*. Similarly, when the Roman spoke of "justice" he used *justus*, from *jubeo*, meaning "order" or "command." The Greek used *dikaiosúne*, from *diké*, meaning "right," the original sense of which was "custom" or "usage." In Hebrew a right or law is a *mishpat*,

from the same root as *mishpaha*, the family or clan; and
the most fundamental of all laws is that of kinship.[9] In the
oldest ethical writing known to us, the *Memphite Drama* [10]
of ancient Egypt, which dates from several centuries before
the Pyramid Age, the writer is reduced to the use of a cir-
cumlocution to distinguish right from wrong. He speaks of
"he who does what is loved" and "he who does what is
hated." It was not until the Pyramid Age that the Egyp-
tians developed an abstract term for "right," in the ethical
sense. They then used the word *maat* which, like the Latin
rectus, was drawn from mathematics. It seems to be clear
that it was only gradually that terms which originally made
explicit reference to conformity to custom came to take on
the deeper and distinctive meaning whereby they could be
used to say that a custom was unjust or wrong; and only
gradually some other words, like the Latin *rectus*, the Egyptian *maat*, and the Hebrew *shalem* (whole) and *yashar*
(straight, righteous) came to have an application to social
behavior which enabled such statements to be made.

The same deficiency thus revealed in the early forms of
these classical languages is also widely manifest in primitive
languages. It is evident that in the early stages of human
society adherence to traditional rules of behavior was so
strongly approved, and departures from them so disap-
proved, and the traditional rules covered so completely all
possible types of behavior, that to describe an action as
customary was equivalent to approval, and an assertion that
it was contrary to custom was sufficient condemnation.

However, the fact that a language does not provide
words with which to distinguish between mere conformity

[9] Johannes Pedersen, *Israel, Its Life and Culture* (New York: Oxford
University Press, Inc., 1926), Vol. I, p. 353.

[10] Cf. J. H. Breasted, *The Dawn of Conscience* (New York: Charles
Scribner's Sons, 1933), chap. iii.

to custom and moral rectitude does not mean that the people who speak that language do not make the distinction in idea, for distinction in idea must come before words are adopted to express it. The lack of verbal distinction in this case means only that they habitually and uncritically accept custom as defining for them their moral obligations so that the need for verbal distinction has not been strongly felt. That need is felt when changes in social conditions make the old customs productive of bad social effects. Then there may arise a critic of the social system who points to these evils and claims that though they appear to bear the stamp of custom or law they are not in accord with the *true* law. His hearers may or may not agree with the critic, but they understand his meaning. And this reveals the deeper signifi- cance that tribal custom or law has always had for them. It was accepted because it was believed to be good. Its basis was never mere habit or authority or social pressure. It was believed to have a valid reason in the welfare of the tribal group. Thus when the critic arises and points to facts show- ing that the custom of the day, believed to be ancient and sacred, has consequences that are not *good*, he can shake the faith of his hearers in it as his own faith has been shaken by recognition of the facts. It is the custom or law of the day but it cannot be the true custom or law of the tribe or nation. For that custom or law is good. This evil law must be a departure from the true law or a misuse or misapplica- tion of it.

The earliest example known to us of this rise of the social critic comes from the feudal period of ancient Egypt.[11] It is typical of many others. In every case there is an appeal to a true law of greater authority than the law in operation among his people at the time. This true, or higher, law is

[11] Cf. Breasted, *op. cit.*

not only claimed to be more ancient, but it is appealed to as having divine support.

The basis of this identification of the true law (the true *maat* or true justice) with the divine will had been expressly laid in Egypt in the philosophy associated with the worship of the sun god Ra, who was always identified in Egyptian religion with the god of the ruling city. This philosophy, contained in the *Memphite Drama* already referred to, taught a religious doctrine which attributed to divine immanence those rational insights of man which had shown him, in Egypt, how to order his society so as to maintain a reign of peace and law over the whole land and to set up an organized economy based on a vast system of irrigation canals. It was a system which only a highly organized central control could maintain, and it endured for nearly a thousand years in the period known as the Old Kingdom, prior to 2500 B.C. Then it collapsed into the disorder of rival and warring feudal principalities. The irrigation canals were neglected. The rapacity of local officials and petty nobles went unchecked. The country suffered from famine, war, mismanagement, and foreign invasion.

The literature of this period manifests two opposed types of reaction to this decadence in human affairs. One is a mood of disillusionment, manifesting itself in religious and moral skepticism. The other is the rise of social critics preaching reform. Probably the most remarkable of the documents of this latter sort is the *Discourse of the Eloquent Peasant*. Here the distinction between the actually existing law and ideal justice is clearly drawn, the higher law being attributed to Thoth, the god of writing and legal procedure.

Do justice for the sake of the Lord of justice, whose justice is indeed justice . . . even Thoth. When right is really right, then it is indeed right. For justice is for eternity. It descendeth with him that doeth it into the grave . . . he is remembered because of right. Such is the uprightness of the word of God.[12]

On a somewhat lower level, but of similar significance as marking recognition of the distinction between the existing law and custom and a more ancient, higher, divinely supported moral law, is Hesiod in the Greek middle ages, the seventh century B.C. In the minds of the people of his day, *diké* (right) and *dikaiosúne* (justice) were still associated with their ancient root reference to custom. Ethical philosophy was as yet unknown and people had not begun to question the justice of their ancient tribal law. But society nevertheless had developed social evils. Population was pressing on the means of subsistence. Land had been subdivided until all too often holdings were too small to maintain a family. The poor man was forced into debt, lost his land and often his liberty, being sold as a slave. The rich were growing richer and the poor, poorer. Petty kings and nobles exploited the peasantry. Bribery and corruption flourished. Against these evils, Hesiod, embittered by a personal experience of injustice, protested. This, said he, is not the true *diké*, the *dikaiosúne* which Zeus upholds. Zeus will punish those who thus violate his laws.

Hesiod's appeal to Zeus as upholder of a higher law did not, however, start a new religious movement of reform. For that his religious ideas were too crude and his moral zeal not sufficiently disinterested or powerful. The ethical distinction he had made, between custom or law as in actual operation and a higher moral law above the law as it is, did not find general acceptance. That had to wait until it was taken up by the philosophers in answer to a skepticism that cut deep into the social, moral, and religious life.

Meantime the growing social evils stimulated the spirit

[12] From "The Discourse of the Eloquent Peasant," translated by J. H. Breasted, and quoted in *The Dawn of Conscience, op. cit.,* p. 191.

of revolt. In the isolated mountain and island communities of Greece no central power was able to make itself strong enough to establish the rule of a dominant class. So, as the dispossessed masses seethed with revolt, they broke through the class rule which had long had the support of custom. They demanded reforms which violated traditional rights of property. But the democracy had no moral philosophy to justify its reconstitution of the social order and the over-throw of traditional rights and privileges. The departures from tradition, unsupported by appeal to religious concep-tions, threw ethical thought into confusion. The Sophists added to the uncertainty with their skeptical inquiries and criticism. It thus became the mission of Socrates to begin to straighten out the confusion of their thought on the meaning of "justice" and preach the reality of a higher moral law. But Socrates, if we can trust Plato's account of his teaching, gave a political interpretation to his theory of justice which was of no help to the democracy. Thus it was not until the rise of Stoicism that Greek thought developed an ethics that could be of any value to the cause of social justice. The Stoics found a ground for the needed distinc-tion in the concept of a universal, divine reason that runs through all things, a reason that can be scientifically found as natural law in the realm of physical things and can be discerned as moral law in the inner life of man.

For one further and very important example of the de-velopment of this distinction, we may turn to the Hebrews. When they come upon the stage of history at the time of the occupation of Palestine they have a tribal law which is identified with the divine law. Their tribal leaders are merely "judges" whose function it is to administer this law, making their decisions in accord with it. Even when they acquire kings, these rulers are also regarded as mere judges, administrators, and military commanders, not legislators.

The law is divine and is embodied in custom and tradition. It is too sacred to be changed.

In the eighth century B.C., however, there developed in the Hebrew kingdoms social evils similar to those of Greece in the time of Hesiod. These became the stimulus for the rise of a galaxy of prophetic stars unequaled elsewhere in human history. They came forth with a conception of God which is unequivocally monotheistic, and a conviction that all God's law is equitable and good. Whatever they saw as inequitable and destructive of human welfare they condemned as unethical and against the divine will. For the most part they did not criticize or reject ancient traditions but reasserted them. In the repudiations of collective responsibility, however, there is a clear departure from an ancient conception of justice expressly embodied in the most important of the earlier codes, and it is put forth as a new revelation. There are other definite advances, such as the forbidding of the enslavement of Hebrews,[13] the frequent condemnation of prostitution, and the condemnation of barbarities committed in war even upon foreigners, for whom there had previously been no signs of compunction. Even more significant than these advances in ethical principle, however, is the intensity of their concern for justice. They not only condemned illegal practices but also the accumulation of wealth and the grinding of the poor by perfectly legal means. Thus the really significant element in their message was the proclamation of an ideal of concern for human welfare, of kindness, brotherliness, and fair dealing, above and beyond the demands of special laws and established customs, an ideal summed up in the great guiding principle, "Thou shalt love thy neighbour as thyself."

This approach to ethical questions lifted the moral ideal

---

[13] This occurs in the Holiness Code, a seventh-century document incorporated in Leviticus. Cf. Lev. 25:45-46.

far beyond that of mere adherence to custom and performance of traditional duties. In the minds of the prophets it
was associated with their new and loftier conception of
God. It is impossible to separate cause and effect between
these two advances in thought—the higher conception of
God and the higher ideal of the moral life. The two ideas
must have acted as influences reciprocal upon each other in
their growth, for they are clearly inseparable in the minds
of the prophets. They argue from examples of what they
conceive as God's love for man to man's duty to love his
fellows, and from examples of human love, such as Hosea's
love and forgiveness of his false and fallen wife, to God's
love and compassion for man. Thus the ideas of a higher
moral law above the law as it is, and the idea of a high God
as source of the moral law, reciprocally support and stimulate each other. For the purpose of our understanding of
the development of conscience, however, the point of greatest importance is this: the recognition of the distinction
between the law as it is and the law as it ought to be (and
of a moral ideal too high to be made a law) is a distinct
advance made by the ethical thought of civilized man over
the vague moral assumptions and confusions of the primitive. And this advance, once achieved and maintained,
opens the way for others.

A Fourth Defect: Limitations of Group Morality

The fourth of the typical defects of primitive morality,
which the thought of civilized man outgrows, is the con-
fining of the concepts of rights, duty, and obligation to the
members of the contiguous or consanguineous group. This
is known as group morality. The rights of the individual
are those he has as a member of a family, tribe, or clan, and

his duties are only to other members of his own group. To the stranger or the foreigner, the primitive may be kind or cruel as his whim pleases. So long as he is not afraid of him, he is usually kind. But except for special cases defined by laws of hospitality (which constitute the earliest breach of this wall of moral indifference to the outsider), the typical primitive recognizes no such thing as a duty to anyone except toward members of his own group as defined by its customs or laws. Civilized peoples recognize a wide variety of special obligations based on group relations, but they also recognize some rights and duties attaching to a human being as such. The special obligations to members of the family, community, nation, or other group are generally regarded as more binding and as justifying certain preferences; but it is not usually regarded as morally correct completely to ignore or deny any rights of the outsider.

The essential difference is this. The moral traditions of civilized peoples recognize certain duties to a human being, as such, because of the values and potentialities of value resident in a human life. The moral traditions of primitive people, on the other hand, recognize only specific duties and rights based on common membership and special position in an organized group. They may be kind, generous, and just to an outsider, but if so it is due to sympathy, fear, or other natural interest, not to explicit recognition of a moral obligation.

The duties of hospitality, recognized among most primitive peoples, are only a partial exception to this rule. The stranger, admitted for purposes of trade or other intertribal communication, must perform or submit to certain ceremonies which give him a temporary status within the group, not as member but as guest. This formal status then defines the respective duties. The motivation for development of this institution is mixed. Probably most basic is interest in the economic exchanges these visitors make possible. Secondarily there is a fear of the magical influence or power of the stranger thus admitted. But hospitality is often extended to strangers found helpless and dying in a desert or wrecked and destitute on an island shore. Here there can be no economic interest, no fear of their physical power, and no fear of their magic, unless it be of their spirits should they be killed. It is therefore entirely probable that natural human sympathy and some moral concern for human values as such, not yet formulated in explicit tribal law, play a part in the decision to extend hospitality in such cases. And similar motives may well have had their influence in the original development of the institution.

This failure to extend the notion of rights and duties beyond the limits of the tribe is, of course, most notable in the conduct of warfare. Among primitives, and also in the early civilizations, the attitude to the foreigner is often simply amoral. More often than not, prisoners are slaughtered. Often they are tortured and their sufferings may be made a means of boasting and display. The women and children may be indiscriminately slain or enslaved. Naga head-hunters in Burma, for example, prized the skull of a woman or baby in arms as a specially valuable exhibit, since it indicated that they must have penetrated the heart of the enemy country to obtain it. The early Hebrews slaughtered and tortured their captives, exterminated whole tribes and cities, ripped up pregnant women of the enemy, with the same moral insensibility as did the nations and tribes with whom they fought, though from the eighth century on we find the prophets protesting against some of these practices. The Greeks, on capturing a city, maintained that it was perfectly justifiable to put the men to the sword and sell the women and children into slavery—as the Athenians did to

Melos, at the height of their power, entirely without provo-
cation and simply in pursuit of a policy of empire building.

Yet examples of rules for the amelioration of warfare are
to be found even among primitive peoples. The Kaffirs, for
example, had regulations requiring an open declaration of
war and forbidding the use of poisoned arrows or the starv-
ing out of an enemy. The ancient Greeks had a tradition
against the cutting off of running water from a Hellenic
city under siege. Such regulations, however, are rare and
usually apply only to warfare between kindred groups.

THE GROWTH OF ETHICAL UNIVERSALISM

It is not until the rise of the great ethical religions,
which transcend tribal limits, that moral ideas make much
progress in extension beyond the bounds of the group. And
even then, of course, there is a great gap between ethical
theory and practice. The credit for the earliest development
of a conscience on the subject of war and the treatment of
foreigners has to go to the religions of the East, not those
of the West. The pacific and universalist trend of Buddhist
teaching, dating from the sixth century B.C., is well known.
It makes the taking of human life a crime under any conditions. But Hinduism was, in this respect, little behind.
Though it teaches the military duties of the warrior caste,
it enjoins a high degree of chivalry in their execution. The
laws of Manu (third century B.C.) forbid the use of con-
cealed, barbed, or poisoned weapons, enjoin the giving of
quarter, and forbid striking a man in his sleep, or unarmed,
or in flight, or when seriously wounded. Confucian ethics
is definitely antimilitaristic, though it does not go so far as
Buddhism in forbidding the taking of human life. It places
the occupation of the soldier at the bottom of the social
scale. Mencius denounces military aggression as a crime,

and asserts that annexation of the territory of a neighbor, except by consent of its people, is inexcusable.

At their best these religions rise to the spirit of ethical universalism. We read in the Confucian classics that "All within the four seas are brethren," [14] and we find the sage propounding the Golden Rule without setting or implying any limits as to its application. He puts it in the negative form, but in expounding its implications he gives positive examples. In India we find the Vishnu Purana, about the fourth century A.D., asserting that "The prudent man should always cultivate that, in act, thought, and speech, which conduces to the well-being of all living creatures, in this world and the next." It is true that the implications of such teaching are not fully grasped. The maintenance of caste distinctions, for example, is still held as a religious duty. But the idea that human life, and even animal life, is a thing of value in itself, and that all such values call for fundamentally equal respect, is clearly present. Even Buddhism, in its revolt against Brahmanism, paid sufficient deference to the social system of India to agree that the layman should respect caste, while abolishing it for the monk. But in its transition to the lands of its missionary enterprise, Buddhism left this incubus of India behind and became an ethic of equal duty to all mankind without distinction of nationality, race, caste, or creed.

In the West, with its turmoil of fierce migrations and the rivalry of great empires which could never impose a peace on the whole area, ethical universalism was a plant of slower growth. It was first attained by the Stoics, whose philosophy of a universal divine reason led to the recognition of a universal and divine moral law which must be the same for Greek and barbarian, freeman and slave. Among the Hebrews, though their concept of duty to one's neigh-

[14] *Analects*, Book XII, Part V, iv.

bor acquired more positive content than is to be found in other scriptures of similar date, the overcoming of their nationalism was slow. They raised the moral idea to its height in the principle of neighbor love, "Thou shalt love thy neighbour *as thyself.*" But they did not extend it in breadth beyond the limits of the consanguineous group. We see this when we refer the text to its context. "Thou shalt not avenge, nor bear any grudge against the children of thy people, but thou shalt love they neighbour as thyself." [15]

It must not be supposed that the Hebrews remained content with this narrow nationalism throughout the pre-Christian era. Long before Christ the question was raised, "Who is my neighbor?" Intimations of the recognition that a universalistic religion should logically imply a universalistic ethic are to be found as early as the Book of Jonah, about 400 B.C. But the question was still merely one for debate when it was submitted to Jesus. His answer, illustrated by the parable of the Good Samaritan, left no doubts open to his followers. Together with the specific injunction, "Love your enemies, bless them that curse you, do good to them that hate you, and pray for them which despitefully use you, and persecute you," [16] it made the ethical idea clear. The fullest measure of concern for the welfare of others, equal to that of one's natural concern with one's own welfare, should be manifested in all human relationships, not only to kindred and friends but also to the foreigner, stranger, and even to one's enemy. The ethical ideal can be lifted no higher and extended no further.

This is a far cry from the limited range of duties to a limited number of persons recognized in primitive ethics. Yet by the first century A.D. an ideal akin to this in range of persons included, and not very different in range of duties

[15] Lev. 19:18.
[16] Matt. 5:44.

recognized, is to be found endorsed by the section of opinion most sensitive ethically in all the three great centers of civilization—in China, in India, and in the Occident. And in each center of civilization it has grown independently. For the intellectual contacts between them have been extremely small; certainly not sufficient for such an idea to be imposed by the one on the other unless that other could find the ground for it in its own experience and contemplation.

Further, it is significant that the ideal has grown, not by rational inquiry into the ways and means for best securing the interests of the individual and the state, but by the self-critical reflection and meditation of the prophet and the seer. The moral insights of the Stoics are the ethical culmination of that religious line of Greek philosophy which runs from Pythagoras, through Socrates and Plato, to Zeno and Cleanthes, whose noble hymn to Zeus was quoted by St. Paul at Athens. Hebrew and Indian thought is religious, through and through, the one monotheistic, the other pantheistic. In China the religious element is not so prominent: but it is there. Confucius claimed no revelation, but acknowledges his thought as derived from earlier sages from whom he has learned his ethical principles and accepted them as "the decrees of Heaven." [17] It is, indeed, a basic principle of the Confucian theory of human nature that moral insight is divinely given to men. "The great God has conferred even on the inferior people a moral sense, compliance with which would show their nature invariably right." [18]

Thus in China, as elsewhere, new and higher moral convictions have arisen and gripped the minds of the sages as they meditated on their own inner sense of right and wrong;

[17] *Analects*, Book II, iii.
[18] *Shu Ching*, Part IV, Book III, ii.

for it is out of such meditation that the religious spirit finds that peculiar illumination and sense of compulsion that is attributed to divine guidance. Such meditation consists not in reasoning about ways and means to accepted ends, but in analysis of the inner process of motivation with its sense of value and obligation. Such analysis penetrates confusions and clarifies the vision of ends. It is the means whereby man comes to an understanding of himself. The significant fact, therefore, which emerges from our study of the development of conscience, is this: that man's reflective analysis of his own moral nature discloses within him something that he can understand only as an inner demand that he concern himself impartially with the welfare of other human beings. And this discovery has been so startling and compelling to those who have made it that they have attributed it to something distinct from their own desire or that of the community, to something, indeed, that is more than human.

For the present it is not with this religious conclusion that we need to be concerned. If we would understand the moral nature of man, we must not too readily jump to the conclusion that in this religious interpretation of their experience the sages are right—or that they are wrong. The important thing is to recognize the nature of the experience and the method of thought and inquiry out of which these moral convictions have come. For such experience is not peculiar to the sages and prophets who first propound these new and higher moral ideals. If it were, then no one would listen to them. The prophets and sages win a following because what they say finds echoes in the breasts of their hearers. These latter find their own moral consciousness illuminated thereby. The ethical and religious literature produced by the prophets and sages becomes classical, and acquires the reputation of inspiration, because it says so

well and clearly what the multitude also vaguely feel. To
many of their hearers, the illumination of the moral consciousness thus induced is disturbing and unwelcome. They
may stone or crucify the prophet in resentment. But those
who come after them and reflect more calmly on the new
moral ideal are won to respect it because it appeals to them
as true. They then build the prophet's tomb, canonize his
writings, and perhaps worship at his shrine.

No explanation of the moral phenomenon in history can
be adequate unless it explains the phenomenon in this
form. It is irrelevant to point out that few persons, if any,
act consistently in accord with such high moral convictions.
This only renders more remarkable and striking the fact
that they have these convictions—for the fact that they do
not act upon them means that wishful thinking would make
them desire to get rid of such convictions if they could.
Yet the uncomfortable convictions persist. It is also irrelevant to point out that many persons do not hold these
convictions and declare that they have no such sense of
obligation as is implied by them. The fact that such obligations are unwelcome is sufficient to explain why many
persons should be psychically blind to them. The further
fact that recognition of these duties or ideals has, historically, been a plant of slow growth, and has always faced
opposition from those whose interests or prejudices are
adversely affected, also explains why it is comparatively easy
for many persons, even in our civilization, to reject them
and deny any experience by which to justify them.

The opposition to these ideals, therefore, and the denial
of their validity, does not lessen our problem. *The fact to
be explained is that moral conviction has, historically, taken
this high and universalistic form, and that such conviction
is widespread and is given almost universal lip service even
where violated in practice;* for this indicates that it is un-

willingly recognized as right. Also to be explained is the manner in which such convictions have grown—by reflective analysis of the sense of obligation and value on the part of individuals deeply concerned with moral issues, and by the more or less reluctant recognition, on the part of those to whom the new concepts of obligation have been taught,, that these insights are right. It is irrelevant for the critic to point out that the principles of love to one's neighbor and equality of rights are all too often violated by individual selfishness and group fanaticism. The fact of significance for an understanding of the moral nature of man is that his conscience, especially as manifest in the teaching of the religions he has accepted as civilization has given him leisure to think, has generally endorsed these principles. The fact that his inclinations so often lead him to violate or distort that conscience only makes its emergence and persistence the more remarkable.

Chapter 2

THE GROWTH OF SKEPTICISM

Skepticism and Wisdom

We have traced the history of conscience to the point where we find that in each of the three great centers of civilization there has independently developed a conviction that man has a duty to concern himself impartially with the welfare of his fellows. This conviction is held in spite of the fact that actual conduct falls far short of its requirements, and even in spite of the acceptance, at the same time, of laws and institutions which conflict with it in practice. And in each case the moral conviction is imbedded in and supported by a religion which declares it to be the will of God or a moral law of the universe—even though other aspects of these very same religions may support laws and institutions which conflict with their highest moral principle in practice.

In view of these inconsistencies of ethical theory, and the conflicts of theory and practice, it is not surprising that, long before the moral ideal had reached its loftiest height and maturity, doubts began to manifest themselves concerning the ideals presented and the religions supporting them.

The wisdom that evolved the moral ideals is not the only kind of wisdom that man possesses. It is a wisdom that *analyzes*, that penetrates the inner distinctions of his hopes and aspirations, his fears and desires, his aims and his efforts. It is the wisdom of insight that discovers the inner connections and directions of his psychic life and propounds

44

them as guiding principles. It interprets man to himself. The other wisdom is that which interprets the outer world to man. Its analyses are practical but superficial, concerned only with the data of sense and the meaning of ideas. It seeks to discover the logical connections of thought and the casual connections of things. Reason, intelligence, and hard thinking are required in the acquiring of both kinds of wisdom, but the subject matter and the aim, and to a great extent the method, are different. The one is the wisdom of human understanding, ethical and religious insight; the other is the wisdom of science and philosophy.

It is a very difficult question as to what kind of intellectual activity is involved in acquiring the first kind of wisdom.[1] When once the idea of the value of a certain object or action, or the obligation present in a certain social relation, is clearly grasped, the question of its further implications and applications is one for use of the same inductive and deductive reasoning processes as we use in science and everyday affairs. But the question is as to whether there is anything unique about the ways in which such ideas are formed. That is the core of the problem concerning the moral nature of man. Whatever the answer to that question, however, it need not affect our recognition of the distinction of two kinds of wisdom, for here there is a distinction of subject matter. A man who is extremely learned and intelligent in the ways of things may be a fool in his failure to understand himself and his neighbors. This will readily be recognized. It will also readily be recognized that it is to the latter type of understanding that the problems of the moral life belong. It is not so generally recognized, but it is nevertheless true, that it is out of thought on these

---

[1] As we proceed, we shall see that there is no radical departure needed from the methods of natural science, only a distinction of emphasis because of a special type of subject matter and aims.

latter problems, rather than speculations on the other phenomena of nature, that religion grows. This has been
increasingly recognized since the days of Kant and Schleier-
macher, and the reasons for it will become clearer as we
proceed. Much of theology is, of course, mere cosmological
and psychological theory. But religion is much more than
theology and its roots lie in insights into the inner life of
the self—insights that are never complete, but more or less
valid, and interpreted with more or less knowledge and
understanding.

It is possible for this type of wisdom to cherish insights
that are self-contradictory and to propound them in principles that are mutually inconsistent, for in this sphere wisdom recognizes that its insights are partial, never sufficiently
clear, profound, and all-embracing. Yet in each case it must
pronounce the truth as it sees it. The result is paradox; and
in personal relations, ethics, and religion, to avoid one
paradox is often to fall into another and worse one. So in
these spheres wisdom has often to tolerate the paradoxical,
hoping that the apparent inconsistency of its insights may
not indicate that either is wrong but only that neither is
sufficiently profound. But this unfortunate necessity tends
to make the thinker in these spheres less sensitive than he
should be to contradiction. He may become uncritical of
what he claims to be his insights and even begin to rejoice
in paradox, laying to his soul the flattering unction that it
indicates his profundity. This is the cherished fallacy of all
too much theology—ancient, medieval, and modern. And it
is not unknown in ethics. Its disastrous effect is to create a
tolerance of inconsistency; and inconsistency breeds doubts
that infest the whole sphere of thought in which it is found.

The wisdom of science and philosophy is always intol-
erant of inconsistency. It demands an ethics (and a religion, if it is to have any) that is consistent with experience

in general and, if possible, free from paradox. In this age of ascendancy of scientific thought, ethics and religion can ignore this demand only at their peril. But since the early days of civilization the demand has been made. Critical common sense and scientific philosophy have challenged the paradoxes and conflicting doctrines of ethics and religion; they have insistently demanded that faith should show a basis in evidence of a kind that reason is impelled to accept. The main attack has been against the dogmas of religion which surround and support the ethical code, particularly when practical experience raises objections to some part of it. Usually the attackers have themselves been anxious to support its main principles and have anxiously striven to find reasons of their own for them to replace the religious props they have torn away; but in this region confusion still reigns. The "scientific" approach has itself developed new dogmas, fiercer than those they have replaced, in the moral teaching of the totalitarians. The skepticism of the newer movements in scientific philosophy is reaching deeper into the foundations of the moral life. In reaction against these movements, the older faiths are proclaiming more boldly the independence of their own sources of insight. The rift between man's two spheres of wisdom grows deeper.

This schizophrenia of our civilization bodes ill for the future. "Whom the gods would destroy they first make mad." Our social sanity and safety therefore require that we insist that "truth is one" and search persistently until we can bring together the two branches of man's wisdom by finding their common root. It is this search on which we are here engaged; but before we attempt the positive task, it will be well to review briefly the principle forms that skepticism has taken, in order to see clearly how far the attack has been successful and how completely the weapons of attack have failed when the attempt has been made to use them as tools of reconstruction. For this purpose it will be sufficient to confine our attention to Western philosophy and to a few of its major figures and movements.

Intuitionism in the History of Ethics

Medieval philosophy developed the conviction that the fundamental principles of morals were not only given in revelation but were self-evident to the natural light of human reason. In early modern times skepticism developed first concerning the detailed claims for revelation. It had long been recognized that moral teaching of the Old and New Testaments could not be taken simply and literally and applied directly to human affairs. The differences between the law in the Pentateuch and the Sermon on the Mount were too obvious to escape recognition. Revelation cried aloud for interpretation. The church claimed to be able to give this with authority but it met with revolt. Protestantism asserted the right of private interpretation, and the dogmatism of sects and individuals replaced that of the ecclesiastical hierarchy. From the confusion of tongues found in revelation, men turned to what was traditionally regarded as the other source of moral guidance, that is to reason. Philosophers sought to base the whole structure of the moral life on a doctrine of self-evident rights.

Outside the Catholic church, religion thus lost its place as the arbiter of moral issues. Revelation, it was agreed, needs interpretation by reason, and the reason of the layman is as valid as that of any other. The moral law, indeed, is a rule of reason which the wise can discover without the aid of revelation. Neither is it the wisdom of science and philosophy that is required for the knowledge of right and wrong, but the wisdom of insight, which is a possession of the pure in heart though otherwise it may be hidden even from the learned. In the eighteenth century, Protestant and secularist alike were usually ready to agree with Bishop Butler that "any plain honest man" who asked himself "Is this right?" would be able to render an answer in agreement with "truth and virtue . . . in almost any circumstance," moral misjudgment being almost always the result of either "superstition" or "partiality," particularly partiality to oneself.[2]

Among religious philosophers the conviction underlying this doctrine of moral insight was that of the philosophy of immanence expressed in the Pauline statement, which Butler takes as the text of his second sermon, that "the Gentiles, which have not the law, do by nature the things contained in the law . . . which shew the work of the law written in their hearts, their conscience also bearing witness."[3] Secularist philosophers, however, sought to explain and justify man's moral convictions by a naturalistic interpretation of human nature. Earlier than Butler, Hobbes had tried to do this on the basis of a purely egoistic theory of motivation. Man's egoism makes him such a danger to his neighbors that his only escape from the turmoil of a constant war of all against all is to set up the authority of the state, contracting explicitly or implicitly with his neighbors to obey whatever laws are made by its sovereign power, and trusting that the self-interest of the ruler will lead him to legislate for peace, order, security, and prosperity. Reason, in the form of enlightened self-interest, then demands of the individual that he fulfill his contract and recognize no moral law above that of the state.

The pessimism of Hobbes's theory of human nature, and the resultant authoritarianism of his theory of the state,

[2] *Sermons*, III.
[3] Rom. 2:14-15.

were a reaction to the period of the wars of religion, including the English civil war. Even the turmoil of his times, however, brought him little agreement among moralists in his low view of man or his authoritarian deductions from it. Soon the relative peace and progress of the eighteenth century restored man's confidence in himself. The Calvinistic emphasis on his total depravity gave way to Butler's emphasis on the inner illumination, and his, and Hutcheson's, insistence on natural human benevolence.

Among secularists the same trend manifested itself in the moral sense philosophy of Shaftesbury and Hume. Rejecting the doctrine of a divinely given rational insight into right and wrong, these thinkers sought to explain the moral life in terms of feeling. Shaftesbury argued that certain types of action, when observed, stimulate an inner sense, which responds as naturally as our eyes do to light, creating emotions of approval; and others have the reverse effect. Thereby we judge the former to be right and the latter wrong. Hume argued that man has a natural tendency to feel an emotion of approval on observing any action or personal quality, in any person, that appears useful to that person himself or any others; and similarly, that we disapprove what appears to be injurious. The function of reason is thus not to form moral judgments by its own analytical insight but to decide scientifically what is really useful and to pronounce as right what our moral sense approves. Shaftesbury was confident that man's social interests, his dependence upon society, and the satisfactions and dissatisfactions of the moral sense mean so much to the joys and sorrows of life that to do what is right would always make for a man's own true happiness in the long run. Hume, more cautiously, said that it would nearly always do so.

It should be noted that all these philosophers are correctly trying to account for the moral consciousness of man in what we have seen to be its fully developed form—a conviction of the obligation of every man to seek impartially the good of all. But the difficulty in claiming any such intuition, whether in the form of a rational insight or as the reaction of a moral sense, is that many deny that they have any such insight or feeling. If it could be claimed that scientifically verifiable facts show that such behavior is essential to the happiness of the individual, or to the full rational development of his personality, then it would not be relevant to point out that some persons cannot see the truth of the matter by direct insight or do not feel the appropriate sense of value. The case would be the same if the principle were established by revelation. But when it is claimed that the only way in which we can know what is right is by an intuitive insight, or by having a certain feeling, then if any principle is to be recognized as universally right, it must be shown that everybody has that insight or that feeling—or at least that he would have it if he gave the necessary attention to the matter. But this claim cannot be made for any of the moral principles traditionally recognized by religion or by these intuitionist philosophers to whom we have referred. Butler and Hutcheson could not claim it for the principle of love to one's neighbor. Hume could not claim it for the tendency to feel approval of whatever is thought to be useful. Neither are there any more specific principles for which it can be claimed. Intuitionism, therefore, in the form of a doctrine of self-evident human rights, or the self-evidence of the principle of universal benevolence, broke down under criticism.

Toward the end of the eighteenth century, Immanuel Kant tried to restate intuitionism in a form he thought less vulnerable. He, too, accepted the conviction that any valid ethical theory must uphold the principle of impartial concern for the good of all, but he was not content to rest this principle on an appeal to intuition or self-interest. Nor was he willing to define human good as happiness. Man's true good, he was convinced, lies in the purity of the moral life, in doing his duty whatever the consequences. Nothing else is intrinsically good. Even happiness becomes evil if it consists in a satisfaction taken in a cruel revenge. But loyal adherence to the moral law is a good that shines only the more brightly if it involves endurance of pain; and though it may fail in its endeavor to produce happiness, the righteous endeavor shines undimmed. Moral goodness, therefore, Kant concluded, is the only true intrinsic goodness. But if so, how shall we define the aim of the morally good act? To say that goodness is the goal of good actions is merely to get involved in a vicious circle.

Kant found his escape from this impasse in another of the convictions of ethical universalism: the same moral law must be valid for all. The principle of impartiality implies that I cannot claim a right for myself which I am not willing to allow to others. This seemed to him self-evident for any rational being. Here, then, he thought, was a criterion for judging the validity of any moral principle. If it could consistently be universalized, it was valid. If one cannot consistently will it to be a universal law followed by everyone at all times, it is wrong. Space forbids a discussion here of Kant's attempts to illustrate the application of the criterion to moral questions, but criticism has abundantly shown that no specific moral principle can be made absolute. In general, it may be agreed, one should not take a human life, or destroy another's property, or break a promise, or tell a lie; on the other hand one should give alms to the poor, help those in difficulties, save human life whenever one can. But circumstances arise in which these excellent principles conflict with one another. Then how shall we decide which is the more important if our only criterion makes them all absolute? Thus the rational intuitionism of Immanuel Kant breaks down. Its brilliant but futile attempt to establish a universalistic and absolute system of morals only strengthened the movement toward thoroughgoing relativism and skepticism.

INTUITIONISM IN CONTEMPORARY ETHICS

The British moralists, like British philosophy generally, have inclined strongly toward empiricism. At the same time they have almost unanimously supported ethical universalism. Both the moral sense intuitionists and the utilitarians have upheld the standard of "the greatest happiness of the greatest number." For the most part the attempt has been made to rest this principle on enlightened self-interest. But toward the end of the nineteenth century, Henry Sidgwick, the great Cambridge moralist, proposed a new combination of utilitarianism and intuitionism. In the preface to the sixth edition of his major work, *The Methods of Ethics*, he tells how he came to see the futility of the attempt to derive altruism from egoism and turned to a fresh study of Butler and Kant. From these he became convinced that there is a genuine intuitional element in morality, though no absolutism can be claimed for any of the ordinary maxims of common sense; but the general principle of impartial concern for the good of all, he saw, is in a different position. Adopted as the supreme moral principle, it can conflict with no other. "I certainly could will it to be a universal law that men should act in such a way as to promote universal happiness; in fact, it was the only law that it was perfectly clear to me that I could thus decisively will, from a universal point of view." [4]

[4] Henry Sidgwick, *Methods of Ethics* (7th ed.; London: Macmillan & Co., 1907), LXX.

We shall see later that it is by no means so clear as Sidgwick thought that no moral requirement can ever conflict with this principle of seeking always to promote the greatest possible happiness. Certainly it removes the greatest difficulty from the Kantian intuitionism. It sets up an intelligible, empirical criterion of good at which to aim, and it offers one supreme principle in the light of which every question can, theoretically, be decided. In claiming, however, that human happiness is the sole good at which all moral endeavor should aim, it raises again that question of the nature of intrinsic good which Kant's analysis had resolved by saying there is nothing intrinsically good but the morally good will. Is a happiness found in lust, vengeance, or arrogance a true intrinsic good? If the goodness of happiness is independent of the moral goodness or badness of its sources and consequences, then is it so clear, so self-evident, that we should promote the maximum of happiness? What if the maximum could only be obtained by some injustice? Furthermore, if happiness is the only good, is it so self-evidently clear that I should always be prepared to sacrifice much of my own happiness for the greater happiness of others? There is nothing in the notion of happiness that logically implies an obligation to pursue it for myself or anyone else. There is no self-evident connection between the ideas of happiness and moral obligation. It may be true that I can will, as Sidgwick says, that the pursuit of the equal and greatest possible happiness of all mankind should be a universal law of human nature—and that I can do this consistently and without contradiction; but that does not prove that I ought to do so, and ought to act on that principle.

Early in the twentieth century another notable Cambridge philosopher, G. E. Moore, sought to remedy the defects of Sidgwick's intuitionism by eliminating its identification of the good with happiness. The notion of "good," said Moore,[5] should be identified with "ought to exist," but further than that it is indefinable. We can see intuitively that many things have this unique character of being good, especially aesthetic enjoyment and personal affection, and we can see that other things, such as the consciousness of bitter pain, hatred of the good or beautiful, and love of the evil or ugly, are bad. We cannot *define* good or bad in these terms, however. We simply have to judge the degree of good or bad in different situations, as we intuitively see it. We acquire skill in such judgment as we attentively practice it, but our judgments are never more than approximately correct, yet we can see intuitively that the good (what ought to exist) is something that we ought always to promote and maximize as much as we are able. The right action will therefore always be that one the total results of which would be the best possible.

Critics have found two main flaws in this argument of Moore's. One concerns the transition from ought-to-be to ought-to-do. Even if we admit that one can see that some mental state such as aesthetic enjoyment or personal affection ought to exist, it does not follow that I, or any other particular person, ought to do whatever is necessary to bring it into existence or continue its existence—or let us take a negative example. A certain sick person may have a pain which can be relieved only by large doses of an expensive medicine. It may be agreed that such a pain is an evil— that, in some sense, it ought not to exist. It may also be agreed that the state could easily afford to supply this medicine and remove the evil. So could any of a number of rich individuals; and even a great many persons of moderate means could do it at the cost of a little sacrifice; but does

[5] G. E. Moore, *Principia Ethica* (London: Cambridge University Press, 1903).

the mere fact of the existence of this evil imply that the state, or any particular person or combination of persons, has a duty to bear the cost of its removal? There is no direct logical transition from the proposition that "This pain is an evil" to the proposition that "Mr. X should pay for the removal of that pain." Obviously some other premises must be added to make the transition, and these premises must say something about Mr. X's *duties*, about what he ought to *do*.

The second criticism of Moore's intuitionism is even more fundamental. It challenges the validity of the concept of good in the sense of "ought to exist." Modern semanticists point out that such a concept has no referent; i.e., there is no entity, and no character of any entity, to which it refers. Personal affection, which Moore regards as one of the chief goods, may exist. It has certain definite characters which distinguish it from hatred and curiosity; and these all have certain characters which distinguish them from faces, bones, birds, and houses. What is the character called "ought to exist?" It is not a constituent part of the mental process called personal affection. Is it a relational character? Does "ought to exist" refer to some characteristic relation which personal affection has to other things or persons or to other aspects of mental life? When we ask this question we see that the "ought" has been misplaced. What we mean by saying that something ought to exist is that it is the sort of thing that someone, or people in general, ought to bring into existence, or keep in existence, when they can. The thing that "ought to exist," and perhaps does not exist, cannot be said to have an obligation. What we are saying is that some person or persons have an obligation in regard to it, to bring it into existence, or keep it in existence, if they can. The "ought" has been transferred, by the figure of speech known as metonymy, from the persons who ought to *do* to the thing which we say ought to *be*.

Moore's intuitionism should therefore be reinterpreted as claiming that we can intuitively see that human beings have certain general obligations to try to produce as much as possible of certain forms of mental life, such as personal affection and aesthetic enjoyment, and to prevent the development of others, such as consciousness of intense pain and hatred of the good or beautiful. This position has the advantage of being in accord with that principle which we have seen to be generally endorsed by the great religions of mankind, the impartial pursuit of the general welfare, but it does no more than claim intuitive self-evidence for this principle. It offers us no criterion by which to decide what forms of mental life are best, for Moore's own high evaluation of aesthetic enjoyment and personal affection is admittedly vague and only the expression of one man's judgment. Nor does it begin to answer the objections of those who deny that there is any self-evident principle of obligation requiring any person to subordinate the pursuit of his own interests to the welfare of another.

The only conclusion, therefore, to be drawn from this brief review of intuitionist ethics is that hitherto the attempt has failed.[6] It has sought to maintain the rational self-evidence of the highest moral ideals developed by religion, but it has failed to disclose any logical ground for such claims, or to show how such moral intuition arises, or to explain why such intuitive insights are not clearly evident to all. Thus far, skepticism has triumphed.

[6] No mention has been made of the intuitionism of the British deontologists but this will be discussed in Chapter 6. For a critique of the intuitionism of Nicolai Hartmann, see my article, "Phenomenological Ethics and Self-realization," *Ethics* (April, 1943).

Naturalism and the Emotive Theory

This failure of intuitionism has led to the development of two different views of the ethical problem. The earlier and still the commoner alternative is that of naturalistic ethics. Here the distinctive ethical terms, "good" and "ought," are interpreted as not having any uniquely distinctive meaning peculiar to ethics, but as equivalent to some other terms having natural, psychological referents. Thus "good" may be taken as equivalent to "pleasure" or to "satisfaction of desire," and "ought" may be taken as equivalent to "required by social demand," or "required by enlightened self-interest." The attempt is then made to explain the growth and expression of the moral convictions of mankind in these terms. In the same terms, those convictions are submitted to criticism, and usually the attempt is made to defend on empirical grounds the principle which asserts man's duty to be impartially concerned with the general human welfare. This attempt of naturalistic ethics to show that it can give rational support to the same ideals of the moral life endorsed by religion at its best we shall examine in the next chapter.

The other alternative is one of more recent development and propounds a more radical skepticism. This is the argument of Logical Positivism. We shall examine it in the forms given it by A. J. Ayer and C. L. Stevenson.

Contrary to the general view of naturalistic ethics, Ayer agrees with G. E. Moore and other intuitionists that ethical statements are not equivalent to statements about natural psychological processes such as pleasure, interests, and demands, but here the agreement with the intuitionists ends. What the Positivists claim is not that ethical statements have a unique and distinctive meaning, but that, strictly speaking, they have no meaning at all. Normative sentences are not a logical use of language. They state no facts. They are merely an expressive or evocative use of language. They give expression to the feelings of the speaker and are designed to stimulate some response in the hearers, but they do not assert anything or deny anything. To say "Stealing is wrong" is merely to say "stealing" and utter an expression of disapproval. Such sentences do not even say that the speaker has a feeling of disapproval. They merely express it, as it might be expressed by the utterance of the word in a scornful tone. And what they express is not an *opinion* about anything but simply an emotional attitude of the speaker toward something.

On this radically subjectivist "emotive" theory of morals, ethics becomes merely that part of the science of psychology which studies that particular set of emotional reactions which we call "moral." Such a science can describe how these reactions arise and the course they take, but it cannot assert any moral judgments to be true or false, or any moral actions to be right or wrong. Ethical philosophy, as distinct from this psychology of the ethical emotions, simply consists in the single statement that all ethical concepts are merely pseudo concepts.

There is, of course, one obvious objection to this interpretation of ethical expressions, and Ayer is clearly aware of it. It means that people are all wrong when they think that they agree on the meaning of ethical terms and statements, and that their disputes on ethical questions are mistaken and meaningless; for if normative sentences have no logical or factual content, then they can be neither true nor false. There cannot even be one opinion expressed by them, let alone two. Yet people certainly do think that they have ethical opinions and that sometimes they agree with one another on ethical questions and sometimes they do not.

Ayer's reply to this objection is that we are simply mistaken as to what it is concerning which we hold opinions. The agreements and differences on ethical questions all concern matters of fact and logic, not norms or values as distinct from facts. They concern such factual questions as: What are the consequences of that action? What was the motive for it? Does it conform to such and such a rule? What are the implications of that rule in these circumstances? What are the consequences of neglecting such a rule or of approving a modification of it? Usually, says Ayer, when individuals are agreed upon such questions of fact and logic, they will experience and express similar emotions of approval or disapproval. If they do, they will regard themselves as in ethical agreement. If they do not, then, if they can find no further facts, useful argument ceases. They may resort to force or they may agree to differ in their ethical expressions. But the remaining difference between them is not a different opinion concerning the truth of a proposition but merely a difference of emotional attitude toward the same set of facts understood in the same way.

It should be noted that this "emotive" theory of ethics asserts that in ethical attitudes and judgments there is an ultimate irrational factor, an emotional element which is apt to differ from person to person, especially if temperament, training, and environment differ markedly. Because of this it must be entirely impossible to prove the validity of any moral rule. Moral rules can never be more than rules approved by the majority (perhaps the great majority) at a certain time and place. The assertion of a moral rule can therefore never be anything more than an expression of the demands of one's own feelings and application of them to one's self, or the imposition of the demands of the feelings of one individual or group upon another. It cannot be

a requirement of anything more significant than the predominant emotional tendencies of a single community.

This implication of the Positivist theory receives frank
and full expression from another member of the school,
C. L. Stevenson.[7] He analyzes ethical sentences as containing both an expression of feeling and a demand that others
shall conform. To say "This is wrong," he says, is roughly
equivalent to saying "I disapprove of this; do so as well."
"This is good" is roughly equivalent to "I approve of this;
do so as well." Like Ayer, he points out that much of our
disagreement on ethical questions is really concerning
matters of fact and logic, but that even when there is agreement on these matters, there may still remain a basic opposition of emotional drive and attitude. This, he insists,
involves a demand that others should agree with us in
their approvals and disapprovals, a demand which can
maintain the ethical dispute even after agreement has been
reached on all matters of fact.

Stevenson recognizes that it is a distinctive type of emotion that is expressed in the use of the ethical terms. Moral
approval and disapproval are not to be confused with mere
liking and disliking, or with the sort of admiration one may
have for something beautiful, skilful, or clever, and the an-
noyance induced by the ugly, clumsy, or dull. The term
"good" may be used in a nonmoral sense as a synonym for
"nice," "useful," or "swell," but its ethical sense, involving
the distinctively ethical emotions, is entirely distinct.

This distinctive nature of the feeling and attitude expressed in the use of ethical terms should be admitted—but
the emotive theorists flatly contradict the assumptions of
both the plain man and the moral sage when they say that
what they call their judgments of right and wrong, of moral

[7] C. L. Stevenson, *Ethics and Language* (New Haven: Yale University
Press, 1944).

good and evil, are merely expressions of private, individual emotions of a certain distinctive type. When an unsophisticated jury agrees on the facts of a case, such as "That the accused killed his victim solely for the purpose of obtaining his money," they would be shocked to be told that it is merely an expression of private emotion to say the action was wrong. They believe that the act would still be wrong even if they were so callous as to feel no emotions about it, and in saying it is wrong they do not merely mean (and with this Ayer and Stevenson agree) that it is illegal, or generally disliked, or apt to have adverse effects upon their own interests.

The emotive theory must therefore maintain that the vast majority of people in all ages, including most of those who have given most thought to the question, are agreed in holding a mistaken view as to what they themselves mean when they use ethical terms. This is an extraordinarily bold position for a philosopher to take, but the Logical Positivists defend it by pointing to the variations and contradictions commonly found in what is said on moral issues. They tend to ignore the broad agreement of the sages upon the principle of seeking impartially the greatest good of all; and they emphasize, as evidence of the irrational emotional surd in man's moral life, the varied moral customs of primitive tribes, the excesses of the Nazis, and the stubborn dogmatism of varying ethical traditions.

CRITICISM OF THE EMOTIVE THEORY

Should we not carry a step further their own argument that difference of opinion on ethical questions is chiefly due to different knowledge and understanding of the relevant facts? This is undoubtedly true, and it is also true that judgments concerning these facts do not constitute the assertion of a norm. On the other hand, it may still be true that the assertion of the norm is not merely the expression of an emotion, but the assertion of what is really a more or less complete and accurate insight into the inner structure of the volitional and rational life, an insight into something common to the nature of all men. It may well be the case that our varying emotional peculiarities tend to obscure and distort this insight, just as our varying views of the facts in any particular situation tend to affect our interpretation of questions concerning the proper application of the insight in practice. However, the broad agreement that the great ethical religions of mankind have attained on the fundamental principle of ethics suggests the gradual discovery of a factor in the moral life that is in some sense objective, universal, and factual, rather than the expression of anything so subjective and variable as mere emotion.

Positivists treat all philosophical questions as questions concerning the uses of language and the analysis of the meaning of terms. All other questions are questions of fact—physical, psychological, and social. Let us tentatively consent to this distinction. Then the question now before us is a question of fact. What is expressed by ethical terms such as good, right, and ought? Admittedly they do not merely express a reference to facts given or indicated in sensation, but they do express something in our experience. We call it conscience, or the sense of obligation, when it applies to our own conduct; and our passing of ethical judgments upon the conduct of others is merely an application to them of what we believe conscience would demand of us in the same circumstances. The question at issue, therefore, is a factual one of a kind which can only be answered by careful analysis of our own experience in the making of what we call moral judgments. It is the question whether there is anything in the experience of conscience or the sense of obligation which distinguishes it from the experience of an emotion or desire. Logical Positivists, who are usually experts in logical analysis, are convinced by their studies of our confused use of ethical language that there is no such distinction. The saints and sages, who have dwelt deeply on the analysis of their ethical experience, are convinced that there is.

The great majority of ordinary people, in spite of the confusions of language, agree on this point with the saints and sages. They speak of their experience of conscience and obligation as a "feeling" of guilt and a "sense" of obligation because these experiences are intimate and immediate, but they do not respond to these moral "feelings" in the same way as to others. This is shown in two ways. In the first place, they treat them with a respect not accorded to emotions generally. This peculiar respect is seen in the following fact. We regard it as a perfectly satisfactory solution for the problem created by any unpleasant emotion, simply to brush it aside and ignore it if we can—provided that it does not indicate an objective state of affairs which our interests require should be remedied. Yet there is something about a sense of obligation which convinces us that to brush it aside and ignore it is definitely not a satisfactory solution of the problem it creates—however unpleasant it may be and however sure we are that it can be ignored without adverse effect upon our other interests.

The second difference between the response to moral "feelings" and to emotions lies in the way in which we generalize the applications of the former. As Immanuel Kant pointed out, the ordinary person believes that whatever would constitute an obligation for one person would constitute an obligation for any other rational being in precisely the same situation. He believes this, not because he believes that the same situation would have the same effect upon everybody's feelings, but because he believes the objective situation can create an obligation for a rational being who observes it, independently of its effect upon his feelings. It may be the case that Logical Positivists and many other intellectuals do not believe this about obligations (though in their nonphilosophical activities they talk and behave as though they do), but the fact remains that saints and sages and ordinary people do believe it. This indicates that their sense of obligation seems to them to be something different from just another emotion.

It is this fact about the sense of obligation that has led intuitionists to say that moral principles are self-evident. This, as we have seen, is a mistake, but it does not follow that the emotive theory is therefore right. It is not the only alternative. The recognition of an obligation is not the recognition of something implied by a general principle. But neither is it merely a recognition of the existence of an emotion or of something required by emotions. It tends to produce certain typical states of feeling, but unless the vast majority of people are entirely deceived about it, the obligation recognized does not itself consist of emotions, nor does its existence chiefly depend upon the emotional states of the person subject to the obligation. In later chapters we shall find reason to believe that a moral obligation is a unique feature of the relational structure of the volitional life. In the next chapter we shall be engaged in showing the failure of attempts to explain moral experience without recognizing that its uniqueness is not merely that of a special kind of emotion, namely emotions of approval and disapproval.

To do this we must examine further the interpretations of ethical expressions offered by the emotive theory to see if they are in accord with the usage which people find intelligible in ethical discussion. For when people continuously use the same terms in talking about their experience, then, if those terms refer to facts of experience, they must fairly consistently refer to the same sort of facts or individuals would not understand one another. If the terms refer to no facts, but merely express emotions, then it must be the case that they feel the same emotions in thinking the same things about the same facts, or again there will be confusion and misunderstanding. According to the emotive theory, when people agree that a certain action is good or right, they are not agreeing about any fact that characterizes the action, though they usually mistakenly think they are. They are merely expressing similar emotions in referring to it. There is really no such factual character of actions as goodness or rightness in the sense implied.

The objection to this theory, however, is that people commonly go on to make, and agree upon, many statements about the goodness or rightness of the action which could not be true unless the goodness or rightness were a fact, and a fact independent of the approval or disapproval of the speakers. They commonly agree, for instance, that it is not their emotions of approval or disapproval that lead them to form the judgment that the action is right or wrong, good or bad. On the contrary, they agree, it is the recognition of certain facts about the action that first leads them to make up their minds, for example, that it is good; and the emotion of approval, they say, tends to follow upon formation of the judgment. If, for some reason, no such emotion were felt, it would not alter the fact expressed in the moral judgment. To say that an action is good is not merely to say "I approve of it." It implies that the action is judged worthy of approval.

Stevenson admits [8] that the statement "This is good" is more nearly approximated in its meaning by "This is worthy

[8] *Ibid.*, p. 107.

of approval," but he says this is merely because "worthy" adds an additional emotive force to the expression of approval. To say "X is worthy of approval," he says, is equivalent to saying "I approve of X's being approved by others." The objection to this analysis, however, may be seen when we try to translate the statement "I approve of X because X is worthy of approval." It would have to be interpreted as meaning "I approve of X because I approve of X's being approved by others"; but this is certainly not what the statement means. It is obvious, therefore, that when people say something is "worthy of approval" they mean to assert that it has some factual characters of the kind that normally evoke approval, characters of the kind they call "good." When a number of people, or a multitude of them, agree that an action is good, they agree that it has such factual characters and that their emotions of approval are merely a normal and appropriate response to recognition of the existence of such characters. The Logical Positivist analysis of the situation is thus seen to be contradicted by the common ethical convictions of mankind.

Another weakness in the emotive analysis of ethical statements is that it does not allow for certain distinctions of meaning to be found in the common-sense usage of the terms "right" and "good." Obviously, if these terms merely express approval, together with a demand that others also approve, there can be no distinction of meaning between them. Stevenson says that the only distinction is that idiomatic usage determines that "good" is applied to persons and things, while "right" is usually reserved for actions. However, even in regard to actions there is a distinction of usage between the terms "right" and "good" which indicates a distinction of meaning, i.e., a reference to distinct factual characters of the action described as "good" or "right." It is generally recognized that an action may be morally right though not morally good. Furthermore we recognize degrees of moral goodness but not of moral rightness; an action is either right or wrong. If a very rich man gives a large donation to a worthy cause from a motive of mere vulgar ostentation, his action is said to be morally right but not morally good; if two persons make the same donation, one giving only what he can well afford and the other making a genuine sacrifice for the relief of suffering, it is generally agreed that both actions are right and good but there is much more real moral goodness in the one than in the other.

This distinction of meaning between right and good is obviously not a distinction between one sort of emotion of approval and another. It is a distinction in the factual character of that which is approved. It indicates again that when we say that an action is morally good, we mean that it has a certain character (obviously connected with the motive) that is worthy of approval; and it also indicates that there is a large measure of agreement as to what this character is. It is evident, too, that when we say that an action is right we are forming a judgment about another character of the action, different from its motive, and that there is also a large measure of agreement as to this character.

The failure of Stevenson, Ayer, and other Positivists to distinguish between the right and the good is apparently due to the same confusion into which G. E. Moore and other intuitionists have fallen—the transfer by metonymy of the notion of "ought" from persons to things, in the form of the pseudo concept of "ought to exist." If we think of the term "good" as equivalent to "ought to exist," then, of course, it does not refer to any factual character of the thing said to be good. To say, with G. E. Moore, that freedom from consciousness of intense pain ought to exist, does not assert any factual character about such freedom. It is merely an indirect way of saying people in general ought to promote such freedom. Such a statement, made in this indirect and misleading way, is easily confused with a mere expression of personal approval and a demand that others also approve. When the term "good," interpreted as equivalent to "ought to exist," is applied to actions, it is true that it is almost equivalent to "right," which is used to designate the sort of action that ought to be done. This accounts for Stevenson's inability to see a distinction between the two terms other than the idiomatic practice of using "right" only to refer to actions. Thus the Positivistic confusion of the meanings of "right" and "good" is due to an inheritance from a false intuitionistic interpretation of "good." The same mistake accounts for the failure to see that both terms have a reference to factual characters of a psychological nature, not dependent upon the emotions of approval of the person using the term, but rather determining those emotions.

The result of this analysis of the development of ethical skepticism is therefore to show that in its extreme form, which identifies ethical judgments with mere expressions of individual feeling, it is not justified; neither is the attempt of ethical intuitionism to establish the universal validity of any system of moral principles. On the other hand we have to look for the foundation of morals in the nature and growth and interrelationship of human personalities. This foundation, it must be admitted, is obscure. The chief question here is whether ethical terms refer to any unique factors in our psychological makeup, or whether they can all be analyzed and defined in terms of feelings, desires, and so forth which are not distinctly ethical in their nature. The latter view is the one held by ethical naturalism and the claim is usually made for it that it is possible to analyze the moral life in such terms, and to deduce from this analysis ethical ideals as broad and high as those of religion at its best, and without the undue rigidity and dogmatism that often characterize the teaching of religion. It is this claim which we must now examine.

Chapter 3

THE FAILURES OF NATURALISTIC ETHICS

Naturalistic Method and Theory

The fundamental principle of contemporary naturalistic philosophy is that the methods of the natural sciences (including psychology and sociology) are the only reliable methods whereby man can discover truth regarding himself and the universe around him. This assumption we shall accept in this book as our own working principle,[1] but most naturalists go on to accept, as a corollary from this, a theory of the nature of man derived from biology which we shall find, as this study proceeds, fails to do justice to the moral life of human beings.

This biological theory of human nature conceives the feeling-striving processes found in living organisms as originating in (and merely developments of) organic reactions tending to restore the equilibrium of the organism when this has been disturbed, and perhaps also involving a tendency to continuous growth. All later developments of feeling-striving must therefore be explained as elaborations of reactions tending to self-preservation and self-expansion. If parental impulses or other animal drives seem to be an exception to this, they must be explained as specific tendencies developed by natural selection because of their value to the species. The organism is not usually, nowadays, regarded as functioning merely as a blind mechanism; but it

[1] It is the difference of subject matter and aim that distinguishes the two kinds of wisdom referred to in Chapter 2.

71

is maintained that its intelligent purposive striving serves only the satisfaction of its desires, and these all have their origin in those reactions whereby the organism maintains its ongoing and expanding life.

Most naturalists today, however, emphatically declare that this theory of human nature does not lead to a mere individualistic egoism in ethics or to a theory of totalitarianism and the will to power in politics. They point to the fact that human nature has been molded by the social environment as well as by animal drives and the blind forces of the physical world. They insist upon the importance of reason, science, and education in enlightening man concerning co-operative as well as competitive ways of attaining his ends. They repudiate the suggestion that the twentieth-century reaction to totalitarianism and barbarism is in any way due to a replacement of the religious by a naturalistic theory of man and the universe among intellectuals, and they claim that naturalistic philosophy can support an ethic which justifies even better than any religious philosophy the ideals of peace, freedom, brotherhood, and good will among men which are cherished in Christian and democratic society. Space forbids any attempt here to review all the varying forms of contemporary naturalistic ethics so we must content ourselves with the study of some typical examples. We shall start with two essays in *Naturalism and the Human Spirit*,[2] a volume written cooperatively to expound the teachings of the school and to defend it against the charge of failing to do justice to the spiritual nature of man.

[2] Y. H. Krikorian (ed.), *Naturalism and the Human Spirit* (New York: Columbia University Press, 1944).

SIDNEY HOOK AND THE NATURALISTIC DEFENSE
OF DEMOCRACY

In this volume, Sidney Hook undertakes a defense of democracy from the naturalistic point of view. He argues cogently that the most essential principle of democracy is that of equality, an equality of opportunity, relevant functions, and social participation. "This principle," he says, "is an ethical one." It "is not a *description* of fact about men's physical or intellectual natures. It is a *prescription* or policy for treating men. . . . It is not a demand for absolute equality of living conditions. . . . It demands that . . . no one should be deprived of necessities in order to provide others with luxuries." [3]

It is to be noted that an *ethical* principle, for Hook, is not a mere *description* of fact. It is a *prescription*, a demand. This is in harmony with the views of the great majority of moralists, from Kant to the Logical Positivists, such as C. L. Stevenson. The terms "ought" and "obligation" refer to some sort of *demand*. The question for naturalism, therefore, is whence does this demand arise and how may we distinguish a genuinely ethical demand from a nonethical or unethical one?

Hook rejects the view that ethical principles (or demands) are grounded in religion or metaphysics or in mere nonrational preference. They are, he says, hypotheses confirmable by methods of scientific inquiry into a distinct range of subject matter, namely, our evaluations. "A moral ideal is a prescription to act in . . . ways that will organize the human needs and wants involved so as to fulfil a set of other values which are postulated as binding in relation to the problem at hand" (page 57). These "other values" are

[3] *Ibid.*, p. 49.

simply other "desiderata" (page 59), but they are not *arbitrarily* postulated. They are brought to the situation as the result of prior experience and are examined and modified in the light of experience of all desiderata that appear to be relevant.

The source of the prescription or demand involved in the statement of an ethical principle is, therefore, found by Hook to lie in "values or desiderata." Apparently what he means is that each person's own desiderata, according as he understands them, make certain demands upon him, prescribing his lines of conduct; and a genuinely ethical demand is to be distinguished from a nonethical or unethical one by its being the result of careful inquiry into the relevant range of desiderata. These objects of desire, of course, need not manifest mere selfishness. The desires of every normal human being include a great deal of concern for the welfare of other people, and selfishness is commonly self-defeating. Hook's defense of democracy very clearly and cogently shows that there is value to every member of society in that recognition of the equal title of all to relevant consideration, which is democracy's guiding principle.

Later in this book we shall see reason to agree that the source of the ethical demand is within the self, but it is seriously misleading to find it merely in an enlightened understanding of one's own desires. The desires of most of us are so much affected by personal ambitions, individual and group rivalries, emotional fixations, and the overcultivation and undercultivation of our various propensities that we cannot assume that even omniscience would disclose that more (and the strongest) of our own desiderata can be realized by giving equal consideration to those of every one else involved. A ruling class or race can exploit the weak for centuries before any nemesis overtakes them; thus generation after generation may live and die in the enjoyment of a greater balance of their own preferred desiderata than they could possibly obtain under a system of equity.

Further, this theory that ethical principles are an expression of a demand issuing from an enlightened consideration of our own desiderata is contradicted by the form taken by ethical principles wherever they come to clear expression. The most elementary ones are negative. They prescribe, for example, that a man should not rob or murder his neighbors. They may make exceptions if this is the only way to avoid still greater evils, but they make no exceptions simply because he may be sure he can do it secretly and profit by it. The reason for the prohibition is not the effect of such behavior on the robber or murderer, but its effect upon his victim. The moral principle is concerned with preserving the desiderata of the *other person*, not with those of the one who contemplates the evil act. Personal moral conviction (however enlightened) likewise takes the form of a felt inner demand that certain rights of others should be respected, even when it seems that there would be a clear favorable balance accruing to one's own desiderata in breaking them.

In brief, the reason why we feel it is wrong to commit murder, cruelty, extortion, and the like is not because we see that these crimes are sure in the long run to be disadvantageous to the total desiderata of the person who commits them, but because we feel it wrong to seek fulfilment of our own desiderata at the cost of so much greater loss or positive evil to others. It may be, and I think it is, true that something in the self sets up an ethical prescription against such seeking of one's own advantage at the cost of others, but an analysis of one's own moral consciousness and of the expressions of the moral consciousness in great literature brings clear conviction that what sets up this prescription is certainly not merely a canny calculation that such treatment of one's fellows is after all not likely to realize the fullest range of one's own desiderata. One does not have to be an absolutist to affirm that some actions are wrong, even if they do bring a favorable balance of satisfied desires to the person who commits them.

But perhaps we misinterpret Mr. Hook. It may be that he finds the source of the ethical demand not in the desiderata of the person upon whom the demand is made but in those of the persons who would be affected by his action. There is, of course, an element of demand that tends to be manifest in all desiderata, i.e., the demand of the persons who have the desires that other people should comply with those desires. This being the case, some naturalists have identified the prescriptive element in ethical principles with the demands implicit in the desires of the community. This places the source of the ethical demand (the ought, or obligation) in the authority of the social group rather than in the structure and process of the self. In its crude form this would involve a relativism giving equal endorsement to the mores of every tribal, racial, religious, or other group; but it may be argued that these *expressed* demands of the group are not the real requirements for fulfilment of its genuine and most important desires—that scientific inquiry into the means of fulfiling these desires will issue in an enlightened set of ethical principles, objective and rationally based, yet tentative and relevant to the varying needs and changing situation of the group. Perhaps this is Mr. Hook's view.

There are, however, two serious objections to this interpretation. In the first place, there is no guarantee that full inquiry will show an ultimate harmony of interests, desires, or needs among the various and rival groups into which society is divided. It may really be the case that a policy of perfectly enlightened pursuit of their own desiderata may, for instance, lead some groups to maintain the power they now hold over others and use it to exploit them. If so, then the above analysis of the meaning of ethical statements would require an admission that in such a case the oppressive policy of that group is ethically right; for this interpretation of the element of demand (obligation) in an ethical principle as the demand implicit in the desiderata of the community does not (as presented by naturalists) offer any reason why the community considered should be inclusive of all persons affected, including strangers, rivals, and enemies, except in so far as they are able to enforce respect for their interests.

The second objection to this interpretation is even more fundamental. There is nothing in the interpretation to show why any one person should *recognize* any demand or prescription in the desiderata of any other person or group except when he is directly and altruistically interested in them, or when he can thereby serve his own interests indirectly, or when they can bring pressure upon him to heed their desires. This situation is frankly recognized by many naturalists, as it logically should be by all who locate the source of the ethical demand or prescription in the desiderata of the group or the other persons affected. Thus Moritz Schlick says:

"I ought to do something" never means anything but "Someone wants me to do it." And in fact the desire of another, directed upon me, is described as an ought only when that person is able to add pressure to his desire and thus to reward fulfillment and to punish neglect, or at least to point out the natural consequences of observance or neglect.[4]

This is the logical implication of the theory that the source of ethical prescription is in the desiderata of those who benefit by the prescription—unless we can point to

[4] Moritz Schlick, *Problems of Ethics* (New York: Prentice-Hall, Inc., 1939).

some other way in which the other person's desiderata become an ethical demand on us. Yet this logical implication
of the theory constitutes its refutation, for it is contrary to
the facts. It is not the case that "the desire of another,
directed upon me, is described as an ought only when that
person is able to add pressure to his desire. . . ." The moral
consciousness of mankind, wherever it has become reflective, analytical, and critical, is almost unanimous that the
sense of obligation makes its demands quite independently
of personal interest and social pressure and often directly
counter to them. It demands loyalty to principles seen to
be for the general human good, even where no pressure can
be brought to bear and where such loyalty involves some
sacrifice. Any theory which repudiates or undermines this
conception of obligation constitutes a surrender of the
hard-won ethical progress of mankind and an admission
that naturalism is unable to sustain the moral ideals
achieved by religion, and that is an admission that the
authors of *Naturalism and the Human Spirit* would be
very loath to make.

Abraham Edel and the Criticism of Choices

Hook's naturalistic defense of a single ethical principle
has illustrated the problems to be faced by a naturalistic
ethics. We find the same problems, with no better solutions, in Abraham Edel's analysis of general ethical theory
in the same volume.[5]

Edel is not quite as definite as Hook concerning the
prescriptive character of an ethical principle, but there is no
essential difference between them. He regards the statement
of an ethical rule, e.g., that "such and such is good," as "an

[5] Abraham Edel, "Naturalism and Ethical Theory," in *Naturalism and
the Human Spirit, op. cit.*, p. 65.

empirical proposition referring to the forms of choice in the conduct and reflection of some implicitly specified individual or group," but adds that "It preserves a normative character because it is a fact that men often guide themselves in present choice by the character of their previous acts of choice and the results of their reflection upon them" (page 71). "Ethical statements are normative to the person or group adopting them as rules of choice" (page 72).

Criticism of choices to decide what is genuinely good or normative proceeds, says Edel, in the light of two criteria. First, "any trend of choice can be criticized in the light of the consistency with the whole body of trends of choice of that individual or group," i.e., those making the choice. Secondly, there is the possibility of "extraneous criticism in the light of the trends of choice of some other individual or group than the one concerned" (page 72).

According to the first of these criteria, therefore, the normative element in an ethical statement (the element of prescription, of demand, of obligation) has its source in *something within the self* rather than in *some other person or group of persons*. Choices are to be critically decided by any individual by consideration of their consistency with "the whole body of trends of choice of that individual," which is certainly something within his self. Similarly, for a group, the criterion is consistency with the whole body of trends of choice established in the collective action of its members.

This is the same criterion (an enlightened view of one's own desiderata), the inadequacy of which we have already seen. The pride, prejudice, and rivalries of all too many individuals and groups is such that decisions made "in the light of the consistency with the whole body of trends of choice of that individual and group" will often be very unfair to other individuals and groups. Edel, however, seems to be clearly aware that this first criterion alone is inadequate. He, therefore, without any logical grounds in his theory, introduces a second line of criticism, namely, "extraneous criticism in the light of trends of choice of some other individual or group than the one concerned." Indeed, most of what he has to say about the criticism of values is based on this second criterion, simply *assuming* that the choices of every individual and group ought to be harmonized as far as possible with those of every other individual and group. He ends his essay with the fine sentiment that "In short, the naturalistic moral philosopher, estimating the values of his group or society, cannot stop short of fashioning a whole conception of good men functioning well in a good society" (page 95). It is evident that he would set no limits to this "good society," but intends it to embrace all the human race.

This universalistic principle of the Christian ethic, however, is one that naturalism has no right simply to *assume* as the initial *basis* of ethical criticism. It is denied by egoists, class theorists, racialists, and nationalists; and it is called in question by positivists and others. The fundamental questions for a naturalistic ethics are these: (1) If the source of the "ought" (of norm, prescription, or demand) in an ethical statement is in the self of the person accepting the statement, then how does his self require of him that he should favorably consider the desiderata and needs of other people *even in many cases where his own desiderata are, on the whole, not served thereby?* (2) If the source of the "ought" is in the desiderata and needs of other people, then how do the needs and desiderata of one person or group set up an ethical demand or obligation for favorable consideration by another, *even in many cases where the desiderata of that other are, on the whole, not served by responding to that demand?*

The crux of these questions is in the "even" clause at the end of each of them. We cannot deny that there are obligations to give favorable consideration to the needs and desiderata of others even in many cases where our own desiderata are, on the whole, not served thereby, for every attempt to do so is either logically or ethically disastrous. If we admit that such cases exist, then it is ethically disastrous to deny the obligation. It is to admit that naturalism cannot sustain or defend the type of moral idealism which is characteristic of religion at its best and which is sorely needed in every society. It is to deny that there is any obligation save that of a prudent regard for one's own desiderata. If, on the other hand, we deny that there are such cases, then our position becomes logically untenable. Either we must affirm that man's altruistic desire for the welfare of all other people is so basic and strong that there can be no cases where a man's own desiderata are not, on the whole, served by giving favorable consideration to the needs and desiderata of all others affected by his actions; or else we must affirm that there is such poetic justice in the world order that no person can ever better promote his own desiderata, on the whole, by refusing to give favorable consideration to the needs and desiderata of others. Naturalism must admit that there is no real evidence for either of these affirmations.

DAVID HUME AND M. C. OTTO

These arguments urged against Hook and Edel could be turned with equal force against other naturalistic writers, such as F. C. Sharp [6] and W. T. Stace,[7] who attempt to de-

[6] Cf. *Ethics* (New York: Century Co., 1928).
[7] Cf. *The Concept of Morals* (New York: The Macmillan Co., 1937). For a criticism of these two writers by the author, see *A Realistic Philosophy of Religion* (New York: Harper & Bros., 1942).

fend a universalistic utilitarian ethic by arguing that the
individual concerned with his own welfare must act in accord with the public welfare also. Naturalists who seek to
maintain this position might well be reminded of the caution of that greatest of all naturalistic philosophers, David
Hume, when dealing with this question.

Hume believed that there is a tendency to general benevolence in man, and he argued strongly and specifically that
man tends to find pleasure in the contemplation of any
action, by any person, which is useful to that person himself or to others. This, he thought, is the basis of all moral
judgment. However, he was too clearheaded to contend
that public welfare and private interest must always har-
monize, without exception. "A sensible knave, in particular
incidents, may think that an act of iniquity or infidelity
will make a considerable addition to his fortune without
causing any considerable breach in the social union and
confederacy." If anyone takes this stand, Hume admits it
would be "a little difficult" to provide an adequate answer.
His only reply is to say that "in all ingenuous natures the
antipathy to treachery and roguery is too strong to be coun-
terbalanced by any views of profit or pecuniary advantage." [8] Hume's argument, therefore, amounts to no more
than a claim that most people are reasonably honest and
humane, and that if a person is so, he will not enjoy doing
things that are the reverse; at the same time he admits that
an intelligent rogue may commit injustice and enjoy the
fruits of it if he can do so with security.

This, certainly, is an altogether inadequate basis for an
ethics of universal good will. Yet a search of the literature
does not reveal any contemporary naturalist who has been
able to say more, and, unfortunately, Hume's reluctant ad-

[8] David Hume, *Inquiry Concerning the Principles of Morals* (Open
Court Edition) chap. ix, pp. 122-23.

mission concerning the "sensible knave" is all too often forgotten. Disciples of John Dewey, in particular, with much less caution than their master, often naïvely combine an advocacy of individualistic freedom in the pursuit of private happiness with a preaching of earnest concern for general social welfare. Apparently, in the warmth of their own social enthusiasms, they find it difficult to believe that any "sensible knave" can really be happy in enjoying the fruits of injustice.

One of the most persuasive writers of this type is M. C. Otto. In one of his most highly regarded essays,[9] he writes: "The goal of life, to put it in a word, is happiness. . . . At bottom the difference between the moral and the immoral or nonmoral attitude is the presence in the former, and its absence from the latter, of scrutiny and appraisal of desires with regard to their effect upon what was just called all-over satisfactoriness." He rejects emphatically the statement of Alexander Meiklejohn that "Many things are worse than unhappiness. But nothing is worse than being contemptible." And he quotes with approval the reply of a student who wrote: "Many things are worse than being contemptible. But nothing is worse than being unhappy. The worst thing about being contemptible is that it makes you so damn unhappy."

So Hume's "sensible knave" who could do things contemptible and happily enjoy the resulting profits, is forgotten. Forgotten, too, is the fact that it does not make a person unhappy to do what is contemptible unless that person first judges the action as contemptible. An act of injustice or spite will not be condemned as contemptible, by the person who commits it, if he applies Otto's criterion and finds its effects manifest what to him is an "over-all satis-

[9] "Scientific Humanism," *The Antioch Review* (Winter, 1943). Reprinted in *Science and the Moral Life* (New York: Mentor Books, 1949).

factoriness." The reference to the so-called "sanctions of conscience," as one of the factors affecting happiness, thus involves this "Scientific Humanism" in a simple fallacy of begging the question.

The naïveté of Otto's genial faith that the intelligent pursuit of happiness must always lead through the paths of justice is also shown in his confidence in what he calls the technique of "creative bargaining" [10] as a method of resolving human conflicts. The essence of this technique is to discover a way in which the underlying purposes at issue on both sides can be achieved, even though the specific form in which those purposes were first cast has to be abandoned. There is no doubt that this can often be done. Persons who have fought each other over an economic issue, for instance, can often be shown that by cooperating instead of fighting they can both get even more than either had at first hoped to obtain by the conflict; but to assume that there is always such a solution for every conflict of desires, even when those desires have been toned down by an examination of their "all-over satisfactoriness," is simply to forget the nature of human desire and the hard facts of life. The places of prestige and power which attract vigorous minds are, by their very nature, exclusive. Ambitions are essentially competitive. Human conflict grows fiercest, not over the things which all can enjoy together, but over those things the value of which is enhanced by their scarcity. Furthermore, human attitudes are often too fixed and human minds too unadjustable to be turned from their set desires, even toward something which really better fulfils their underlying purpose. In the impasses thus created there is no solution in which both can find happiness. It is then that the pursuit of happiness leads each party, by subtilty or by sheer

[10] See M. C. Otto, *The Human Enterprise* (New York: Appleton-Century-Crofts, 1945), chap. iii.

assertion of power, to do that which is contemptible—unless, by some standard other than the pursuit of private happiness, they have learned to recognize the contemptible for what it is and firmly put it from them.

Ralph Barton Perry and the Interest Theory of Value

Many naturalists, today, are keenly aware of the weakness of the sort of arguments we have been considering. For this reason, there is, at the present time, a widespread tendency among them to surrender the attempt to provide an objective basis for ethics. The Positivists, as we have seen, are declaring ethical statements to be mere expressions of emotion. Others are content to say that ethics must find its basis in mere postulates, adopted by an individual or group. Others, again, insist that there is no meaning to moral judgments outside a reference to the customs and demands of a particular social group. All these positions, of course, involve a surrender of the claim of naturalism to provide objective support for ethical ideals adequate to replace those of the great religions. On the other hand, the maintenance of such ideals as a basis for democratic equality of rights is recognized as so important that many naturalists still cling to formulations of objective naturalistic ethics put forward in the early part of the present century. It is therefore necessary for us to examine such of these as are still most influential.

One of the most notable of these is that of Ralph Barton Perry.[11] He defines a value as "any object of any interest," and then argues that we can obtain an objective measure of the value of any object simply by examining the extent of

[11] Cf. R. B. Perry, *A General Theory of Value* (New York: Longmans, Green & Co., Inc., 1926).

the interest taken in it. We may pass over difficulties in doing this arising from the incorrectness of the judgments involved in some interests and from the incommensurability of the intensity and preference of different interests. We can take the simple case of two objects of interest, where all the interests involved are correctly based and have equal preferential status and intensity. Then, says Perry, the object of the greater number of interests has greater value than the other, whether these are interests of different persons or different interests of the same person. If A is an object of interest to Peter only, and B is an object of similar interest to both Peter and Paul, then B has greater value than A.

The triviality of the conclusion derived from this way of stating the matter appears, however, when we ask the question "Greater value to whom?" Then we discover that B does not have greater value to Peter simply because Paul also has an interest in it; it only does so if Peter has an interest in Paul's interests. If he does, however, says Perry, then B acquires an increment of value for Peter. It is, first, a direct object of his own interest; and, second, it is an indirect object of his interest, through his interest in Paul's interest. Thus, by acquiring an interest in the development and satisfaction of other people's interests, we can make the values of their lives our own. Thus by love of our fellow men, we share their values and enrich the values of our own lives; and this is better far than competing with them and destroying their values simply to save our own. An "all-benevolent will" would thus acquire the values of all other persons whose interests were known, and it would attain for itself the greatest possible richness of values. Alas! says Perry, none of us attains to this desirable state of benevolence; but it is clearly the path of wisdom to cultivate it as far as we can. In any case it has been shown that there is no incompatibility between seeking the greatest possible

range of values for oneself and also seeking them for everyone else.

It may be agreed that, granting his definition of value,
Perry has shown this. He has shown that "it is more blessed
to give than to receive"—if one loves the one to whom one
gives, more than one loves the satisfaction of one's other
interests. He has shown that the person who possesses an
"all-benevolent will" could find happiness in keeping the
golden rule. But he has, perforce, to admit that most people do not have an all-benevolent will and have no real
chance of developing it; indeed, for most of us it is only
toward a very limited range of people that we can develop
such an interest in their interests that we can obtain as
much satisfaction from the satisfaction of their interests as
we can from the direct satisfaction of our own. Perry's
analysis of value, therefore, provides no ground for saying
that an enlightened view of an individual's own interests
will always direct him to do that which seems to him most
conducive to the best interests of all concerned.[12]

JOHN DEWEY: THE GOOD AND THE RIGHT

Probably the most influential of all the supporters of naturalistic ethics has been John Dewey. The principal theme
of his voluminous writings throughout his long life has been
the contention that objective criteria of moral values can be
established by the methods of scientific examination of
natural phenomena, broadly conceived. His analysis of
human motivation insists upon the interpretation of the
volitional life as a continuum of means and ends. There are
no fixed ends, no final goals, no intrinsic goods, but each

[12] For a criticism of DeWitt Parker's variant of the interest theory of
value, see A. C. Garnett, *Reality and Value* (New Haven: Yale University
Press, 1937), chap. viii.

desire pursues its end-in-view, which in turn becomes means to another. Every problem is, in the last analysis, simply the problem of how life may go on—developing itself in richness of experience and power to solve its further problems. A good choice is the one that, in the circumstances, serves the most inclusive range of desires, avoiding the defeat of life by adverse circumstances and avoiding self-defeat resulting from the cultivation of incompatible desires. The interests thus served are always, of course, the interests of a particular self, but Dewey insists emphatically that they are not merely interests *in* the individual self. Man is a social animal. He is dependent upon the cooperation of others at almost every point, and his desires and aims are for the most part a reflection of the aims and desires of the society in which he has grown up. His satisfactions have, therefore, to be sought chiefly in cooperation, rather than in competition, with the other members of his social group. His happiness is bound up with theirs, and his moral conscience is a reflection of their expressions of approval and disapproval.

Dewey's clearest statement on the distinctive nature of "good" and "right" is to be found in the 1932 edition of his *Ethics*.[13] Here we find the succinct assertion that "the Good is that which satisfies want, craving, which fulfills or makes complete the need which stirs to action" (pages 204-5). This, however, needs qualifications which are stated as follows:

Not every satisfaction of appetite and craving turns out to be a good (p. 205). Impulse and desire . . . become evil in contrast with another desire whose object includes more inclusive and more enduring consequences (p. 201). There is, accordingly, a conflict brought about within the self . . . between two objects present in thought, one corresponding to a want or appetite just as it presents

[13] John Dewey and James H. Tufts, *Ethics* (New York: Henry Holt & Co., 1932).

itself in isolation, the other corresponding to the want thought of in relation to other wants (p. 200). Wisdom . . . is the ability to foresee consequences in such a way that we form ends which grow into one another and reinforce one another. Moral folly . . . is snatching at one satisfaction in a way which prevents us from having others and which gets us subsequently into trouble and dissatisfaction (p. 288).

The moral problem, as thus presented, is the problem of how to get for one's self the most inclusive range of satisfactions and the least dissatisfactions within the span of one's life. The welfare of other people is, thus far, an object of ethical consideration only in so far as one happens to have a direct interest in their welfare and so can find immediate satisfaction in achieving or contemplating it, or in so far as it is an indirect means to satisfaction of some of one's other wants.

There are, furthermore, two subtle dangers in Dewey's analysis of the moral situation which he fails to see. The first lies in the analysis of every problem of choice as fundamentally a problem of how life may go on. The solution of the problem comes thus to be depicted as the acquiring of power, the securing of control of the means which make it possible to do what one wants to do. The aim of life is simply "to get on in life"; and to get on in life means merely to acquire more power. This interpretation of human motivation is not much improved by emphasis on the fact that specific desires are, for the most part, shaped by group influence to conform to those of the social group; for the group that shapes our desires is always a narrow group—family, class, nation, and race. The pursuit of individual power is thus transformed into the pursuit of group power. Power for life to go on is still presented as the ultimate goal. This is a consequence far from what Dewey intended, but it is the conclusion which issues logically from his analysis of the roots of human values.

The second danger in Dewey's analysis arises in what he has to say about "right."

Right is only an abstract name for the multitude of concrete demands in action which others impress upon us, and of which we are obliged, if we would live, to take some account. Its authority is the exigency of their demands, the efficacy of their insistencies. There may be good ground for the contention that in theory the idea of the right is subordinate to that of the good, being a statement of the course proper to attain good. But in fact it signifies the totality of the social pressures exercised upon us to induce us to think and desire in certain ways.[14]

This insistence that, in practice, might makes right is not intended by Dewey to be accepted as final. It is rather a part of his argument in rejection of the authority of all standards of conduct, leaving the individual free to pursue whatever he finds good, as opportunity offers; but such a repudiation of specific principles, taken in conjunction with an interpretation of human good as the acquirement of power by the individual to obtain the widest range of satisfaction of his desires, is full of dangerous possibilities. And, when allied with the conception that the individual can best seek such power by participating in the common pursuit of it by his group, the conception of right as being in practice but another name for what the group demands becomes still more insidious.

These consequences are far from what Dewey himself sees in his analysis; but they are, nevertheless, its logical outcome. Writing in 1922, the danger of such implications was not as clear as it later became. Perhaps it was the effect of the portents of totalitarianism that induced Dewey to make

[14] John Dewey, *Human Nature and Conduct* (New York: Henry Holt & Co., 1922), p. 326.

a new statement concerning the "right" in the 1932 revision of his *Ethics*. It is a revision, however, which succeeds in improving the ethical content of the concept only at the cost of the logical consistency of his argument.

> The *concept of Rightness*, in many cases, is independent of the concept of satisfaction and good . . . introduces an element which is quite outside that of the good. This element is that of *exaction, demand* (p. 234). The Good is that which attracts; the Right is that which asserts that we *ought* to be drawn by some object whether we are naturally attracted to it or not (p. 235). Right, law, duty, arise from the relations which human beings intimately sustain to one another, and . . . their authoritative force springs from the very nature of the relation that binds people together (pp. 237-38). Any *particular* claim is open to examination and criticism. . . . A criterion for the rightness of particular laws and obligations has to be found. The essence of the claim which Right puts forth is that *even if the thing exacted does not appeal as his good to the one to whom it is addressed,* [italics ours] he should voluntarily take it to be a good (p. 250).[15]

This states the issue clearly. The transition from the notion of Good to the notion of Right is presented as a transfer from consideration of how best to achieve one's own satisfaction to that of obligations or demands which *may* conflict with one's own good thus conceived. The ethical claim or demand comes from other persons, from the social group. This raises the crucial questions. Which of their claims are right, and why should I accede to them if they differ from those of my own most inclusive and permanent desires? Dewey's answer is a very instructive case of begging the question.

> The person upon whom the duty is laid, himself makes claims upon others. . . . If the claim is, then, of the kind which he himself puts forth, if it serves a good which he prizes for himself, he must,

[15] John Dewey and James H. Tufts, *Ethics* (rev. ed.; New York: Henry Holt & Co., 1932).

in the degree in which he is fair-minded [italics ours] acknowledge it to be a common good, and hence binding upon his judgment and action (p. 251).[16]

Thus from the *fact* that a certain claim or demand which others make on me is of the same sort as I make on them, the argument passes to the *ethical* judgment that I "should" or "ought" to acknowledge this claim, that it is "right." It is true, as Dewey points out, that this is in accord with the "principle of reciprocity" (page 252), but by what intuition does our leading naturalistic empiricist claim to see that reciprocal acknowledgment of claims is a moral obligation? He tells us that a man must acknowledge it "in the degree in which he is fair-minded," but if "fair-minded" merely means "inclined to grant reciprocity to others in claims made upon them," then by what intuition do we see that all men *ought* to be so inclined? On the other hand, if "fair-minded" means "ethically just or right," then by what intuition do we see that the principle of reciprocity is one to which all men *ought* to adhere?

Obviously the argument begs the question. Dewey's attempt to pass from what is desired to what ought to be desired is no more successful than that of John Stuart Mill whose fallacies at this point in his "proof of Utilitarianism" are favorite examples in almost every logic textbook. It is strange, but not without significance, that both these brilliant logicians of the empirical tradition should have fallen into simple logical fallacies in seeking to defend their genuine and praiseworthy ethical convictions.

There must be a reason why keen and logical minds become insufficiently critical of their grounds when considering a basic ethical principle of the kind that wins almost universal assent among thoughtful people, such as the principles of reciprocity, impartiality, and the common good;

[16] *Op. cit.*

the reason would appear to be the same as that which has persuaded so many thinkers that such principles are intuitively given or self-evident. The explanation, I suggest, can be found in recognition of the fact that when civilized human beings reflect on those closely related phases of experience we commonly call "the sense of value" and "the sense of obligation," they *tend* to experience a distinctive sort of *constraint*, not quite the same as a desire, to direct or adjust their conduct to whatever appear to them to be the conditions of general human welfare. This is only a tendency. It is not felt unless we reflect, and it is all too easily obscured or repressed by special interests, emotions, and prejudices.

I think that all readers of this book will agree that they have this experience. Moral philosophers tend to experience it strongly because they reflect a great deal on these matters; and the result is seen in the trend of their writings toward ethical universalism. Among naturalists this "sense of obligation" is generally ascribed to social conditioning, which deprives it of most of its ethical significance. It may be questioned, however, whether this explanation adequately accounts for the universality and persistence of the experience and its historic tendency to issue in universalistic and absolute ethical judgments. Probably the ablest and most thorough attempt to explain away these difficulties of the interpretation in terms of social conditioning is that of G. H. Mead.

G. H. MEAD: THE SOCIAL THEORY OF MIND

Mead has been the principal influence in developing what is today called the social theory of mind, a theory which insists most strongly on the influence of society in shaping the mind of the individual. The moral conscience, according to this view, is a reflection in the individual of the reactions of society. But we will let Mead state his own theory.[17]

The organized community or social group which gives to the individual his unity of self may be called "the generalized other." The attitude of the generalized other is the attitude of the whole community. . . . Only by taking the attitude of the generalized other toward himself . . . can the individual think at all; for only thus can thinking—or the internalized conversation of gestures which constitutes thinking—occur. . . . The self-conscious human individual, then, takes or assumes the organized social attitudes of the given social group or community (or of some one section thereof) to which he belongs, toward the social problems of various kinds which confront that group or community at any given time (pp. 154-56).

Ethical ideas, within any given human society, arise in the consciousness of the individual members of that society from the fact of the common social dependence of all those individuals upon one another. . . . Every human individual must, to behave ethically, integrate himself with the pattern of organized social behavior which, as reflected or prehended in the structure of the self, makes him a self-conscious personality (p. 319).

It should be noted that this interpretation of the source of the ethical demand derives it from both something within the self and the demands of society. The self is an entity so constructed in interaction with society that the social demands have entered into its own structure and are felt by the individual as arising from within himself, not merely from the social group. This saves Mead's theory from attack with the semantic weapon which points out that the demand of conscience cannot simply be identified with social demand because "I ought to do that" does not have the same meaning as "Society demands of me that I do that." Mead also avoids the identification of moral obli-

[17] Quotations are from G. H. Mead, *Mind, Self and Society* (Chicago: University of Chicago Press, 1934).

gation with the most inclusive interests of the person, for
the moral demand is interpreted as a reflection of the social
demand which the individual has made his own by a process
of unintentional absorption. He has learned the nature of
the demands, felt himself subjected to them, echoed them
and joined in impressing them on others until they have
become a part of himself. He does not merely endorse them
as a means to his own long-run and inclusive interests. He
does not feel that this is the reason why he accepts them
and must obey them. Such arguments in support of them
are an afterthought, a rationalization and a defense of demands that he feels within himself he knows not why; he
feels these demands even when they run counter to what
he believes to be his own most inclusive interests. It is only
the social psychologist who can see that their real origin
and source are the demands of the social group in which he
has been brought up, the group whose thought has entered
into the structure of thought of all its members.

The social psychologist who thus explains the origin of
the sense of obligation feels that he is performing a valuable
social service in emancipating humanity from the trammels
of outworn ethical creeds. He assumes that when people
clearly recognize that a specific ethical principle, such as
that of an unbreakable marriage bond or sacred right of private property, has its origin merely in the specific demands
of a specific community in a specific period, they will cease
to think of such principles as having general and absolute
validity and will be free to reshape the social demands and
laws in more suitable form. Strangely enough, most of
those who use this explanation of the sense of obligation as
a weapon in a campaign against moral absolutists do not
expect their hearers to carry the theory to its logical conclusion and repudiate the whole idea of any obligation of one
person to another, or of the individual to society. They

suggest, instead, that all traditional moral principles should be critically examined in the light of their effects on the community, and that those found generally beneficial (such as impartial justice and freedom of speech) should be retained. And, strange to say, this salutary but utterly illogical reaction is the commonest effect, at least in our American society, of the growth of the idea that the sense of obligation is due to social conditioning.

Now it is certainly true that any belief that is merely due to social conditioning will tend to be undermined (and its emotional effect diminished or lost) by growth of the knowledge and belief that this is the true explanation of its origin. So we may take it as indicated that those features of common moral conviction that plainly tend to be undermined by the belief that all moral conviction is due to social conditioning are really due to it, and those features of moral conditioning which tend to resist this undermining influence are not due to social conditioning. This would indicate that *specific* moral principles (such as the prohibitions against theft, manslaughter, adultery, and the like), and the sense of obligation to adhere to them as moral absolutes, are due to social conditioning; but the general conviction that one has an obligation to his fellows to consider and respect impartially the conditions of their welfare is not. For the explanation of this we must look deeper.

Furthermore, it becomes clear that the specific injunctions, and the sense of obligation attached to them, are only partly due to social conditioning. They are adopted as special cases of, or means to, the fulfilment of the general obligation to respect the conditions of general welfare. Social conditioning has merely inculcated the conviction that this is the case, and the sense of obligation attaches itself to them as part of the general obligation. To shake the conviction of their validity, it is necessary not merely to show that they have been adopted merely as an effect of social conditioning, but also that in their effects they run counter to the general obligation to promote human welfare.

Our American society is so pregnant with the spirit of democratic ethical universalism and social meliorism that the full logical implications of the theory that the moral conscience is basically an effect of social conditioning have not been widely adopted in the minds of those students of the social sciences who have accepted the theory. In nondemocratic and less pragmatically minded countries, however, the logic of this conception has been more fully recognized and more effective. Its various presentations (usually less penetrating and guarded than Mead's) have been a commonplace of the naturalistic outlook for half a century or more. The logical outcome of the theory is a complete rejection of the validity of all moral principles, except so far as the society that has impinged them upon us exerts pressure enough to arouse our enthusiasm or compel our compliance. In this situation the more universalistic ideals are the first to go. The pressure and call of race, class, and nation is acceded to as inescapable. What is left of the ethical life thus becomes an acceptance of the demands of the narrow group. The broader sense of obligation to respect the general human welfare is repressed, and the repression creates a certain fanaticism in loyalty to the narrower conception of the moral life.

The practical effects of adoption of the theory that moral conviction is basically an effect of social conditioning are, therefore, not what one should expect if it were true. This indicates that the theory is false; and we have also seen that it is dangerous. The plausibility of the theory and its limited value as an argument against making absolutes of specific rules of conduct are due to the fact that it does constitute an explanation of how such specific rules come to be regarded as morally absolute, instead of being recognized as subordinate to the general principle of respect and concern for the conditions of human welfare.

Social Theory of Mind and the Sense of Obligation

A further criticism of the theory, however, may be developed by showing that it is theoretically inadequate to explain the phenomena of the moral consciousness as manifested in ethical history. The conspicuous feature of that history is the ethical advance from primitive tribalism, with its limited range of duties to the members of a limited group, to that ethical universalism which knows no boundaries of nation, race, class, or creed and calls for a high devotion which counts no personal sacrifice too great provided that it is genuinely needed for the greater good of the whole. If the sense of obligation is a reflection within the individual mind of demands made by the social group, then how has this advance occurred? For it is certain that the new moral ideas have, in general, arisen first in the minds of individuals who have felt themselves bound by them and called to expound them to a society at first unaffected by them and even hostile to them. The prophets of new and higher moral ideals, so far from echoing the group mind, have all too often been persecuted, stoned, or crucified for their opposition to it. Further, since the groups that shape the individual mind are always narrow groups (family, local community, tribe, nation, class, race, etc.), and since the groups are often antagonistic to other groups, it is natural that they should impinge upon the minds of their members an ethic of narrow loyalties and a spirit of contest and rivalry. How, then, is this overcome in such a way that ethical thought tends increasingly to condemn the pride and selfish-

ness of the group and teach impartiality and an equal concern for the good of all? Thus the first question concerns
the tendency of individuals to rise above the group ethic.
The second concerns the tendency of ethical thought to expand beyond and in opposition to the interest of the group
which is supposed to have shaped its demands.

Mead's answer to the first question is that individuals
rise above the inherited ethic of the group by working out
more fully and more logically what is already implied in the
principles and institutions endorsed by the group.

> The attitudes involved are gathered from the group, but the
> individual in whom they are organized has the opportunity of giv-
> ing them an expression which perhaps has never taken place before.
> (p. 198).
>
> An individual of the type to which we are referring arises always
> with reference to a form of society or social order which is implied
> but not actually expressed. Take the religious genius, such as Jesus
> or Buddha, or the reflective type such as Socrates. What has given
> them their unique importance is that they have taken the attitude
> of living with reference to a larger society. That larger state was one
> which was already more or less implied in the institutions of the
> community in which they lived. Such an individual is divergent
> from the point of view of what we would call the prejudices of the
> community; but in another sense *he expresses the principles of the
> community more completely than any other* [italics ours, p. 217].
>
> Jesus generalized the conception of the community in terms of
> the family in such a statement as that of the neighbor in the para-
> bles (p. 216).[18]

Thus it is argued that the prophet or philosopher who
teaches a new and higher moral principle is never really
contradicting the true meaning of those obligations which
his mind has absorbed from his community. He is merely
working out more fully and logically what is already implied
in those obligations. If this were so, it would explain the

[18] Quotations from *Ibid.*

conscience of the moral innovator in harmony with the theory that, basically, the sense of obligation is always produced by social conditioning. But is it always so? Let us look more closely at Mead's own example. Is the principle that one ought to love one's neighbor, and even one's enemy, logically implied by the principle that one ought to love the members of one's own family? Obviously not. Is the concept of the "larger state" or world community implicit in that of the Greek city state? Certainly not. The family is one group, with certain relations established between its members and demanding the fulfilment of certain obligations by those members according to their status. The state is a wider and different group, its members sustaining a different set of obligations and different relations. The world community is not an organic group at all, but a set of more or less interdependent and more or less rival groups. There is no logical argument, but only a false analogy, in the contention that the duties which hold among the members of the one group should also hold among the members of the other. What Mead's thesis really suggests is that the ethical advance of mankind from acceptance of a limited range of specific obligations to members of the same family and tribe to a universalistic ethic is the effect of an ever increasing acceptance of a very obvious logical fallacy.

But if it is not to be explained as reasoning by analogy, why is it that such metaphors as that of the brotherhood of man have made such a wide ethical appeal? Not because the acceptance of the narrower institution (the family) is logically seen to imply that the relations and attitudes recognized as appropriate within it must also be appropriate in the larger institution, but, rather, because the response to the thought of human need demanded of us by something within the self is essentially the same whether that person in need be a brother or a stranger. It is first recognized in the case of the brother because the needs of those so close to us are first and most commonly and strongly called to out attention. But when we do, at length, think of the stranger's need, we see that essentially the same response is demanded.

Some may be inclined to argue, in defense of Mead, that the reason why something within the self demands of us that we make helpful responses to human need wherever it is found is because this principle has been inculcated by the family and the local community in relation to its own members, and thoughtful persons, seeing the stranger and enemy also in need, apply the same principle to him. This, however, is to misunderstand the nature of such principles of obligation as operate among primitive peoples. They do not inculcate a duty to man as man, a duty to relieve suffering as suffering, but a duty to brother, kinsman, tribesman, *et al.* And they equally emphatically inculcate duties to support kinsman and tribesman *against* their rivals. "Thou shalt love thy neighbour and hate thine enemy." Duties are specific and limited in regard to the persons to whom they apply. It is this that makes it impossible for ethical universalism to have arisen by any *logical* explication of the notions of obligation implicit in the institutions of primitive man. From the obligation to love one's neighbor and one's kinsman there is no logical transition to the idea of an obligation to love the foreigner or enemy.

Mead, therefore, has failed to explain the emergence of the moral innovator in terms of his theory of conscience as basically a product of social conditioning. Can he do any better with the second question, which concerns the tendency of ethical thought to expand beyond and in opposition to the interests of the group which is supposed to have shaped its demands? His explanation here bases itself on the fact that communities which have at one stage had, or recognized, no common interests, and have therefore shaped their mores without concern for one another, often grow to discover or develop common interests and thus learn to reconstruct their moral principles and social order with a wider scope of concern for the common good.

Any such social reconstruction, if it is to be at all far-reaching, presupposes a basis of common social interests shared by all the individual members of the given human society in which that reconstruction occurs; shared, that is, by all the individuals whose minds must participate in, or whose minds bring about, that reconstruction. And the way in which any such social reconstruction is actually affected by the minds of the individuals involved is by a more or less abstract intellectual extension of the boundaries of the given society to which these individuals all belong, and which is undergoing reconstruction—an extension resulting in a larger social whole in terms of which the social conflicts that necessitate the reconstruction of the given society are harmonized or reconciled and by reference to which, accordingly, these conflicts can be solved or eliminated (p. 308).

The question whether we belong to a larger community is answered in terms of whether our own action calls out a response in this wider community, and whether its response is reflected back into our own conduct (p. 271).[19]

Thus Mead, consistently with his theory, urges that common interests and reciprocal interaction between the members of a wider community must actually exist in fact before they can issue in a social demand for appropriate behavioral response and before these demands impress themselves in acceptance of a new set of moral rules and institutions which eliminate the old conflicts. The extension of the abstract idea of the community is a consequence and effect of the growth of community of interests in fact. In illustration, he points to the way in which modern nations are

[19] All quotations are from G. H. Mead, *Mind, Self and Society* (Chicago: University of Chicago Press, 1934).

gradually coming to recognize a system of international institutions because the facts of economic and political life have already created a certain world community of interests.

The actual history of the development of ethical ideas, however, refutes this theory that they grow to recognize obligations only after the actual development of common interests. The fact is that the great ethical religions made the outward leap to assert obligations of universal good will far ahead of the development of any community of interests. They continuously assert that man's obligation to his fellows is quite independent of the question whether his own interests are in any way bound up with their welfare, and these obligations are just as clearly felt as those where duty and self-interest are conjoined.

This idea of an equal and universal obligation to respect the conditions of welfare of all mankind is, of course, given logical support by the concept of a universal deity. It may have been, and probably was, that concept that first suggested that even the complete stranger and one's enemy should be an object of good will; but it is certainly true that acceptance of this ethical universalism and the feeling of the obligations it entails is not merely a product of, and not entirely dependent upon, such theological belief. The best in the ethics of the high religions is still accepted by many who have given up the theology. It is thus neither universalistic theology nor an actual universal system of common interests creating an embryo universal community that accounts for the emergence of universalism in ethics. For an explanation of it we shall have to look for something deep-rooted within the self that is more widespread than either ethical monotheism or the recognition of a world community of interests.

The social theory of mind therefore fails to explain the

presence and operation of that distinct feeling of constraint to concern one's self impartially with the general welfare which is characteristic of the developed moral consciousness. We must therefore seek its explanation in some other interpretation of mental life. That is the major task of this book: but before we turn to it we will do well to devote a chapter to clearing up the existing confusion in the use of ethical terms which we have already seen to be the root of much fallacious ethical thinking.

Chapter 4

THE PLAGUE OF SEMANTIC CONFUSION

THE SIGNIFICANCE OF AGREEMENT AND DISAGREEMENT

Perhaps the most remarkable thing about all this philo-sophic diversity and skepticism is that, in spite of it, there is so much agreement about practical questions of human values and obligations. There are some important differ-ences in the evaluation of ends between the judgments of primitive man and civilized man, but relatively few among civilized men themselves—and such as there are are chiefly due to the surviving influence of primitive tribalism and superstition. There are important differences among civi-lized men as to the best means of pursuing commonly acknowledged ends—and these differences lead to support of different institutions and laws—but there is much less difference in the evaluation of the ends themselves. In practical judgments of value, therefore, agreement is much more in evidence than difference; but in the theory of value, the situation is reversed. Our disagreements are not so much as to the ends we ought to aim at, as about why we ought to aim at them.

This situation indicates that there needs must be some common elements in our experience of value and obligation, or such practical agreement could not be maintained. The ethical inquiry is therefore not the pursuit of a subjective will-o'-the-wisp. There must be some referents, largely common to the experience of all, for our fundamental ethical terms. This, however, does not carry us far. It leaves open the question whether those referents consist entirely or partly of emotional states, sensations, thoughts, volitions, rational principles, inner relations of psychological structure, external relations of social structure, or some combination of these. All these seem to play some part in the constitution or conditions of values and obligations, and many of them are vague and obscure. It is not surprising, therefore, that there should be much difference of opinion in the analysis of these factors and the attempt to construct a theory of their place in life. Indeed, the surprising thing, when we consider the nature and complexity of the data, is that there should be so much agreement as to the practical responses appropriate to situations involving such subtle and elusive factors.

The differences of opinion, however, also indicate that some of the more subtle and elusive of these suggested factors are really among those involved. If morality were merely a matter of seeing and applying self-evident principles, then its issues should be much clearer than they are; but the fact that some of the more elusive psychological factors, such as emotional states and volitions and inner relations of psychological structure, appear evidently to be involved in the constitution and causation of values and obligations, does not necessarily indicate that these latter must be devoid of common principles. It may only mean that the application of common principles must take account of individual differences. It is, however, only too clear that the search for any such principles is fraught with difficulty, and that even when there is agreement on a principle there may be disagreement about the ground upon which its acceptance should be advocated.

Yet if our society is to enjoy the orderly progress and stability that come from recognition of common ethical principles, and if we are to have the capacity to criticize and improve traditional principles and adapt their application to new circumstances, we must have agreement, not only upon some accepted body of principles but also upon the reasons for them; for without an understanding of the reasons, and agreement upon them, a body of principles becomes a bondage to tradition, a set of absolutes removed beyond intelligent criticism, adaptation, and reconstruction.

The complexity and elusiveness of the psychological facts involved in our experience of value and obligation have resulted in serious confusion in the terms we use to describe them. This confusion is an important factor contributory to the mood of skepticism concerning the validity of any ethical principles. Much of the disagreement in the history of ethics is due to differences in the use of terms. When Thrasymachus says justice is the interest of the stronger, and Socrates says it is the true health of the soul, each seems to the other to be talking nonsense because they are using the same term for different things. One is speaking of the established social order, and the other of the answer of a good conscience within the self. When Bentham says that pleasure is the only good, and Kant that nothing is good in itself save the good will, the difference in meaning of the term "good" is more subtle but very important. Bentham is using the term to refer to the appropriate objective of right action, Kant to designate the peculiar value character of moral rightness itself. When G. E. Moore says "good" is synonymous with "ought to exist," and Dewey says it means that which satisfies desire, the former has included the notion of obligation in his concept of good and the latter has excluded it for separate consideration.

These examples should be sufficient to indicate the need for a preliminary set of definitions before venturing further upon analysis of those factors in human experience that are referred to as values and obligations. It must not be expected, however, that we can begin with a complete set of definitions, for the definition of what value and obligation *are* is the most fundamental object of our inquiry; and, indeed, one of the most basic issues in contemporary ethical theory is just the question whether ultimate ethical terms are definable at all. One, at least, of our most basic terms must, therefore, for the present, remain undefined, its meaning or referent simply being broadly indicated by examples. The preliminary task which now faces us is to make distinctions between various shades of meaning among ethical terms which refer to different factors, phases, and relations of the moral life. In doing so, there are two principles which must guide us. The first is to make a distinction in thought wherever there is a difference in the data referred to, and to mark it with a clearly defined term. The second is to keep our definitions and our usage of terms as close as possible to the common usage while clearing up sources of ambiguity and confusion. At this stage of our inquiry, therefore, we shall have to pay attention to what people say on ethical questions without stopping to inquire whether what they say is correct: for the different things that people say call attention to the different facts, often rather obscure psychological facts, to which they refer. It is our task to find these different facts, to distinguish them and label them as different. The choice of terms to mark the necessary distinctions must be somewhat arbitrary, but that is not important. What matters is that we should develop a set of terms which will enable us to avoid confusions in our thinking.

THE CONCEPT OF OBLIGATION

We shall take as our key concept, which for the present, at least, must remain undefined, the idea of obligation. It is the name of a relation. We say that a person is under obligation to pay his debts, to refrain from injuring his neighbor, to obey the law, to provide for the needs of dependents, and so forth, or we say that he ought to do, or ought not to do, certain things. These statements obviously affirm the existence of a distinctive type of social or interpersonal relation. We also say that a man may have obligations to himself, indicating that we think of the relation as one that can exist within the life of a single individual, between his present person and some future state of his person. The relation involves a requirement to do, or not to do, something. It is thus understood to be some sort of demand or constraint or requirement upon the will, the voluntary behavior, of the individual; for we do not say that a person has an obligation to do something that is physically or psychologically impossible. The relation of obligation is therefore understood to be psychological in its nature, and in general also social. It is a sociopsychological relation.

We take the concept of obligation as our central, or key, concept because it is much less ambiguous than the concepts of "good" or "ought." The former is extremely vague and, as we shall later find, the distinctive concept of "morally good" cannot be defined without reference to the idea of obligation. The word "ought" is equally vague and has a wide variety of uses that have no necessary reference to moral issues, and in the distinctive sense of a *moral* "ought" we have the concept of obligation. A recent psychological study by H. L. Hollingworth [1] reveals the ambiguity in the use of "ought." He gathered a large number of statements containing varied uses of the word and asked his subjects to classify them according to the different meanings they found in them. He was given a considerable variety of

---

[1] H. L. Hollingworth, *Psychology and Ethics* (New York: The Ronald Press Co., 1949).

classifications and finally concluded that the consensus of opinion among his most sophisticated judges distinguished ten different categories: (1) The ought of logical inference, or drawing the correct conclusion. (2) What is required to give completeness to a pattern or organized whole. (3) The aesthetic ought, or what is required for beauty. (4) What is required for social welfare. (5) Requirements of utility. (6) Requirements of duty. (7) Requirements of safety. (8) Requirements of custom or convention. (9) Requirements of justice. (10) Requirements of law.

It may be noted that in each case the "ought" refers to something needed to fulfil some requirement—of validity, of completeness, of beauty, of personal or social need or desire, of social demand, or of ethical principle. But they do not all present the individual with an obligation, with something he ought to do. The category of duty is a distinct category among the ten. Hollingworth argues that all the "oughts" refer to something that could be called a good, and that a complete ethical vision requires attention to all of them. This is true, but clarity will be attained by keeping these "oughts" distinct rather than fusing them. The "ought" of duty is that of personal obligation, implying something I ought to do. The "oughts" of law, justice, social welfare, and safety refer to matters which are commonly a part of duty, but they allow of exceptions. A man may conceive it his duty to break a law, to commit a specific injustice for the sake of social welfare, or to uphold individual rights (justice) at some cost to social welfare, to violate the rules of safety and of convention, to destroy a thing of beauty or an organized whole, to do what is worse than useless, or to deny what he knows to be a logically sound conclusion. More often than not the ought-to-do of duty or obligation is in harmony with the other "oughts." Always they seem to have some relevance to it, but there is no doubt that it is distinct from them and may be opposed to them. It is the "ought" in this sense that is central to our conceptions of moral right and wrong.

As our primary ethical concept, then, we shall take the notion of "ought to do" in the sense in which it is equivalent to "under obligation to do" or "have a duty to do." We shall not yet discuss what our obligations or duties are, or how they are determined, or whether there are any universal principles of obligation. We shall simply assume something that very few will deny—that some human beings, in some situations, are under obligation to perform or refrain from performing certain actions, or to try to bring about certain results affecting the future state of themselves or of other persons. This means that an obligation or duty is a relation between a person as voluntary agent (the person under obligation) and some possible line of action which, in certain circumstances, he is under obligation to perform or refrain from performing. It is a psychological or social relation.

It is certainly true that human beings in all stages of society have asserted the existence of relations of this sort, and that there is a large measure of agreement as to specific cases in which they occur. There is also sometimes disagreement, but such disagreement can often be resolved by further discussion or by investigation which brings a fuller understanding of the circumstances. It is therefore wildly improbable that all this agreement and discussion could concern a type of relation which does not exist at all. The only questions that arise must concern, not the existence of obligations, but their nature and the circumstances that determine their existence.

These certainly are difficult questions, but at least it is clear where the answer is to be sought. It must be found, if at all, in an examination of the cases in which there is wide agreement that an obligation exists. We must discover precisely what it is concerning which this agreement arises. Then we must take the particular and typical cases of recognized obligation and examine them to discover what factor or factors they have in common. Thus we may be able to formulate, more or less precisely, some general principles descriptive of cases of obligation, as recognized at least by certain groups and types of people. It may be possible to find some principle or principles sufficiently generally recognized to enable us to dismiss the dissidents as mistaken in their judgment of the elusive factors involved, or as manifesting some sort of moral blindness conditioned by habit, tradition, or emotional abnormality. For such a principle or principles we could then claim that it defines what people in general claim to discern when they say they can see that a certain person is under an obligation, or when they agree that certain types of human situation involve certain specific duties.

For the purpose of clarifying a further system of definitions of ethical terms, it is not necessary, however, that this search for general principles should first be carried out. Indeed, we need to clarify our definitions before we can hope to attempt that task with success, and for the present we need not even assume that the task can be carried out to the point of showing that there are any general principles of obligation. All we need is a recognition that there are cases where obligations exist, cases where it can be said, with a significant agreement and understanding among a number of individuals, that a certain person has a duty to act in a certain way, or has a certain obligation. The notion of duty, obligation, ought-to-do, can be taken as the sole and central distinctively ethical term, and all other ethical terms can be defined by using it together with terms having natural psychological or physical referents. The question as to whether the central and distinctive ethical term "obliga-tion" can also be analyzed and defined in such nonethical terms can be postponed for further inquiry along with problems concerning the nature, sources, and criteria of obligation.

Ethical, Moral, Right, Wrong, and Cognate Terms

We may take first the term "ethical." It is sometimes used in a generic sense and sometimes in a specific and posi-tive sense, as distinct from its contradictory, "unethical." In its specific and positive sense, "ethical" means "in ac-cord with existing obligations," and "unethical" (the nega-tive form) means "not in accord with existing obligations." In its generic sense, the term means "having direct rel-evance to obligations," without implying that what is referred to is in or out of accord with existing obligations. We use the term in this generic sense when we speak of an "ethical theory," or an "ethical problem," or the "ethi-cal sense" of a term. Its contradictory is "nonethical," i.e., "having no direct relevance to obligations." We use the term in its specific (positive and negative) senses, however, when we speak of conduct as ethical or unethical. In the specific sense, "ethical" is equivalent to "ethically right," and "unethical" to "ethically wrong."

It should be noted that all human conduct (behavior subject to voluntary control) is either ethical (in the spe-cific sense) or unethical, either ethically right or ethically wrong. Behavior that is not subject to voluntary control, however, is neither; it is nonethical. Thus *conduct*, being behavior subject to voluntary control, is either ethical or unethical—it is either in accord with existing obligations or out of accord with them; but *behavior* is subject to a dual distinction. If not subject to voluntary control, it is non-ethical (has no direct relevance to obligations); if subject to voluntary control, it is ethical in the generic sense (has relevance to obligations) and then it is either ethical or unethical in the specific (positive and negative) senses, according as it is in or out of accord with existing obligations.

It should also be noted that "conduct" has been defined as "behavior subject to voluntary control." This is, obviously, the only sort of behavior that can be ethical in the generic sense of having direct relevance to obligations. It is irrelevant to speak of an obligation to do something that is not within the voluntary capacity of the person said to be so obligated, but it should further be noted that not all involuntary actions are completely beyond voluntary control and so nonethical. An action may be involuntary at the time it occurs, but it may be the consequence of an action, or failure to act, which was subject to control. In its larger setting, therefore, even involuntary action may have direct relevance to obligations. For this reason "conduct" (the behavior that is ethically relevant) is not defined simply as "voluntary behavior" but as "behavior subject to voluntary control."

The term "moral" is best taken as an exact synonym of "ethical." Some philosophers use the two terms in different senses to mark certain distinctions. For example, "moral" may be defined as referring to traditional views of right and wrong, and "ethical" as referring to ideally correct views, but such usage is confusing. The two terms come from Latin and Greek roots, respectively, which refer to what an ethnic group upholds as its traditional and approved customs, customs regarded as right. Taken into English, the terms are used interchangeably in common speech, and it only creates confusion to try to draw a distinction between them. The two terms even have the same ambiguities.

"Moral," like "ethical," is used both in the generic sense, "having relevance to obligations," and in the specific positive sense, "in accord with existing obligations." "Immoral" is equivalent to "unethical." "Nonmoral," "amoral," and "unmoral" are all synonyms equivalent to "nonethical." It should be noted that "unmoral" is not equivalent to "unethical," the former being a negative of the generic sense and the latter of the specific sense.

Between the terms "ethics" and "morality," the only distinction is that one refers to theory and the other to practice. Very appropriately, the Greeks have provided us with the former and the Romans with the latter. Since we have taken the terms "obligation" and "duty" as containing our key concepts, "ethics" must be defined as "the theory of obligation or duty" and "morality" as "the practice of obligation or duty," or more specifically, "conduct in accord with existing obligations." Since contradictory theories are all a part of ethics, but contradictory practices are not all a part of morality, we need a negative for the latter term, though not for the former. So we have "immorality" to refer to "conduct not in accord with existing obligations."

The terms "right" and "wrong" are used both in an ethical and a nonethical sense. In all cases the terms refer to consistency or inconsistency with some facts or principles that set a standard. The question of the right road is determined by consistency with the facts of geography, that of the right pronunciation of a word by the conventions of language, that of the right answer to a problem in arithmetic by the principles of mathematics. Similarly, a question of right moral conduct must be settled by reference to the facts of obligation existing in the time, place, and circumstances referred to. It is the facts of obligation that constitute the standard. The terms "ethically right," "morally right," "ethical" (specific sense), and "moral" (specific sense) are therefore synonyms equivalent to "in accord with existing obligations"; similarly, "ethically wrong," "morally wrong," "unethical," and "immoral" mean "not in accord with existing obligations."

When we speak of a moral rule, law, or principle as right or wrong, we must distinguish whether it refers to some specific time, place, or circumstances or is alleged to be of universal applicability. If the former, its rightness consists in its consistency with the obligations existing in the time, place, and circumstances referred to. If the latter, it asserts the existence of some obligation or obligations attaching to all behavior subject to voluntary control, and the question of the rightness of the rule is the question whether such obligations do actually exist. It should be noted that a moral rule does not *create* obligations. It simply states that certain obligations exist. What creates obligations is another and very difficult question which we shall discuss later. It would be generally agreed that some of the factors that enter into the creation of obligations are the making of laws by legislative authorities, the existence of customs, the existence of human needs and interests; and the existence of obligations is affected by the *knowledge* of moral rules and of the factors that enter into the creation of obligations. Ultimate questions concerning the creation of obligations and how we know of their existence take us into the theory of human nature and the fields of metaphysics and religion.

A distinction should be made between "morally right" and "obligatory." The former means "in accordance with existing obligation," the latter means "required by existing obligations." Many things are right (we need not always explicitly say *ethically* or *morally* right) that are not obligatory. It may be right for a man to make a handsome donation to a certain charity or to treat himself to a vacation in

Florida, although neither may be obligatory. Any action is right which it is not wrong to do. An action is obligatory only if it would be wrong not to do it.

Another, and much more important, distinction is that between what is objectively right and what is subjectively right. This distinction arises from the difficulty of knowing with certainty what our "existing obligations" are. The most that any person can do to fulfil his obligations is to try his best, with an open mind and all available information, to find out what his obligations are, and then make his best effort to fulfil what this inquiry leads him to think are his obligations. And since there can be no obligation to do the impossible, this must be recognized as the full extent of each person's obligation. If a person does this, then, from the subjective standard of his own capacity to know and do, he does right.

The subjective standard of morality, therefore, which is ultimate for each person, can be described with complete clarity, exactness, and fullness. It is to do one's best to find out what one's obligations are, and to do one's best to fulfil them. To that extent the course of the moral life is unambiguous and clear; and if this subjective standard of obligation has been maintained, it is entirely illogical to blame any person, or for any person to blame himself, for doing wrong. The objective standard of morality, however, is another matter. That is determined by the facts of existing obligations. It is this objective standard that, according to the subjective standard, it is our first duty to discover. If a person, although making his best effort to find out what is objectively right, mistakes the objective standard (misunderstands his existing obligations) and violates or fails to fulfil them, his moral judgment may be criticized as mistaken but he should not be blamed for moral failure. If he has, like some conscientious objectors in wartime, become

convinced after honest inquiry that a small minority opinion on some moral issue is correct, and courageously takes
a stand against the majority at considerable self-sacrifice, he
should be admired for his loyalty to the subjective standard,
even though his opinion may still be regarded as mistaken.
The important point to be emphasized in this connection
is the need for full, critical, and open-minded inquiry into
the facts that constitute objective obligation. It is this inquiry which constitutes the first part of our subjective obligation, and the most fundamental part of this inquiry is
that involved in the problems of ethical theory with which
we are now concerned.

The Definition of Good

We now come to the most vexed question in the whole
of ethical theory, the definition of "good." The hedonists
have identified it with pleasure or happiness; others, including Spinoza and Dewey, with that which satisfies desire.
For Kant, the only intrinsic good is the will to do one's
duty. G. E. Moore declares that the term is indefinable,
but takes it as synonymous with "ought to exist." A. C.
Ewing, another distinguished British philosopher, takes it
as equivalent to asserting that there is a peculiar moral fit-
tingness in adopting a favorable attitude toward the object
in question; i.e., to say "X is good" is to say "X is a fitting
object of a pro attitude." The Logical Positivists have denied that the term says anything factual about any object
at all. It is, they say, an expressive or evocative, not a
logical, use of language. Some say it merely expresses personal approval, others an approval mingled with a demand
that others also approve.

One of the reasons for this confusion is the failure to
make an initial distinction between the concepts of right

and good. There is certainly a close connection in human experience between whatever is referred to by these concepts, for it is constantly assumed and agreed that statements about the one enable us to infer statements about the other. This has led some philosophers to assume that the connection is one of logical entailment and that these concepts must be defined in such a way that one at least implies the other: but all such efforts lead to conclusions that contradict some general and deep-rooted convictions concerning either what is good or what is right, and these contradictions have led other philosophers to ethical skepticism, subjectivism, and extreme relativism. It is for this reason that we chose to take as our key concept the notion of obligation and leave it undefined except by demonstrative reference to the situations in which obligations are commonly recognized. We shall now proceed to adopt a definition of good which contains no direct reference to what is right, or what ought to be, or ought to be done. The relation of the two concepts we shall then proceed to find, not in their definition, but in the practical relations of the facts to which they refer. By this method of approach we can not only avoid smuggling in a whole ethical theory in our initial definition, but we can also find a definition that is in harmony with general usage and one which will enable us to develop the distinctions necessary to clear up the chief sources of confusion.

Apparently the one point of agreement among the varied definitions to which we have referred (and they are typical of the whole history of ethics) is that the term "good" is used as an expression of approval. It is also clear, however, that the person who says a thing or action is good means that it possesses characters which make it reasonable for himself and others to approve of it. When a person decides that something is good, he thereupon expects that other persons who have the same knowledge of it will also see that it is good, in the same way and in the same sense. If another person questions whether the thing is good, then both assume that the way to bring agreement is by a reasoned inquiry into the true characters of the thing, and by both parties being reasonable in their attitude toward it.

These facts therefore indicate that a definition of "good" which would be in harmony with general usage would be as follows: "X is good" is equivalent to "X is a reasonable object of a favorable attitude," or more fully, "X is an object toward which it is reasonable to adopt a favorable attitude." By a "favorable" attitude we here mean an attitude inclined to keep, preserve, or promote the thing, or the kind of thing, in question. By saying that an attitude is reasonable we mean that the attitude is such as would arise from an enlightened understanding of the object and of one's self and of the relation of the object to one's self. We might express this by putting the above definition in a third alternative form. "X is good" means "X is an object toward which enlightened understanding tends to develop a favorable attitude." [2] More briefly: good is that which reason-

---

[2] This is an example of what G. E. Moore, in his *Principia Ethica*, calls a "naturalistic definition." All such definitions, he says, are fallacious because it is always possible to ask of any natural property, such as "pleasant" or "satisfying," "Is it good?" and it is not self-contradictory to say of any natural property that it is not good. The plausibility of this argument, however, rests on the usage of "good" in the sense of "ought to exist," which in Chapter 2 we have already shown to be a figurative way of saying "ought to be preserved, promoted, and so forth," i.e., "ought to be an object of a favorable attitude." Our definition, therefore, simply replaces "ought to be favored" with the statement that it is so if our attitude is "reasonable." This change allows for the distinction between "natural" and "moral" good drawn later in this chapter. The use of "ought" in the definition makes it applicable only to the latter. If the definitions of these two kinds of good offered on page 124 are examined, it will be found it *is* self-contradictory to say that moral good (as defined) ought not to be favored, but it is *not* self-contradictory to say this of a natural good. The criticism of our definition as an example of Moore's "naturalistic fallacy" is therefore seen to rest on the confusion in the con-

ably determines a favorable attitude toward itself. The definition of "bad" follows from that of "good." "X is bad" means "X is a reasonable object of an unfavorable attitude" or "X is an object toward which enlightened understanding tends to develop an unfavorable attitude." "Evil" is simply a stronger synonym for "bad." Between good and bad there is, of course, a neutral ground consisting of objects that reasonably determine neither a favorable nor an unfavorable attitude.

These definitions, it should be noted, leave open the question whether a thing that is good at one time or place, or to one person, will be good at every time or place or to all persons. In the sense defined, it is possible to say, "This is a good to me but may not be a good to everybody," or it may be claimed that something is universally good, that it is something toward which it is reasonable for all people to adopt a favorable attitude. It should be noted, too, that we are not defining goodness as consisting in the character of actually being the object of a favorable attitude by anybody or everybody. A thing can be good, even if nobody has a favorable attitude toward it. Its goodness consists in its having characteristics which make it *reasonable* that some person or all persons should have a favorable attitude toward it; if only one person, then it is to that person a good; if all persons, then it is good in general.

This definition does not tell us what things are good or what makes them good. It merely tells us what people generally mean by saying that something is good. And our claim in putting forth this definition is that if we adopt it, and use the term accordingly, we shall find that we can use it thus consistently, unambiguously, and intelligibly, and that from this starting point we can go on to unravel other

---

cept of "ought to exist" and the failure to distinguish between natural and moral good.

confusions in the use of the term. It will readily be seen that the definition fits general usage. When the hedonists claim that pleasure or happiness is good, and when other philosophers say that moral conduct or the will to do one's duty is good, they mean to affirm that these things are reasonable objects of a favorable attitude. Perhaps some of them intend to convey something else as well, but this at least they all mean, and when the ordinary citizen says that health, wealth, peace, and freedom are good, he means to assert the same thing.

DIFFERENT KINDS OF GOOD

The reader, perhaps, may be somewhat disappointed that the definition of good tells him so little about it. He wants to know what things are good and what makes them good. Those are further questions and very difficult ones, but our definition at least tells us what to look for in the search for the good. We are to look for those things toward which a favorable attitude is adopted when there is enlightened understanding of the self and when the attitude is determined by an enlightened understanding of the things in question. Such things will be good, at least in the view of the person whose favorable attitude is thus determined. If we can find some things toward which such attitudes are universally favorable, then those things will be universally good. We shall therefore make a first distinction, within the general concept of the good, between that of universal good, or good in general, and a particular good, a good only for some individual or group.

A second important distinction is that between intrinsic good and extrinsic or instrumental good. Most of the things toward which we regard it as reasonable to adopt a favorable attitude are so prized, not for what they are in their own intrinsic character (i.e., apart from their causes and future consequences or use) but for their extrinsic relations, such as the good effects they tend to produce or can be used to produce. These are instrumental or extrinsic goods. They are good in the sense of being "good for" something else. But a cause or instrument is good only if it is good for something that is itself good. And we are lost in an infinite regress unless we recognize something that is not merely "good for" its future consequence or uses but good as something immediately contemplated or presently enjoyed—good in itself, an intrinsic good.

It is very difficult to decide what is intrinsically good, and because of this difficulty Instrumentalist philosophy has denied that there is any such thing, asserting that all goods are instrumental, instrumental to the solution of problems and thus to the ongoing of life. This, however, is merely to smuggle in an intrinsic good without acknowledging it. It treats the solution of problems and the ongoing of life as intrinsically good in the sense of our definition. We shall have to inquire later whether this interpretation of what is intrinsically good is sound, and we shall find that as a description of intrinsic *natural* goods it is fairly near to the truth; but we must insist upon the importance of making the distinction between instrumental and intrinsic good, for much that may be truly said of the one is not true of the other, and the concept of intrinsic good is constantly assumed in ethical thought and, indeed, is necessary to make that of extrinsic or instrumental good intelligible.

A third and still more important distinction, which needs to be made within the concept of the good, is that between moral good and nonmoral or natural good. In the case of actions subject to voluntary control, and the agents of such actions, moral considerations are relevant to the reasonable determination of a favorable or unfavorable attitude. Outside human conduct itself, however, there is a vast range of things and events which, in themselves, are nonmoral; and the question whether a favorable attitude to them is reasonable has to be decided on other grounds. These things and events are usually not irrelevant to moral choice. They are the things concerning which, in our conduct, we have to make moral decisions, but we cannot decide what our conduct toward them ought to be until we have decided whether it is reasonable to adopt a favorable attitude toward them as nonmoral entities. Thus the grounds on which we decide that a nonmoral entity is good are very different from those which determine the decision in the case of a voluntary action. An act of heroism, for example, may be considered morally good, although it may be unsuccessful, painful, and injurious to health—all characteristics which, in considering it as a nonmoral event, would reasonably determine an unfavorable attitude toward it.

We shall therefore distinguish the terms "morally good" and "ethically good" as meaning "having moral properties which, apart from other considerations, constitute it a reasonable object of a favorable attitude"; and "nonmoral good" or "natural good" we shall define as meaning "having nonmoral properties which, apart from moral considerations, constitute it a reasonable object of a favorable attitude."

It should be noted that a moral good is always an intrinsic good. It is the intrinsic character of the act as a right choice that makes it a reasonable object of a favorable attitude. But a morally good action may have effects which are predominantly bad and may therefore also be pronounced an instrumental evil. This would be true of a justifiable but unsuccessful act of heroism which resulted in the loss of the hero's life. But this instrumental evil is a natural evil. The act is good in one sense and bad in another, but there is no contradiction in saying it is both good and bad. There are also actions which are morally (and intrinsically) bad but are natural (instrumental) goods, as when an act of spite turns out to produce unintended good consequences, making it beneficial on the whole. In general, however, morally good actions are natural instrumental goods and morally bad actions are natural instrumental evils. Whether an intrinsic natural good can ever be an intrinsic moral evil, or vice versa, we shall have to wait to decide after we have inquired into the nature of the former.

Our definitions of "morally right" and "morally good" now enable us to make clear what sort of action is morally good. In the first place, it is an action which has moral properties; in the second place, its moral properties must be such as reasonably to determine a favorable attitude. I think it will be generally agreed that, if attention is confined to the moral (as distinct from the nonmoral) properties of an action, then, in the normal human being, an enlightened understanding of those properties determines a favorable attitude toward those actions we believe to be right and an unfavorable attitude toward those we believe to be wrong.[3] This means that whatever is thought to be ethically right action functions as a good in general human experience; i.e., it is a general good, not merely a good to a limited number or special groups of people. This is a very important fact but it is so commonplace that it is usually taken for granted without its importance being recognized, and I do not know of any thinker who has challenged it.

To be morally good, therefore, an action must be right. But must it be objectively or subjectively right? Obviously it is the subjective standard that is here revelant, for objec-

---

[3] Of course it does not follow that a favorable attitude thus generated will issue in action. That will depend upon whether there are other motives in operation at the time when action is called for.

tively right action may be nonmoral or immoral. It is generally agreed that a mistaken or unsuccessful action may be admirable in its moral intention, but the intention to do something that the person himself believes to be wrong is never morally admirable even if the majority judge it to be right. To be morally good, therefore, an action must be subjectively right.

Judgments of moral goodness and badness are, for this reason, always hazardous. We have to know what the person *thought* was right and whether he did his best to find out what was right and to do it. This is difficult enough. But the *degree* of moral goodness also depends on further factors still more difficult to assess. Subjectively right action reasonably determines a favorable attitude, but how favorable depends on other factors besides subjective rightness. We give our higher praise and admiration to actions where we believe considerable voluntary effort was required to maintain that subjective rightness. We most strongly blame and despise those actions which are subjectively wrong despite obvious obligations of a kind normally supported by powerful motives. Since the good is defined as that which reasonably determines a favorable attitude toward itself, the very good must be that which reasonably determines a very favorable attitude toward itself, and the very bad that which reasonably determines a very unfavorable one. What makes an action very good (morally) is therefore its being right under conditions requiring great effort to do right; and what makes another very bad is its being wrong in spite of what should normally be very strong motives to do the right. Thus the widow's mite, the publican's repentance, or a heroic self-sacrifice in the course of duty is admired as having an element of nobility, while the rich man's extortions from the poor or a murder committed for petty monetary gain is regarded as peculiarly despicable.

There are only two types of entity that can be morally good or bad. These entities are actions subject to voluntary control, and character, or personality, which is in part an effect and, in turn, in part a cause of voluntary actions; but there is a very great difference in what affects the degree of goodness of these two things. An action is morally good if it is subjectively right; a character or personality is morally good if it tends to produce actions that are subjectively right; but an action has great moral goodness if it requires great effort to do right, while a character or personality has the greater moral goodness the less the effort it requires to do right. There is no paradox here, but much confusion will be avoided if we keep clear the distinction between the moral goodness of an act and of a character. It explains, for example, why we can reasonably admire the attempt of the person of weak or bad character to turn over a new leaf, while it would be foolish to praise the ordinary decent citizen for maintaining his ordinary decency and honesty. The ordinary good citizen's character is probably much more admirable than that of a reformed thief for he feels no particular temptation to steal; but that he should refrain from an opportunity to make a dishonest profit with safety to himself is not so admirable, as a moral achievement, as it would be for a man who in all his previous life had practiced larceny.

One must not, however, deduce from this that a good character is likely to produce fewer actions of high moral value than a bad or indifferent character. With the latter, any great effort to do right is rare. With the former, though ordinary action is maintained without effort, there is usually a consciousness of a higher standard of obligations which is only maintained by constant moral thought and effort—and which indeed may be too high for even the best of men constantly to maintain. At the lower stage of character development, the individual's best efforts to discover his existing obligations may not enable him to see the high duty that is envisioned by the person of finer sensibility and more fully developed character. Moral achievement in practice not only makes similar moral achievement the easier in the future but it also tends to clarify the moral vision. Ethical ideals tend to grow by geometrical progression, while moral practice advances by arithmetical progression. Thus at every stage of moral development there tends to be a recognition of obligations which the individual finds require a moral effort to make himself willing to fulfil; and at the highest stage there is a clear consciousness of falling below the ideal. The only exception to this rule is where the development of good character has been accompanied by a development of spiritual pride which blinds the individual to his remaining moral deficiencies and stultifies the further growth of his moral ideals. This condition we shall have to examine further when we come to discuss what religion calls "sin."

Summing up the results of this analysis, we find that in all instances "X is good" is equivalent to "X is a reasonable object of a favorable attitude," but beyond that the statement is highly ambiguous. It may have any one of five more precise meanings, and the same object which is good in one of these more precise senses may be bad in another. The five possible meanings are found by working out the combinations of the three distinctions pointed out above. A good may be general or particular, intrinsic or instrumental, moral or natural. This would yield the theoretical possibility of eight different kinds of good. However, we can limit moral goods to one kind, namely, general intrinsic moral good, for it seems to be generally agreed that it is only of subjectively right actions and the characters that produce such actions that we can say that they are reasonable objects of a favorable attitude by reason of their *moral* properties and apart from other considerations; and the moral properties of an action or character are intrinsic features of it—those features of an action which constitute it a piece of voluntary conduct that is subjectively right, and the tendency of a character to produce such actions.

In addition to (1) moral good (which is always a general and intrinsic good) there are, however, four other possible types of good. These are (2) particular intrinsic natural good, (3) general intrinsic natural good, (4) particular instrumental natural good, (5) general instrumental natural good. In the sense of (2), "X is good" means "To A, at time T and in circumstances, C, by reason of its intrinsic nonmoral properties and apart from moral considerations, X is a reasonable object of a favorable attitude." In the sense of (3) it means "To all people at all times, and in all circumstances, by reason of its intrinsic nonmoral properties and apart from moral considerations, X is a reasonable object of a favorable attitude." In the sense of (4) it means "To A, at time T and in circumstances C, by reason of its instrumental properties and apart from moral considerations, X is a reasonable object of a favorable attitude." In the sense of (5) it means "To all people, at all times, and in all circumstances, by reason of its instrumental properties and apart from moral considerations, X is a reasonable object of a favorable attitude." It will, however, I think, be generally agreed that there are no instances of a general instrumental natural good. This reduces our practical concern with different kinds of good to four. This is sufficient, however, to create most of that confusion for which ethics and value theory are notorious. Most of the rest of the confusion comes from the failure to recognize that in none of its commonly intelligible senses is "good" equivalent to "right" or "obligatory."

VALUE AND ITS COGNATE TERMS

Before passing from these questions of semantics, something should be said about the uses of the term "value" and its cognates. The term is almost hopelessly ambiguous and should be avoided except where the context makes its shade of meaning perfectly clear, or where vagueness is an advantage in covering a broad field, as when we speak of "the general theory of value." It has all the variety of meanings of "good" and some of its own. We must distinguish between particular and general values, between instrumental and intrinsic values, and between moral and nonmoral values. We must also recognize that "value" sometimes refers to the abstract character of goodness, and sometimes to the concrete good thing or good action; i.e., there is no verbal distinction between the concrete, the thing that has value, and the abstract, the values that it has. Both are "values," and this causes much confusion of thought. In economics the term is further confused by its equivalence in some of its uses to price (which itself has several meanings) and its use in another sense more akin to that of utility. In some other fields it is used still more vaguely as a synonym for "quality," "quantity," or "meaning," as when we speak of "color values," "mathematical values," or "the precise value" of a word in a sentence.

The verb "to value" and the adjective "valuable" have further ambiguities of their own. The verb sometimes means "to prize or cherish" and sometimes "to evaluate, or to estimate the value of something." The adjective, "valuable," means "having relatively high value," either in one of the economic senses, or in the sense of being a natural good, or in the sense of the instrumental value of a moral good. In brief, "valuable" is an emphatic synonym for the adjective "good" in every sense but that of intrinsic moral good. For example, we do not speak of an act of heroism as a valuable action if it resulted in nothing but loss. Yet we may speak of it as a morally good deed and as having intrinsic moral value.

Chapter 5

WHAT OUGHT WE TO DO?

The Quest for Intrinsic Natural Good

What is the chief good for man? This was the form in which Aristotle framed the problem of ethics. It assumes that the individual cannot reasonably be expected to do anything nobler than pursue his own chief good. It is significant of the influence of Christianity that for Immanuel Kant the question had become transformed into "What ought we to do?" Christianity had taught that man's "reasonable service" might present him with a duty that, so far as this life is concerned, might mean the sacrifice of his own chief good. In his effort to lift ethics above a concern with pleasure and the satisfaction of desire, Kant went on to attempt to define man's duty without reference to his good. As we have seen, this effort fails. Kant was not able to give an account of man's duties without reference to the consequences of his actions for good or evil.

A brief review of what are commonly recognized as obligations will show clearly that in most cases, if not in all, they are obligations to produce good consequences and avoid bad ones. This is true of the general principle of impartial concern for the good of all, expressed in the duty to love one's neighbor or obey the golden rule. It is true of the injunctions against stealing, murder, and adultery. It is true of the duties of family relationship—of parents to children, of children to parents, and of husband and wife to each other. It is true of the reciprocal duties of employer and employee, of buyer and seller, of government and people. Even where the duty is directly to obey a specific law, the purpose of the law is to produce good consequences and avoid bad ones. Some problems arise, as we shall see later, if we say that every ethical question can be decided by a weighing of the consequences for good or evil of the various possible lines of action. This raises some confusing questions about means and ends, but these can be postponed for the present. It is clear that duties are concerned with requirements to seek to produce good consequences and avoid bad ones, both for others and for ourselves.

Furthermore, the good that is involved in these consequences is natural good. Moral good, as we have seen, consists in the effort to find out what we ought to do and to do it. To say that a man ought to do that which will produce as much moral good as possible is, therefore, simply to say that he ought to do that which will produce as much as possible of the effort to find out what he ought to do and do it. This, however, does nothing to direct that effort. We are lost in a vicious circle unless we find some other sort of good, besides moral good, at which we ought to aim. The principle which says that we ought to seek impartially to produce the greatest possible good must, therefore, if it is to mean anything specific, refer to natural goods, and certainly most of the specific principles concerning the obligations of parents, citizens, and so forth refer directly or indirectly to natural goods.

We cannot, therefore, escape the need for an inquiry into the nature of natural good and the means whereby we can measure one natural good against another; for often an obligation to produce one good is incompatible with an obligation to produce another, and we must choose between them. If we recognize the obligation to pursue impartially the greatest possible good, then that becomes the ground of decision between conflicting obligations; but we cannot decide which of two goods is the greater unless we can reduce them to a common denominator. Instrumental goods must be judged by their contribution to production of intrinsic good, but we still have no means of comparison unless we can agree upon what constitutes an intrinsic good and find some common and approximately measurable character of all intrinsic goods which constitutes their goodness. Our question then is a threefold one: (1) What sort of things are intrinsic natural goods? (2) What is the common feature of all of them that makes them good? (3) How do they differ so as to possess different degrees of goodness? The same questions arise concerning the bad or evil.

A direction for this inquiry is given us by our definition of natural good. An object is a natural good if, when considered apart from its ethical significance, it reasonably determines a favorable attitude toward itself, and it is an intrinsic natural good if it does this when considered for what it is as immediately experienced or presently enjoyed, apart from its further consequences. Our first question, therefore, is this. What is there that, considered in and for itself as immediately experienced or presently enjoyed, determines a favorable attitude toward itself when clearly distinguished and understood?

In the first place, the very form of the question, which comes from our definition of intrinsic good, makes it clear that intrinsic good does not belong to anything as existing outside of and independent of all experience. This may be brought out in another way by first considering instrumental goods. If we think of something that does not affect the experience of any person, and postulate that it cannot possibly ever affect the experience of any conscious creature, then its instrumental properties, thus limited, cannot be said to render it a reasonable object of either a

favorable or unfavorable attitude. In this I think there will
be general agreement. Nothing, then, is instrumentally
good or bad except as it affects experience, but instrumental
value arises from the effect on intrinsic value. Nothing
therefore has intrinsic value (goodness or badness) except
some phase of experience.

In the second place, we can narrow down our inquiry to
the subjective phase of experience—the mode of experienc-
ing rather than the perceptual entity experienced. The
same perceptual entity changes in value with a change in
the subjective attitude toward it. The food we are eating,
as tasted and enjoyed, changes in value from good to indifferent and to bad as we reach and pass the stage of reple-
tion of appetite. The same music, heard one day in one
mood, may be good; heard another day, in another mood,
it may be bad—irritating, boring, or depressing. The goodness or badness of perceptual entities is thus seen to be
instrumental rather than intrinsic. They change in value
with their changing effect on the subjective attitude, the
more or less active response, of the perceiver. Perceptual
entities, therefore, which are complexes of sensation and
meaning, are instruments affecting the value of the subjective response. It is the subjective response itself that has the
character of being intrinsically good or bad.

Our question as to the nature of natural good therefore
narrows down to this. What is the difference between one
subjective response and another, considered in and for itself
as immediately experienced or presently enjoyed, such that
the one sort determines a favorable attitude toward itself
when clearly distinguished and understood, and the other
an unfavorable attitude? In order not to confuse the issue,
we shall have to consider this question from the standpoint
of a good-to-me, for each person has immediate experience
or enjoyment of his own subjective responses only. But, on

the assumption of an essential sameness in this basic matter between one self and another, we can conclude that the distinction in intrinsic good and intrinsic evil in the subjective response is the same for one person as for another. If it is not, then to that extent human beings must completely misunderstand one another on the most important subject of intersubjective intercourse—the distinction between intrinsic natural good and bad. The only way to tell whether there is such basic and hopeless misunderstanding is to examine the course of such intercourse to see how far it is successful. Since human beings usually understand each other in this matter so long as they use terms in the same way, we may conclude that we are justified in assuming that in this basic matter their experience is the same. Each of us can therefore ask the question for himself. What do I find as the essential distinction between my subjective responses whereby I characterize the one sort a natural good, and the other bad, in the sense above defined?

Put this way, the question looks easy, but it is still somewhat elusive. Historically and popularly, two answers have been given, both of which are closely related though neither of them is entirely satisfactory. Unfortunately the inquiry has usually been confused by a failure to make an initial and adequate distinction between moral and natural good. With this source of confusion out of the way, we will try again. The very closeness of the two historic answers is encouraging, for it suggests that both approximate to the truth. The first of these answers is that natural good is pleasure, the second that it is satisfaction of desire. We must examine both in turn.

THE PLEASURE THEORY OF NATURAL GOOD

The view that pleasure alone is a natural good is known as hedonism. It takes three forms. In its least plausible form it simply identifies good with pleasure. It says that to say a thing is pleasant is to say that it is good, and vice versa; but this means that the statement "Pleasure is good" is a mere tautology. It is to say, "Pleasure is pleasure." Most hedonists, however, do not fall into this error. They use the term "good" in a sense much more akin to the way we have defined it. Let us see, therefore, whether pleasure can plausibly be said to be the only thing that is good in our adopted sense of the latter term.

This leads us to the second and traditionally the most popular interpretation of hedonism, which claims that pleasure alone is good because it is the only object of desire. If this were the case, then it would certainly be the only thing that is good, in our sense of natural good, because it would be the only thing that could determine a favorable attitude toward itself, whether reasonable or unreasonable. This hedonistic theory of motivation (usually known as Psychological Hedonism) is, however, nothing more than a common psychological mistake resulting from failure to analyze properly the nature of desire. It glibly says that all human interest is directly or indirectly self-interest because, of course, satisfaction of an interest is to some extent satisfaction of a self. In part this is a sheer fallacy of equivocation. Every interest is self-interest in the sense that it is the interest *of* a self, and its satisfaction therefore brings satisfaction *to* a self; but it is simply not the case that every interest is an interest *in* the self or in its state of feeling. Man is not so completely self-conscious. Interest *in* the self is a relatively late development. Most of our interests, even in maturity, are interests directly in objects for their own sake. For the most part we forget ourselves in our interest in objects, and if we are to obtain much pleasure in the objects, we have to do so. The Greeks long ago discovered the paradox of hedonism. "To get pleasure we must forget it."

Another way of arriving at this same result is to analyze the sources of pleasure. We find that they can be divided into three: (1) Pleasures of sense. (2) Pleasures of pursuit. (3) Pleasures of satisfaction. Pleasures of sense are, of course, direct objects of desire, but pleasures of pursuit and of satisfaction are merely incidental effects of the progressive fulfilment of a desire. In most cases the object desired is not a pleasure. The pleasure of reading comes from progressive fulfilment of an aroused curiosity, an interest in knowing the solution to a problem or the further course of a series of events. Our social pleasures come largely from satisfaction of our desires for attention and prestige and from the added stimulus accruing to any interest by sharing it with others. People desire power, revenge, prestige, knowledge, affection, and a host of things in which sensory pleasantness plays only a small part or which may even be unpleasant in sensation. It is only because we *first* desire the goal that we obtain any pleasure in the pursuit or in attainment of the end. And the desire of the goal is a response to a drive that is somehow part of our nature, though conditioned by prior experience of its exercise and successes and failures. Pleasure and pain function as factors affecting the shaping of these drives. When we have found ways in which the drives may be stimulated, and find pleasurable response, we seek out these stimuli, but the root of the motivation is in the natural human drives and the objective interests they have created rather than in the pleasure and pain of sense or the incidental pleasures of pursuit and satisfaction. Among our drives, it should be remembered, are those which impel us to social associations and develop our objective interests in other human beings.

It is evident, then, that pleasure is not the only object of desire and, indeed, is the primary object of comparatively few desires. This kind of hedonism puts the cart before the horse. Pleasure is usually not the goal of desire but the incidental consequence of the fulfilment of desire for something else. Every fulfilment of desire is more or less pleasant. Some, however, bring less pleasure than pain—usually earlier pleasure and later pain. This situation is recognized by the third type of hedonism which declares that it is only reasonable to adopt a favorable attitude toward those desires and ends which bring more pleasure in the long run than pain, i.e., that a positive balance of pleasure over pain is good, and the only good, in the sense of our definition.

This position, usually known as Ethical Hedonism, is much more defensible than the others. Most of the traditional criticisms of it come from confusion of natural with moral good—for example the criticism that a crime may bring a positive balance of pleasure over pain to the person who commits it. The Hedonist may answer that the crime may well be a natural instrumental good to the criminal. That is why he commits it: but it is still a moral evil. Or, again, it is argued that pleasure cannot be an intrinsic good because certain actions, such as an act of cruelty, are made more evil if the person who commits them has pleasure in doing so. Once again it is the moral evil of the action that is here referred to. Considered apart from moral issues (as a natural good, by definition, must be considered), the pleasurable act of cruelty, lust, or vengeance may be a natural intrinsic good.

It is certain that, where no moral evil enters in to confuse the issue, experiences that are, on the whole, pleasurable are rather generally regarded as reasonable objects of a favorable attitude, and painful experiences as the reverse. Whatever is pleasurable may therefore be regarded as a natural good, and whatever is painful as a natural evil. We may even go further and agree with the Hedonist that, apart from the existence of pleasure and pain in our experience, we would not regard anything as either good or bad. A world devoid of hedonic tone would be devoid of value. If there could never be the slightest degree of joy or sorrow, of happiness or unhappiness, or any other kind of pleasure or pain in human experience, then it would not matter what happened.

Having made this concession to the Hedonist, we need not go all the way with him. This concession only means that pleasure and pain are necessary constituent elements in what makes the difference between good and bad in our experience. It does not mean that they are the sole determining factors. Pleasure, we may agree, is a factor in the constitution of natural good, but it is not the only factor; something else is involved too.

There are two main reasons for refusing to go all the way with this third type of hedonism. The first is that degrees of pleasure and pain do not seem to vary consistently with our common judgments of degrees of goodness and badness, indicating that there is another factor involved. It is true that this is in part due to the fact that our common judgments often confuse natural and moral good, or intrinsic and instrumental good, but even when we keep these distinctions clear and concentrate on intrinsic natural good, the criticism still holds. To judge the issue, we must compare two brief experiences, one involving a high intensity of pleasure but exercising only a limited range of our faculties, and those of the simple, elementary type such as perception and motor control; the other involving positive pleasure, though of somewhat lesser intensity, but exercising a much fuller range of our faculties, including our higher mental capacities. Then we must abstract from moral issues and the further consequences involved, and ask ourselves whether a favorable attitude toward the former experience would be more reasonable than a favorable attitude toward the latter. By a favorable attitude in such a case we should mean that, in so far as moral values and further consequences are not affected, the one should be prolonged and repeated rather than the other. I think that consideration of such examples will show that, even apart from moral issues and future consequences, we tend to regard it as reasonable to adopt a favorable attitude to the exercise of our higher and fuller capacities, even if this involves some loss in the intensity of the accompanying pleasure. If so, we must recognize activity also as a factor in the constitution of the good.

This is more decisively brought out in our second reason for rejection of Ethical Hedonism. Pleasure alone would not constitute a good; it must involve activity. To test this we must make another psychological experiment. Imagine a single intensely pleasant moment of experience. Then imagine that such an experience could be continuously repeated, without change and without any activity, through the full time span of a normal life. Would that be what we agree to call a good life, the sort of life which we would reasonably favor, or choose, if we could, in preference to a life with normal change and activity but less pleasure? I think there is no doubt but that choice of a time span of repetition without change or activity would be regarded universally as unreasonable. Repetition of pleasure without change and activity, therefore, does not make life or experience a natural good. So hedonism, even in its most plausible form, must be abandoned as not more than a half-truth.

The Satisfaction Theory

We turn, then, to the theory which says that it is satisfaction of desire that makes experience good. Here we have a subjective process involving both pleasure and activity, for the process of satisfaction includes a successful course of achievement as well as its consummation. It is certain that, looked at as an intrinsic natural good (i.e., apart from moral considerations and further consequences), we should always regard it as reasonable to adopt a favorable attitude toward the process of satisfying any desire, and an unfavorable attitude toward denying it satisfaction, i.e., that satisfaction is good and dissatisfaction is bad. We may also agree that life without desire would be neither good nor bad. Even pleasure and pain would be of no importance if we did not desire to have the one and avoid the other.

There is, however, one objection to the view that it is simply the process of satisfaction of desire that constitutes a natural good. This is the fact that, even apart from moral considerations and future consequences, such satisfactions do not seem to be all on the same level of goodness, i.e., their goodness varying only with the strength of the desire. If we have to choose between the cultivation, increase, intensification, and satisfaction of desires expressing and utilizing the higher mental processes, and doing the same with those utilizing only the lower mental processes, then I think most persons would say it is reasonable to adopt a favorable attitude to the former rather than the latter—apart altogether from consideration of moral issues and future consequences. This means that the process of satisfaction of what we call the higher desires is commonly recognized as a greater intrinsic natural good than that of satisfying the lower.

The following illustration will give point to this issue. Suppose a scientific dictator should discover a drug which, if given to the 90 per cent of the people outside the party, would make them perfect servants, all their desires directed to serving the state, but incapable of any exercise of their higher mental faculties except in performing the purely economic functions assigned to them. He could argue that, if natural good is the fulfilment of desire, then this would be the ideal way to secure that this 90 per cent of the people had the maximum of good in their lives, for their lives could be filled with satisfied desires on the lower level of mental activity, in the enjoyment of adult appetite and childish play; but even granting the attainment of a maximum of satisfaction of desire in this way, I think very few of us would agree that it constituted a maximum of natural good. It therefore seems clear that the factor which makes an experience an intrinsic natural good is not to be found simply in the satisfaction of desire.

Natural Good as a Form of Activity

These inquiries, however, have brought us close to the solution of our problem. It is evident that that which is either good or bad (in the sense of intrinsic natural good and evil) is subjective activity. It is also evident that its goodness depends upon its being positive in feeling tone, i.e., pleasant, although the degree of goodness does not depend solely upon the degree of pleasure. To be good it must also be positive in form, i.e., it must be an activity in pursuit of some desired goal and successfully moving toward its goal; otherwise it is not pleasant and it is not a process of satisfaction of desire; a subjective activity may be said to be negative in form when it is directed not toward some desired goal but to the mere avoidance of something or to the mere removal of an obstacle. Positive form expresses appetition; negative form expresses aversion. A natural good is therefore a forward-moving and pleasant, appetitive, subjective process. This may be briefly expressed by saying it is a conscious life-activity that is positive in form and quality.[1] This is the answer to the second of the questions raised early in this chapter. The answer to the first question told us that it is only subjective activities that can be intrinsically good or bad. The second asked what makes them good; and we have learned that the difference between good and bad is due to the difference between being positive or negative in form and quality. Positive form and positive quality go together, as do negative form and negative quality.

Our third question concerns the degrees of good and bad. What accounts for the difference between good and better, and between bad and worse? Here part of the answer, but only the less important part, has to do with differences of intensity. The moment of intense subjective activity will be either more pleasant or more painful than the moment of less intense activity and, considered in isolation from other moments, will be pronounced better or worse, a great good or a greater evil, accordingly. A reasonable view of our subjective activity, however, even if confined to its purely intrinsic character, does not take brief moments in isolation. It views a span of subjective activity, an interest process taken as a whole, in its working out from beginning to end; and it is then seen that intense activity (with intense pleasure) must be compensated by interim

---

[1] This is not another definition of natural good, but a brief description of the constitutive properties that give to a subjective activity the relational property of goodness.

periods of lax interest, dullness, or boredom; or there must
be a complete change of interest. The value of a unit of
subjective activity (an interest process taken as a whole,
from initiation to satisfaction) therefore cannot be judged
by its moments of maximum intensity. This alone reduces
the importance of degrees of intensity in assessing values.
Further, since intense interests are apt to be short-lived,
this also lowers their intrinsic value as a whole. When we
go on from the intrinsic value of an interest process to take
cognizance of its instrumental value, we find again that the
intensity value of a subjective process has often to be dis-
counted by its effects in lowering the intensity of subsequent interest processes or in causing those of negative
value. For all these reasons, the intensity of pleasurable
experience is of less importance than at first appears in
making it a good, i.e., a reasonable object of a favorable
attitude—the attitude that chooses to cultivate and promote
it.

But subjective processes vary in another way besides that
of intensity. They vary in complexity or degree of development. The higher level subjective processes are built upon
the base of the lower levels and include them. We should
distinguish three levels, the third of which is capable of
great elaboration. The lowest level is that of mere sense
awareness without awareness of meaning. It is only theoretically distinguishable from the second level, the level of
perceptual intelligence, which involves awareness of the
meaning of objects and adjustment to them, without abstract thought about them. Third is the conceptual level,
the level of thought, which uses general terms and is capable of imagination and inference. Only at the third level
do we rise to the grasp of values, whether moral or aesthetic.
It requires imagination to appreciate beauty, realize the
significance of truths, and evaluate conduct; and the latter

two processes also require logical inference. These higher processes also involve the lower, i.e., sensation, perceptual meaning, and memories and images of these.

Thus in our higher subjective processes there is actually more subjective activity in any one moment than in the lower. That is why, moment for moment and hour for hour, so far as they are positive in form and quality, we evaluate the higher subjective processes as greater goods than the lower. They actually contain more of that which is good, i.e., more subjective activity which is positive in form and quality. These higher subjective processes can also contain more of that which is intrinsically a natural evil, i.e., subjective activity which is negative in form and quality. Our deepest and bitterest sorrows as well as our highest joys and greatest happiness are those of our subjective activity at its richest and fullest.

Thus far we have attended almost exclusively to intrinsic natural good and evil; but every moment of subjective activity is also an instrumentality productive of consequences for future good and evil. In evaluating the total goodness or badness of an action or experience, we take its whole natural value together, intrinsic and instrumental. In such evaluation the instrumental value is usually overwhelmingly the more important, and here, obviously, the value for good or ill of the higher mental processes usually outweighs that of the lower. In particular, the activity of the higher mental processes tends to enlarge our capacity for further subjective activity and for control of that activity in ways which make for good rather than bad. We call this growth of our subjective capacity the development of personality.

Thus we see that our analysis of intrinsic natural good leads us to recognition of the validity of one of the most widely accepted criteria of the distinction of true good and evil—the criterion of personal development. Broadly speaking, intrinsic natural good consists of subjective activities of the sort which constitute a part of the process of personal development; and the higher the personal development expressed in them, the better those subjective processes are. Instrumental good consists of those factors, physical, intellectual, and social, which contribute to the development of personality. To sum it up in a word, natural good, intrinsic and instrumental together, consists in human welfare and whatever contributes to it.

This may seem to some of our readers a trite and common-sense conclusion to come out of an elaborate analysis. Since the conclusion is so simple, why all the bother of the analysis? The reason is that the analysis, if correct, makes clear in what human welfare consists. It consists in those conscious life-activities of the sort which constitute a part of the process of personal development, and the richer the elaboration of those life-activities, the better. Such development and opportunity require security of access to the physical means of life and growth, educational opportunity and stimuli, freedom as wide as is consistent with the good of others, and an environment which demands from each the expression of the best within him.

It should also be clear wherein our analysis agrees with, and differs from, the frequently adopted view which simply identifies good with the process of satisfaction of desire. It agrees with this view in finding intrinsic natural good in the positive, or appetitive, feeling-striving process, and evil in activities predominantly expressing aversion: but there are two differences. First, it does not regard the feeling-striving process as always expressing one or more specific desires, responding to specific stimuli and tending to specific ends. It looks on the life-process as essentially creative and free, constantly ongoing and seeking new expression.

Specific desires are simply the special canalizations of

the life-process, responding to the stimulus and pressure of specific types of situation in ways found satisfactory in the past. Merely to fulfil such desires is to remain bound to the past, dominated by the achievements of earlier stages of development. Only the generalized, nonspecific urge to creative and experimental living really manifests the upward and onward thrust of life; and this upward and onward thrust is a *gratifying* process but not a *satisfying* one, not a process of moving toward satisfaction. It is never satisfied. In this it differs from desire, properly so called. If we speak of the good as the process of satisfying desire, we place the emphasis on the canalized and stereotyped goods. If we say, instead, that the good is conscious life-activity that is positive in form and quality, we open the way to the discovery that the chief emphasis must be laid on the onward and upward movement of life and mind; and this discovery is made when we observe that the greater goods are not merely the most intense satisfactions but the richer and more fully developed phases of mental life.

The second difference between our theory of the good and that which identifies it with satisfaction of desire lies in the important distinction we have drawn between moral and natural good. When good is simply identified with the process of satisfaction, without this distinction, then the difference between right and wrong has to be identified with the difference between the more satisfying and the less satisfying. The effort has to be made to show that self-sacrifice for the greater good of the community is not really self-sacrifice but a way of attaining true satisfaction, or it has to be admitted that no real self-sacrifice is ever morally required of anyone. The former of these alternatives, however, as we have seen in Chapter 3, is contrary to the facts; and the latter is contrary to the moral idealism of mankind.

It is important, therefore, to recognize that satisfaction

of desire is only a partial phase of natural good, and that moral good consists in the effort to do what one thinks is right, i.e., to fulfil obligations. It must be clearly recognized that the sense of obligation is not itself a desire. To be aware of an unfulfilled or violated obligation may make us uncomfortable, and this mental discomfort may arouse a desire to be rid of it, which may lead to fulfilment of the obligation or to an attempt to make reparation. However, the awareness of an obligation is not an awareness of a sensation or emotion. It is the awareness of a relation which sets up an inner constraint or tension in the organization of our structure of purpose; and it is linked with awareness of interpersonal relations in the social structure. It arises only at the level of self-conscious purpose and is discerned by intelligent thought rather than by feeling. The obligation reveals itself as a relation constraining us to do something that is often opposed by predominant desires; and its importance is recognized as quite independent of any desires in its favor, or any desires to be rid of a sense of guilt occasioned by it. The goodness of the process of fulfilling an obligation is therefore something quite distinct from the goodness of the process of fulfilling (i.e., satisfying) a desire. One process is good in one sense, that of natural good, and the other is good in a different sense. It is a moral good.

OBLIGATION: ITS RELATION TO DESIRE

Our next problem, therefore, is to analyze the nature of obligation. We have already seen that this is generally recognized to be something of the nature of a demand or requirement. It is a relation within the interwoven structure of the self and society. It exercises a constraint upon the individual but is not sufficient of itself to determine his behavior. To be aware of the obligation constrains him, but its fulfilment also requires his assent and often some effort. Our study of naturalistic ethics showed the failure of persistent attempts to explain man's sense of obligation as it has evolved and come to clear and strong expression in the moral consciousness of the acknowledgedly great moral leaders of society. It there takes the form of a sense of obligation to be impartially concerned with the welfare of all who can be affected by our actions, and this ideal is endorsed as ideally expressive of our obligation by a general consensus of civilized mankind. It is this widespread phenomenon—the sense of obligation in this form—that has to be explained if we are to understand the moral nature of man.

This phenomenon naturalistic ethics seeks to explain as arising from a rational consideration by the individual of the problem of securing fulfilment of the completest possible range of his own interests, or desires, as operating in the social matrix and subject to social pressures. We have seen how various forms of interpretation of this view all break down. All these interpretations, however, we have also seen, are based upon a certain biological theory of human nature. This theory regards the feeling-striving processes, out of which our mental life has evolved, as originally and essentially reactions of the organism tending to maintain and restore its equilibrium and expand its growth and power. All later developments of these processes, therefore, have to be explained as elaborations of reactions tending to self-preservation and expansion. It is this naturalistic theory of human nature that has confined naturalistic ethics to an attempt to explain the sense of obligation as arising both from a more or less enlightened pursuit of self-interest and the effect of social pressures, resulting from the group's pursuit of its own common interests. The failures of efforts to explain the moral life within the limitations of this theory of human nature, therefore, call for a critical re-examination and reconstruction of the theory.

To begin with, we should note that the theory is not based on empirical considerations but on the naturalistic assumption of the primacy of matter—which is a metaphysical dogma without basis in empirical facts.[2] Empirical considerations suggest that the feeling-striving process is primarily active (not merely reactive) and directed upon objects beyond itself, not primarily concerned with restoration of the internal status quo. This is indicated by the following facts: (1) Animal life is essentially active, going out to impinge itself upon its environment, not merely reacting to effects of the environment upon it so as to restore equilibrium. (2) Feeling-striving is directed primarily upon external objects, not upon an inner state of pleasure. Pleasure or satisfaction is felt when the objects are controlled and adjusted in ways we want them to be. It is the *wanting the objects to be thus and so* that is primary. (3) We are not content with sameness of objects, however comfortable we are internally, but experience an urge to manipulate and change them. (4) The sort of change which, on the whole, we strive to create in objects is the sort that makes it possible to control and readjust objects more and more effectively. Thus that state of objects is regarded as good which is seen as serving the expansive movement of life. (5) Although the young child at first necessarily judges objects as good only as they are seen as gratifying the expansive movement of his own life, yet it seems evident that, as soon as he becomes clearly aware of the existence of other centers of such life and gratification, he judges objects as good if seen as gratifying the life activity of those others; he then

[2] For the evidence for this assertion, see two articles by the author in the *Journal of Philosophy*. (1) "Naturalism and the Concept of Matter" (August 26, 1948); (2) "The Naturalistic Concept of Mind" (October 21, 1948).

manifests spontaneous interest in these goods, though such interest is not at first strong enough to counteract established interests in the goods that are seen as more immediately gratifying.

These facts indicate that the feeling-striving process is not merely a reaction tending to restore the equilibrium of the organism. It is an expansive and *creative* activity, driving the organism to impinge itself on its environment. It reacts selectively to the environment in ways which are found to increase the malleability of the environment to life-activity. When it acquires the capacity to think, it draws the distinction of good and bad (in the instrumental sense) among its objects, good being those that tend to increase the malleability of the environment to life activity and bad those that have a reverse effect. Because the primary nature of its drive is upon the world of objects (not reactively upon itself), and its selective choice is primarily directed to increasing the malleability of objects (not to increasing its own power over objects), its primary aim, as it discovers its world to be a world containing many such lives as its own, becomes that of increasing the malleability of its world to such life as its own. Thus life below the human level is incapable of being self-regarding (because incapable of an idea of the self), and at the human level it is not *primarily* self-regarding. The feeling-striving process is still directed upon the objective world, and its selective preference is for forms of that world that seem to it to be malleable to life activity—to life activity *such as* it intimately knows in itself, *but not only to its own* life activity.

Thus the feeling-striving processes that enter into the structure of the human mind are *primarily and basically disinterested*. The self-interested processes of mind are a later development, coming only after the idea of the self has been clearly developed. They never, even in the fully developed consciousness, form a large part of the total mental activity, for most of our purposive striving is directed upon external objects as its final goals, without explicit thought of self-satisfaction or its reverse. If self-interested processes tend to predominate in the personality, we have the maladjustment known as an excessive introversion. Extroverted interests are those in which the individual's own body and empirical self are seen as means to the shaping and reshaping of the objective world beyond the embodied self. Introverted interests are those in which this is reversed—the world of things and other persons has become a means to ends found within the embodied self. In the normal, well-integrated personality, it is the extroverted interests that must predominate.

Feelings of satisfaction and dissatisfaction are, however, the phenomena that primarily determine that distinction in meaning among objects which we call good and bad (in the instrumental sense), and the organism develops habits of directing its activities toward creation of objective situations that thus seem good. Since the goods (instrumentally good objects) that directly affect the individual himself are the only ones of which he is aware in his early years, and since these goods always play the largest and most vivid part in his experience, *habit tends to be chiefly directed upon the goods that are good for the individual himself* (or herself) rather than upon what is good for other persons; the same is true of appetites and other inherited drives.

Thus the *set tendencies*, or *specific drives*, of the personality are chiefly of the kind we call egoistic rather than altruistic; yet the *primary or basic tendency* of the feeling-striving process as a whole is a disinterested striving to produce what seems to the individual objectively good. The striving processes of the individual can only constitute an integrated whole so far as they are directed objectively toward what appears to be the greatest possible good. Any specific drive which, by force of habit, appetite, and the like, produces a choice of some lesser good rather than a greater, must involve a loss of integrity, of personal integration, and this must be true even though the individual sees the lesser good as a good for himself and the greater as a good only for other people. Reflection on such a choice therefore tends to discover a peculiar sense of constraint—something different from desire, but nevertheless a motivation—toward choice of the greater (or greatest possible) good. This is the sense of obligation. It is the inner demand of the self for maintenance of its own personal integrity.

This fact that the feeling-striving process (the sort of process by the multiplication and elaboration of which a mind is constructed) is primarily disinterested has been obscured by the fact that habit and native impulse are so largely matters of individual or private interest. It is habit and native impulse that control conduct in our earlier years and it is only very slowly that conduct comes to be modified by reflection on the sense of obligation and by the later-developing social interests. To the person with a zeal for righteousness, therefore, man presents a rather sorry picture. To the religious mind, in spite of a genuine good will toward men, man is thus apt to appear chiefly in the role of sinner. Human nature is interpreted as basically evil. It is thought incredible that the natural human will, the feeling-striving process in its essential nature, could be a disinterested tendency creatively seeking to mold its world in ways that seem good. The same facts make a similar impression on the naturalistic philosopher—added to which his conception of the primacy of matter and of the feeling-striving tendency as an organic reaction growing out of organic needs also tends to blind him to the primarily disinterested nature of purposive striving.

The facts of human selfishness and pride, however, should not blind us to the primarily objective and disinterested character of the feeling-striving process—a fact which discloses the real basis of the moral life in human nature; for the reason for the egoism and egotism of human beings is perfectly clear. They are due to (*a*) the initial infantile blindness to the existence of other lives, (*b*) the establishment during this period of blindness of strong habits and drives to pursue goods of immediate concern to its own life, (*c*) the inheritance from its ancestry of tendencies to other drives equally blind to the welfare of other persons. Primarily, though, the feeling-striving process is neither egoistic nor altruistic in its conative tendency. Its aim is creative in the sense of tending to choose whatever seems to promote the expansive movement of life.

OBLIGATION: THE CONSTRAINT TOWARD IMPARTIALITY AND OBJECTIVITY

It thus comes about that when we reflectively analyze *what we really want* and draw conclusions as to what we call a "reasonable" choice, then (*a*) if the choice is between a lesser but immediate and a later but greater and equally certain good (both being merely one's own goods and indifferent to the welfare of others), then it always seems "reasonable" to choose the greater good, even though we may have a stronger desire for the more immediate one. We say we *ought* to choose the greater good in the long run. If, however, (*b*) the choice is between a lesser good seen as "good for me but not for others" and a definitely greater good seen as "good for others but not for me," then, unless strongly affected by desire for the former good or prejudice against the other persons, we tend to feel it is "reasonable" to put the greater good of others ahead of our own lesser good. Unless there is some specific and fixed notion of a moral rule or "right" involved to affect judgment to the contrary, we say we *ought* to give preference to the greater good even though it is not a "good for me."

Reflective analysis of any situation in which a choice is involved, even though it may reveal that some egoistic desire is the strongest, yet, if it also reveals that this is in conflict with some greater good of other persons, then it tends to reveal an interest in that greater good and to present that interest as more "reasonable," more in harmony with the essential nature of the feeling-striving process as creative effort to modify the environment in ways found good. There is thus set up a relation of constraint within the self between (*a*) the habit-strengthened desire for some familiar good that is one's own good and (*b*) the interest in the greater good, which is more representative of the true nature of the self as a system of essentially creative and object-centered feeling-striving processes. The more thought dwells on this situation, the stronger the desire for the greater good (for others) becomes because it finds its integration with the basic character of the whole creative process that constitutes the self. Satisfactory integration of the self in decision is not possible unless either the thought of the greater good is stifled or the desire for the lesser good (for self) is subordinated. The former solution brings only temporary satisfaction unless it purchases integration and decision at the price of psychological repression and stultification of rational self-development. The period of adolescence, when the new interests in the welfare of others are clear, spontaneous, and unrepressed, and the old egoistic drives strong, yet not well organized or controlled, is a period of moral conflicts. Gradually the two types of interest, egoistic and altruistic, find an accepted place in a set of habits. Some place is given to altruism, but some of its further reaches are stifled; the compromise is made comfortable by establishment of some mild but sufficient repressions so that the sense of obligation is not too disturbing but functions to play a part in maintaining a "reasonable" (not uncomfortably vigorous or far-reaching) concern for the general welfare.

Thus most of us adopt, and adapt ourselves to, the moral standards of our time, pitying or scorning the poor sinner who is not able to do so, and disliking the prophet, the saint, and the moral critic whose nobler ways and ideals disturb our comfortable repressions. Yet the prophet, saint, and critic are able to disturb such morality of mediocrity because, if they can only drive the morally self-satisfied mediocre person to think and think hard about his senses of value and obligation, they force him to penetrate his crust of habit and discover the inner constraint to be concerned impartially with the greatest possible good. The prophet, saint, and critic are persons whom the circumstances of life have made sufficiently self-critical to discover that constraint for themselves—a constraint which, oftentimes in history, the discoverer has found so foreign to his familiar self and the demands of his society that he has believed it must come from a superhuman source. If it be true that the life of man, the creative impulse which thus unfolds itself in moral sensitivity and spiritual aspiration, is in some way derived from the divine, "begotten of God," then the prophet's conviction on this point is sound. The prophet and his followers find support and courage in this conviction; but it is important to note here that the moral conviction does not rest on the theological, but on the inner experience of moral constraint.

If this analysis is correct, then "obligation" is the name

of a psychological relation that exists and may be vaguely or clearly felt as a constraint within the structure of that system of interest processes (conscious and unconscious) that constitutes a self or personality. The constraining element within this complex is the need of the self for unity or consistency of its purposive life. The elements under constraint are the impulses and desires which drive toward specific goals determined by habit and inherited constitution. The ultimate direction of the constraint is determined by the basic tendency of every feeling-striving process, so far as it is conscious of its end, to direct itself primarily upon the objective world beyond it (rather than introvertedly upon its own feeling-states or idea of the self) and to seek to shape that objective world in ways that seem to it to be good. This inner constraint is not itself a desire, although the discomfort it engenders may stimulate a desire to solve the problem in some way; but the constraint may be effective in stimulating an effort to achieve personal integration, "to obtain control of one's self," and make a decision in the direction indicated by the sense of obligation. In that it also stimulates further thought, it also functions to bring other desires into focus, thus tending to restrain the desire that is out of harmony with the major trend of personality.

The fundamental constraint of the sense of obligation, if clearly envisioned, must always be to direct us to do what is for the greatest good of all concerned. The fundamental principle of ethical right therefore must be first to *discover* how to produce this maximum good and then to *do* what is thus required. Particular moral principles, such as the preservation of life, property, freedom, truth, and the like must be subordinate. The sense of obligation often attaches mistakenly to such principles as moral absolutes because of the failure to distinguish means and end, making

the common means an end in itself. The only moral absolute (or unconditional, categorical obligation) that is demonstrated by this analysis is the obligation to use one's best
efforts to discover and produce what would be best for
all concerned, but it is important to recognize that this
is an absolute, unconditional, or categorical obligation. It
is a demand, the source of which lies in the essential nature
of the feeling-striving processes that constitute the self.
Thus something in the self that is more than any one desire
or set of desires demands of us that we consider and pursue
the greatest possible good of all concerned. This fundamental principle thus becomes the criterion for the settle-
ment of all ethical disputes. By it every specific ethical
question, and the validity and applicability of every principle of secondary generality, such as those of the Ten Com-
mandments, must be tested.

This, then, is the fundamental *objective* principle of
right and wrong; but we must not forget the distinction
between the subjective and objective standpoints in regard
to obligation. From the subjective standpoint, it is right to
do one's best to find out what one ought to do, and then
to do it. The person who has understood and accepted
the above objective principle will therefore be subjectively
right if he does his best to find its application to each specific situation and acts accordingly. The primitive, or other
person, who has not understood and accepted this principle,
may experience a different obligation. This is the inner
constraint toward integrity of his personality, impelling him
toward a different action because of his different personality
and limited outlook. If he acts accordingly, his action is
subjectively right and praiseworthy. He will feel moral satisfaction in so acting, but if he open-mindedly considers the
fact that he has destroyed greater values (for certain other
persons or groups) than those he has produced or main-

tained, then his satisfaction is apt to be disturbed by a shadow of doubt and inner tension. He may dismiss this as foolishness or disloyalty to his own group, but if he lets his mind dwell upon it, seeking, as one must do to be subjectively right, the answer to the question as to what is really objectively right, then the doubt grows. It is in this way that at length the insight dawns that it can really be objectively right only to seek impartially the greatest possible good of all concerned. It is thus that loyalty to the subjective standard led at last, in the long history of ethical inquiry, to the discovery of the objective. And, in the lives of those brought up to respect the objective standard, loyalty to it, as subjective standard also, develops an increasing conviction of its subjective value and objective validity.

The sanction of this fundamental objective moral principle is that adherence to it is the price of personal integration with self-understanding. If we depart from it, mental peace and strength can only be maintained with more or less repression and loss of inner integrity. Thus it is *in general* the most fundamental condition of happiness, though it may *sometimes* require the sacrifice of much of one's own happiness for that of others; but we must not confuse the sanction with the source and ground of the moral demand. It is not *because* it makes for inner peace and happiness that we ought to abide by the principle. The moral *ought* is a requirement that issues from the teleological, creative, and object-directed or self-transcending character of the processes that constitute the self, and it is independent of the effects of its demands upon the happiness of the person required to fulfil them.

Further sanctions of the ethical principle come from society, but society, because of the persistence of infantile egoism, native impulse, and social tradition, does not always shape its sanctions in true accord with the principle. It often condones selfishness and endorses sectional favoritism and even hatred. There is a sanction that hangs over society, however, if it does not shape its special moral principles in accord with the requirement of ethical universalism; for a society with a narrow or inadequate ethics is one that is exerting the weight of its influence in ways that stultify and distort the personalities of its own members. It impresses on them certain repressions and disintegrity. It may flourish for a time, but it contains the seeds of inner decay. Thus any society that takes a long view of its future must set up its special principles and sanctions in accord with what we have seen to be the basic ethical demand of human nature.

The Two Elements in Conscience:
Critical and Traditional

This analysis, finally, enables us to clarify the status of conscience, both as to the respect due to it and as to its limitations. We can see that it contains two elements, one of which is, in a sense, innate, and the other the effect of external influences, particularly social conditioning. The innate element derives from the fact that it is the natural tendency of the feeling-striving process, as it becomes aware of alternatives, to respond positively to the one that appears to be characterized by the greatest value. This establishes, as a basic requirement for integration of the purposive life, the need that activity should be maintained in harmony with the principle of impartial concern for the greatest possible good. The inner constraint in this direction must always be present, though its nature, extent, and importance are only slowly realized. It is this element in conscience that accounts for its persistent thrust toward the ethic of the brotherhood of man and the dramatic and revolutionary advances of prophetic reformers beyond the limits of tribal codes and traditional creeds. It is the basic element in the *critical*, as distinct from the *traditional*, conscience.

Concerning this element in conscience, religion may, with reason, acknowledge the claim that "the voice of conscience is the voice of God"; for if there is any truth at all in a theistic interpretation of the universe and the doctrine of divine immanence, then the feeling-striving process, which is the essence of life, must owe its essential nature to the divine being. The natural tendency of that feeling-striving process, which expresses its essential nature, is to strive creatively to realize larger and larger possibilities of good wherever they may be found. That element in conscience which demands of the individual that he concern himself impartially with the welfare of all must, therefore, be recognized by religion as of divine origin, clearly expressive of the divine will.

There is, however, another element in conscience for which the religious interpretation (unless it adopts a complete theological determinism) can make no such claim. A religion which recognizes human moral responsibility must assert that much in individual character is due to personal choices and social conditioning. The demands of formed character constitute the second, and often the most pressing, element in that inner constraint toward maintenance of personal integrity which is described as conscience. These demands of formed character may or may not be in harmony with those arising from the general tendency of feeling-striving to respond to what appear to be the possibilities of greatest good. If they are not, then a contradiction will be felt within conscience until either character is adjusted to the fundamental ethical demand, or that fundamental ethical demand, as expressing itself in this connection, is repressed, or the two are harmonized by discovery that the conflict was due to mistaken ideas as to what really constitutes the greatest good in such a situation.

Because of the fact that formed character (as well as the general tendency to pursue the greatest good) exercises its constraint for maintenance of its integrity, conscience is subject to inner conflicts that appear as conflicts of principle, as well as to questions as to what really constitutes the greatest good. Even when there are no such inner conflicts and doubts, the felt constraint of conscience may be out of harmony with what would really be required by the principle of impartial pursuit of the greatest possible good. This happens when there is a mistaken judgment concerning the means to the greatest good, and when established habits and loyalties to social groups and accepted principles and institutions create a conscientious constraint so strong as to repress the constraint arising from recognition of the greater values lost or destroyed by rigid adherence to the established code.

Conscience, therefore, considered simply as the felt inner constraint of our moral structure, is an unsafe guide. It requires illumination arising from an intelligent understanding of its dual nature and multiple sources; and it requires always an intelligent inquiry into the nearer and remoter consequences of each contemplated action. An uncritical assumption that conscience is always "the voice of God" is therefore both foolish and dangerous. The same is true of a nonreligious uncritical conscientiousness or moral dogmatism. It is true that loyalty to conscience, in the sense of maintaining the integrity of one's ethical convictions and the doing of one's duty as one sees it, is the essence of the moral life. But the first principle of such conscientiousness must be the maintenance of a constant critical and openminded inquiry into what is really good and really right.

Without such a critical (and, indeed, *self*-critical) and

open-minded inquiry, it is entirely possible for a person to be selfish, proud, and prejudiced, and yet well extroverted and possessed of an easy conscience. The psychologically "normal" person is by no means devoid of repressions, and the tendency to take an interest in the welfare of others, since it develops only after the habits of pursuing many other satisfying goals are already well formed, is not very difficult to repress. Thus where there is little tendency to reflective analysis of one's own motives and values, the sense of obligation may do little to disturb selfish complacency and strong prejudice. Integration of personality is then purchased cheaply at the price of this lack of self-understanding. Borrowing a term from William James, we may call these persons the healthy-minded sinners—and the world is full of them; but the roots of the primary and critical conscience in the tendency of human interest to become positively concerned with the welfare of others are revealed when the analyzing intelligence is turned inward upon the experience of motivation, valuation, and the sense of obligation. Complacent selfishness and prejudice are then inevitably disturbed; and the person who is in earnest about such self-understanding discovers more and more clearly that the price of peace in his inner life is the cultivation of attitudes of impartial concern for the welfare of all.

The integration of the "healthy-minded sinner" is therefore something far short of genuine integrity of personality. It is a relatively unstable equilibrium achieved only at the cost of stultification of personal development in its most distinctive form—growth in the discernment and attainment of values. If by "integrity of personality" we mean not merely a psychological integration which comfortably adapts the individual to cope successfully with his environment, but an integration which frees his energies for the fullest possible measure of coordinated growth, then the requirements of such personal integrity can be seen to be equivalent to those of the most enlightened moral conscience. The vital energies of the personality, straining to maintain such conditions of free and intelligent development, can be seen to be the source of that inner constraint toward choice of the greatest possible good which we recognize as the sense of duty growing gradually to a more and more complete understanding of its own essential demands.

Finally, this enables us both to offer a definition of the term "obligation," which was left undefined in our discussion of semantic problems in Chapter 5, and to state broadly the fundamental principle of obligation. An obligation is the relation of a voluntary agent to an action or restraint of action required of him by the conditions of his personal integrity, understanding by that integrity the integration of his purposive life in a way which frees his energies for the fullest possible measure of coordinated growth. The basic principle of obligation is the requirement to do one's best to discover and fulfil the conditions of the greatest possible natural good for all who are or can be affected by one's conduct. Our analysis of the problems of ethics has therefore led us to an ethical theory that is naturalistic in the sense that all ethical terms, even including the term "obligation," have now been defined in terms referring to natural psychological processes; but this has involved a rejection of the common contemporary naturalistic theory of human nature which interprets all human motivation as directly or indirectly derived from the biological tendency of the organism to react to its environment in ways which tend to restore its own equilibrium and facilitate the expansion of its own ongoing life.

Chapter 6

PUBLIC GOOD AND INDIVIDUAL RIGHTS

The Conflict of Ultimate End and Specific Duty

Our analysis has led us to a teleological ethics, an ethics which says that questions of right and wrong must be judged by their consequences for natural human good. Our next problem, therefore, is to guard against certain dangers and difficulties which history has shown to be inherent in such a position. The dangers arise not only from the blindness of prejudiced and selfish persons but also from the ruthlessness of clear-sighted and well-intentioned persons. There are those who think they know better than others what is for the public good and have a program for its realization. All too often such persons think they are justified in ignoring common ethical principles and violating the rights of individuals in pressing their great program to its grand conclusion. Thus a Communist justifies violent revolution, treachery, assassination, and the "liquidation" of opposing groups as means to his Utopian end; Puritans justified the burning of alleged witches; the Catholic church has justified torture for the saving of souls and the glory of God; and the Prophet of Nazareth was crucified by those who judged it better that one man should die than that the established order should be imperiled. These are notorious examples; but in a host of minor cases the ruthlessness of well-intentioned persons dressed in a little brief authority reveals the need of an ethic which demands respect of principles as well as an impartial effort to produce the greatest possible good.

Not only is it dangerous in practice to maintain an ethic that pays exclusive attention to consequences. The position is also faced with certain theoretical difficulties. The appeal to the general consensus of ethical judgment makes it clear that there are some specific obligations that the moral consciousness affirms in apparent independence of any appeal to consequences for good or evil.

In the first place, there are specific obligations which are due directly to specific past actions or continuing attitudes of the person obligated rather than to considerations arising from the consequences of the action that would fulfil the obligation. Promises, contracts, pledges, sales, and other business transactions create such obligations. Society puts itself under certain obligations by promulgating laws granting certain privileges or opportunities and guaranteeing the performance of certain functions. The assumptions of social intercourse and communication create obligations; and so do the accepting of favors and the committing of acts which directly or indirectly injure another person. Altogether apart from any calculation of benefits in consequences, these acts result in obligations; they give the other person what we call a "right" to expect something. Yet these rights are not absolute. Where a serious balance of evil or loss of good would result, they are set aside by the obligation to produce the greatest possible good; but the point is that they do have some degree of independence of that general and ultimate obligation.

In the second place, we must recognize that these specific rights and obligations sometimes seem very clearly to maintain themselves in apparent opposition to the general and ultimate obligation. This is clearest in the case of an obligation to make reparation for an injury. Suppose an impecunious family man should have his car skid on an icy road into another car, parked and empty. No one has seen the accident and he drives off, having recognized the damaged car as belonging to a man earning twice his own salary, and aware that he has done it a hundred dollars' worth of damage more than his insurance will cover. He might argue that a greater total good would be done by leaving the hundred dollars in his own bank account than by acknowledging the accident and paying for it. But it will generally be agreed that this does not affect his obligation to pay. A more serious and even clearer example is the following. Suppose a respected family man had committed a murder to defend himself against blackmail arising from a crime in his youth. He then finds a lonely and friendless hermit charged with the crime and condemned to death by strong circumstantial evidence. He might argue that justice would be served in the eyes of the public as well by this man's death as his own, and less harm would be suffered by family and friends. But would this balancing of good over evil justify the guilty man in allowing an innocent person to die in his place? Again, the general consensus of opinion supports the specific principles of the rights and duties of the individual against an argument based on total consequences for public good.

These cases of the apparent primacy of a specific duty to an individual over the duty to produce the greatest total good could be multiplied indefinitely. It is, in general, true of all promises, contracts, debts, and the like. If it can be proved that some slight balance of general good would result from repudiation of a contract or a debt, we still do not regard that as justifying the wrong involved to the individual who loses by it. Sometimes we may say that an individual is selfish to insist upon his contractual right when it is clearly against the public interest. But we still recognize that he has the right, and that private rights should not be set aside except to avoid very serious public loss. The obligation to produce the greatest possible good seems thus to be made to take its place as merely one obligation to be balanced against others. In the case where specific injury to some individual is involved, it always seems particularly clear that a mere cumulation of good consequences to *other* persons does not readily justify the action, even though the amount of good seems definitely to outweigh the evil. Probably the clearest cases of this kind are those where an innocent person is made to suffer for the guilty. All these cases seem to come under the heading of specific obligations, such as the implicit contractual obligations of society established by law and the obligation of a man to save another whom he has put in danger or injured by his own action. They are thus cases where a specific obligation seems to hold good against the general obligation to produce the greatest possible good.

Another instance where the obligation to produce the greatest possible good seems to be challenged is that where an unequal distribution of good seems to promise the greatest total amount of good, and yet a more equal distribution seems more just and therefore right. In a country where the farmers are one third of the community, and the poorest class, would it be fair to adopt a tariff which would further depress the condition of the agricultural community but benefit the more prosperous and larger section engaged in commerce and manufacturing? Would such a tariff be right if it could be shown that it definitely increased the prosperity (and presumably the good) of the community as a whole, even after making allowance for the loss and added discontent of the agricultural section? Or would the inequity be wrong in spite of the contribution to the greater good? Most persons seem to agree that the increase in inequity would not be justified unless by a very great contribution to the good of the already favored section or a very slight loss for the less favored. If it would be unjust, and therefore wrong, then we have here a further case of the obligation to justice apparently outweighing that to produce the greatest possible good—for we cannot accept the way out of the difficultly adopted by those who say that equitable distribution in itself constitutes an intrinsic good of such high value as to turn the scale. Only conscious life-activities are intrinsically good; so the mode of distribution can only be an instrumental good. Our example presupposes that its effects are taken into consideration when we say that the inequitable measure still produces a balance of good over evil.

Do Specific Duties Have an Independent Basis?

All these are cases where an injustice to an individual or group is considered a wrong in spite of the fact that it is instrumental to a greater balance of good over evil than could have been produced without the injustice. The argument that the injustice is justified in such cases is commonly referred to as assuming that the end justifies the means. Those who have insisted that the only moral principle that has ever to be taken into consideration is that of producing the greatest possible good have often argued that the end does justify the means and that nothing else but good ends can justify anything. This, for example, is explicitly stated by G. E. Moore,[1] though he is careful to show that the calculation of ends (or consequences) must include the means.

On the other hand, cases of the kind to which we have

[1] *Principia Ethica,* (London: Cambridge University Press, 1903), p. 147.

been referring have led another important group of British philosophers to develop the thesis that the obligation to do good is only one of a number of obligations, none of which can be formulated as a principle, but each of which can be discerned in the specific situation where it arises and must be intuitively weighed against any other obligation in the same situation. Thus W. D. Ross argues that there are two distinct types of obligation:[2] First, a general obligation to produce all the good we can. Second, three specific obligations arising in each case from a specific past action: (1) The obligation to keep a promise. (2) To make reparation for injuries. (3) To make return for benefits received. He has then to admit that ethical theory cannot help us further in deciding which of these obligations is most important when they conflict. We are told that we must then rely on our own intuitions. This is the great practical objection to the theory, but the theoretical objection to it is its incompleteness. It does not bring together the two types of obligation to show their unity, as obligations, in a common ground.

In our analysis developed in the preceding chapter, it may be claimed that this is done. The sense of obligation we there saw arises from the self's own need of inner integrity. This integrity is threatened by any inconsistency in the volitional life. That is why we feel that the making of a promise places upon us the moral demand that we keep it. Similarly, the acceptance of social status and social responsibility as individuals who make claims upon others places upon us the obligation to acknowledge their claims upon us. So, since we expect others to make reparations for injury and to return benefits received, we must do so also. Likewise, since we expect others to tell us the truth,

[2] W. D. Ross, *Foundations of Ethics* (New York: Oxford University Press, 1939), chap. iv.

to respect our person and property and character, and to bear the consequences of their own misdeeds rather than seek to impose them on others, we must do the same. Being social individuals, maintaining a certain social "front," the adherence to the general principle of reciprocity is as much a necessity of our own inner integrity as it is of the integrity of the social order. Thus all the specific principles of ethics, including many which Ross does not mention, arise from this inner need of personal integrity. We have already shown how the general principle of impartially doing the greatest possible good arises from the same inner need.

Thus our interpretation of the roots of the moral life succeeds where Ross's fails. It shows the common source of both types of obligation. Both are requirements of inner personal integrity. We can see why specific requirements of integrity should arise from specific actions like making a promise, without reference to the general requirement of producing the greatest possible good, but we can also see why the principle of impartial concern for the greatest good should, in general, present itself as the ultimate criterion whereby to decide every moral question. It is because the pursuit of what seems to it good expresses the essential nature of each and every feeling-striving process that enters into the constitution of the life and mind of man. This, however, still leaves on our hands the problem of explaining what appear to be the exceptions to this general rule. It brings us back to the problem of the relation of the rights of the individual to the principle of doing that which will produce the greatest public good.

Moral Rights and Legal Rights

In each of the cases referred to above, we are faced with the notion of something specifically *due* to a particular individual or group. Some person or group has certain "rights" which must not be set aside, even for the sake of producing a greater good on the whole. This usage of the term "right" as a noun should be carefully distinguished from its use as an adjective. The adjective "right" means "in accord with existing obligations," and this includes the ultimate and general obligation to produce the greatest possible good; but the noun "right" always refers to something more specific. It is the name of a relation which is conversely implied by the existence of a specific obligation. If A is under obligation to perform the act X, which confers a certain benefit on B, then B has a right to have A perform the act X. B's "right" is his relation to the non-existent but specifically indicated act X, which it is A's obligation to perform.

Rights are of three kinds: rights to services; rights of possession; rights of action. A right to a certain service implies that certain persons are under positive obligation to perform that service. A right of possession or of action means that others are under the merely negative obligation to refrain from interfering with a certain person's use of certain goods in certain ways, or with his doing certain things. In each case the right and the obligation are reciprocal. The one implies the other.

Another important distinction is that of legal and moral rights. Law defines and stipulates certain obligations of the members of a community. It then becomes the right of each member to have others obey the law as it affects him, and it is the duty of certain officers of the state to

uphold the rights of each member by requiring (if necessary by force) that other members perform their obligations. The law may either state the obligations directly by
saying that certain persons shall or shall not do certain
things, or it may indirectly imply the obligation by stating
that certain persons have certain rights. In any case, obligation is implied, and this obligation is regarded as not
merely a demand of certain public authorities having power
to enforce it but also a *moral* demand; for the lawmakers
are regarded as having a moral right to make laws.

Thus a legal right is always regarded as presumptively
a moral right on account of the obligation of everyone to
obey the law. Even if the law is a bad one, a law that
ought to be changed, it is usually assumed that it ought
to be obeyed until it is changed; so the legal right, on this
assumption, is still a moral right. Only when it is maintained that the law is so bad, or so wrongly made or en-
forced, or the circumstances so peculiar or so changed, that
it is actually wrong to recognize or uphold the law, can
it logically be claimed that the legal right is not a moral
right. Where the obligation to obey the law is in such
cases denied, the right it claims to confer must also be denied. The legal right is then not recognized. Logically, it
must be denounced as a pseudo right, no real right at all.

Thus interpreted, legal rights are not a coordinate classification with moral rights, but merely a subordinate class
within the category of moral rights. The only real rights
are moral rights, for they alone imply obligation. Legal
rights are such moral rights as the law singles out to define
and support by its sanctions, or such rights as lawmakers
create by rightfully exercising their right to command and
stipulate the obligations of members of the community.
But lawmakers can create obligations within certain limits
only, and only within those limits can they create rights.

To deny this is to make the lawmaker morally absolute; it is to make the moral standard a creation of the state instead of making the state an instrument for the maintenance of the moral standard.

To assert that the moral standard, or moral law, is above the law of the state and may render it morally nugatory is not to say that there is no moral obligation to obey a morally mistaken or bad law. The public order established by law is established for the common good. It can never be perfect, but its authority must be upheld for the common good. To admit the right of private judgment as to when we should and when we should not obey the law certainly tends to undermine its authority and power to protect society. Yet that right of private judgment cannot be denied without making the state absolute above the moral standard itself. For the sake of the goods that depend on the existence of a legally ordered society, the right of private judgment, however, must be exercised with extreme care. The decision that it is right to disobey the law (the denial of a legal right) must be made only after every relevant factor affecting the right and wrong of the situation has been considered as fully as possible. When this is done, it will often be clear that it is better on the whole, and right, to obey and uphold a mistaken and bad law rather than injure the social structure by breaking it.

What those factors are which may sometimes justify the decision that an alleged legal obligation and legal right do not hold good morally is part of the problem of this chapter. Our present point, in clarifying the meaning of the concept of "a right," is to note that there *are* limits to the power of lawmakers to create rights—otherwise the state would be the creator of the moral standard instead of an instrument for its realization. It is thus morally and logically possible to deny that certain privileges which the law declares to be rights really are rights. This means not only that it is possible that certain alleged legal rights never were rights at all, but also that certain rights once established and morally justified by existing conditions have ceased to be morally justified, by reason of changed conditions, and that it is even wrong any longer to recognize them; or it may mean that a legal right which is morally justifiable in normal conditions is morally unjustifiable in certain special conditions to such an extent that it is wrong to claim or uphold it.

The category of moral rights is therefore wider than that of legal rights and includes all true legal rights. It is also wider than that of "recognized rights." In legal circles there is a tendency to confine the notion of a moral right to whatever is generally recognized as such. Thus a standard British textbook of jurisprudence defines a right (in the general, nonlegal sense) as "the name given to the advantage a man has when he is so circumstanced that a general feeling of approval, or at least of acquiescence, results when he does, or abstains from doing, certain acts, and when other people act, or forbear to act, in accordance with his wishes; while a general feeling of disapproval results when any one prevents him from so doing or abstaining at his pleasure, or refuses to act in accordance with his wishes." [3]

This limitation may be justifiable in legal practice. The judge and lawyer must be sure of their ground when they step beyond legal rights to recognize moral rights. But ethics cannot admit that rights do not exist until generally recognized, nor is such limitation practiced in general discussion of moral and social issues. We speak of "the rights of women," "the rights of labor," "the rights of small nations," and "the rights of backward peoples and oppressed

[3] T. E. Holland, *The Elements of Jurisprudence* (New York University Press, Inc., 1916), pp. 81-82.

classes," not merely in appealing to what is generally recognized as their rights but in asserting what ought to be recognized. This is justified by our definition of a right as the relation of a person to that which he may claim by reason of the specific obligation of some person or social group.

Whenever conditions create a definite obligation to do something, the person who would benefit from that action may, therefore, claim it as a moral right. Wherever we can point to a definite principle of obligation having a certain degree of generality, we can point to those who would benefit from its observance as having a specific moral right to those benefits. If the rights are not recognized, then, by pointing to the obligations, we can show that they ought to be recognized. On this ground, claims to changes in the law and in social attitudes can logically be put forward as matters of justice and right, even when not supported by any important section of public opinion. The claim can be made rationally effective if the alleged right can be shown to be logically implied by some recognized principle as applied to existing conditions. In this way, the principles of equity and the greatest good of all concerned can be made the basis of an appeal for many reforms. The reform can be presented as required as a matter of right and justice and not merely as gratuitous charity or starry-eyed idealism.

We can agree with the ancient Greeks and Romans that justice means the giving to every person whatever is his right or due. We have begun to clarify this conception of justice by defining a right as the relation of a person to that which he may claim by reason of the specific obligation of some person or group. Thus the ground upon which a right rests is always the fact that someone is under obligation to do something, and obligations in turn, as we have seen, rest upon what is required for the integrity, the integrated whole-ness, of the self.

Finally, the integrity of the self requires two things. It requires, that, ultimately and in general, voluntary conduct shall direct the best efforts of the self to produce what seems to promise the greatest possible good in all concerned. It also requires that consistency be maintained in the pur-posive life of the self, and this requirement of consistency is the source of certain specific obligations that are not di-rectly dependent upon the general obligation to produce the greatest good. Thought must be brought into harmony with action, and action into harmony with thought. This requires truthfulness and the maintenance of pledges. It requires that behavior must accord with the idea of the self, and of society, and of the status of the self in society. It thus requires the fulfilment of social responsibilities, the maintenance of self-respect and the respect of the commu-nity. On these conditions rest the obligations to return favors and make reparation for injuries.

It is on these general and specific obligations that spe-cific rights are grounded. Even the general obligation be-comes the source of specific rights in specific situations. It demands that we endeavor to do what is best for all con-cerned; and in specific situations it becomes clear that cer-tain specific things are, or would be, best. These things, then, become obligations and thus establish rights. It even becomes clear that certain specific *rules* of conduct would be best for all concerned; and it then becomes a general ob-ligation to uphold and obey these specific rules; and thus, again, those who benefit may claim a right to the benefits created by observance of the rules.

The Basic Obligation and Apparent Exceptions

This analysis of the situation reveals two ways in which what is logically recognized as a specific right may sometimes come into conflict with the general obligation to produce the greatest possible good. In the first place, the right may be one created by law or sanctioned by custom. Such rights are given specific form by the more or less explicit pledge or contract involved in law and custom. Society is pledged, and thus obligated, to do or not to do certain things; and these social obligations are legally undertaken, or obtain customary recognition, because they are thought to be conducive to the common good. These legal or customary rights thus rest indirectly upon the general obligation, but directly upon specific obligations involved in pledge and contract. In most cases the exercise of such rights is in harmony with the general principle of pursuing the greatest possible good, but occasionally there is conflict. Even a good law may have harmful effects in special instances, or it may have become out of date and so support special rights which no longer serve a useful social function; it may have been a bad law or custom from the beginning. Yet law and custom create rights: and thus specific rights sometimes conflict with what would seem to be required by an application of the principle of the greatest good.

In the second place, the right that apparently conflicts with the principle of the greatest good may be one which (apart from law and tribal custom) rests purely on specific obligations created by the individual's own action, such as the obligation to keep promises. These obligations rest on the requirement of inner consistency which is essential to the integrity of the self. When we see a situation in which this requirement of inner consistency is plainly involved, such as in the case of a promise, we immediately recognize a prima facie obligation and a right of the other person to the benefits deriving therefrom. Usually, of course, such an obligation and right are in harmony with and supported by the obligation to produce the greatest possible good. But sometimes this is not the case.

In cases of conflict between general and specific obligation, the latter, because clear and specific, is apt to receive more attention and be supported by habit. The recognition of the former requires calculation of consequences and is more easily ignored. However, where every factor has been taken into consideration (including the injury to social confidence in general and that of the disappointed person in particular, the loss of self-respect and other subtle psychological disturbances, the uncertainty of future good consequences and the possibility of miscalculation), and there still appears a clear balance of good in favor of the breaking of the specific obligation, then the reflective moralist will generally agree that the obligation to produce the greatest possible good must take precedence over the specific obligation and the specific right.

If our analysis of the nature and ground of obligation is sound, then the general obligation to produce the greatest possible good must be regarded as ultimate, *providing everything is taken into consideration*. The integrity of personality requires the consistency of thought and action involved in telling truth, keeping promises, accepting responsibility for injury to others, and maintaining status by returning favors, but the deeper and more far-reaching requirement is that of keeping *all* activity in harmony with the general tendency of will to pursue the greatest possible good. To be false to that is to be false to the deepest and most constant demand in the structure of personality. To maintain consistency of conduct at the price of this deeper rift is essentially destructive of integrity. To put up with the discomfort and ignominy of failing to fulfil a specific prima facie obligation for the sake of a clearly greater good, on the whole, may hurt one's pride, but it is right; for it is the only way to maintain the real integrity of a life that finds its deepest fulfilment in the disinterested pursuit of the good.

We must, however, note the provision that *everything* must be taken into consideration. This leads to an important point. When the issue is one which concerns our own obligation as against our own apparently greater good, the situation is not the same as that of our own obligation as against the apparently greater good of others who do not benefit from the obligation. I may feel justified in neglecting to fulfil a prima facie obligation (thus depriving someone of his right) in order to save someone else toward whom I have no specific obligation from a distinctly greater loss. Should I neglect such an obligation in order to save myself from a similar loss? Here three other factors enter. In the first place, I can be more sure of the soundness of my judgment in the former case where my own personal advantage is not concerned. In the second place, where the loss is my own and I determine to take it rather than fail in my obligation, there is another compensating factor present— the good I thereby do to the strength of my own personality and the inner satisfaction of having done a difficult duty. In the third place, the likelihood that the person whose right is ignored will misunderstand the motive, feel personally injured, lose faith in the moral trustworthiness of his fellows, and even be encouraged to avoid obligations himself, is much greater in the latter case. For all these reasons, therefore, the cases where one is justified in failing to fulfil an obligation in order to preserve one's own greater good are very much less frequent than those where it is the good of others that is at stake. We need to be sure that there is a much wider margin between the good involved in keeping our obligation and that produced by breaking it when the latter good is our own. However, such cases do arise. Who will deny that a man may break a promise to pay a small debt on a certain date if he can keep his word only at the cost of his life?

Some may feel that, in resting rights on obligations and obligations on the requirements of personal integrity, we have not considered the matter sufficiently from the standpoint of the person who has the right and may be deprived of it for the sake of the greater good of some other persons. Does not the right really rest, it may be asked, on the ground that the person who has it has been led to expect certain benefits and is injured by being deprived of them? And why should he be injured to produce some other person's good? The answer to this must admit that the right may, and often does, rest on the fact that expectations have been aroused and injury would result from deprivation of the right. It is these facts that create the obligation. They do so by reason of the general obligation to produce the good (and so to prevent injury) and the specific obligation to fulfil the more or less explicit pledges that have aroused the expectations. It is only because these facts create specific obligations that they create a *moral* right. We therefore do not weaken the significance of the right when we turn attention from the need of the person who has the right to the source of obligation in the person who should respect it. We merely show why the claim based on need, contract, law, and the like has a *moral* force. It is a claim that the other person needs must respect or suffer loss of his own integrity.

When there is an apparent conflict, therefore, between specific right and the general good, we have to take *every-*

thing into consideration that affects the good of all concerned and then pursue the line that promises the greatest
good. Specific obligations (and therefore specific rights)
must give way before the obligation to pursue the greatest
possible good. If the party deprived of his rights complains
of injustice, he must be reminded of the fact that no specific rights are absolute. He may also be reminded that he,
too, is under obligation to do that which will produce the
greatest possible good. This may include the voluntary surrender of a specific right, or at least a submission to the loss
of it without protest. However, the emphasis in the statement at the beginning of this paragraph is upon the word
everything, and that leads us to a consideration of the reasons why certain cases of specific rights (such as those referred to at the beginning of this chapter) seem to be
exceptions to the ultimate criterion of the greater good.

Means and Ends: The Importance of Principles

When, in pursuit of an end involving some allegedly
much greater good, lies are told, pledges broken, property
is destroyed or stolen, pain inflicted, or life taken, the protest is commonly raised that the end does not justify the
means. Even if it is admitted that the good results eventually achieved for certain individuals outweigh the losses
or injury inflicted on others, the protest may still be made
that it is not justice to deprive some persons of their rights
in order to bring benefit to others. That is exactly what
Kant meant by saying that we should never treat any person
as a mere means to another's ends, but treat everyone as an
end in himself. Kant meant that the end never can justify
the means if the means is a specific breach of obligation.
Most persons do not go quite that far, but agree that the
mere fact that a greater good in the end is wrought cannot

always justify a specific wrong—especially when the person who suffers the wrong himself receives no sufficiently compensating good.

If we press for the reason for the assertion that the end cannot justify the means, we find two different types of answer. Some simply assert that it is always wrong to break certain specific principles. Truth, life, property, the pledged word are sacred. Certain rights and moral commands must never be set aside. This, of course, is pure formalism. Its rigor results in inevitable contradictions. It is not always possible to save both life and truth or to preserve both property and the pledged word.

But there is another line of defense of the assertion that the end does not necessarily justify the means if the means itself is unjust. It may be pointed out that to admit that it is always right to commit any injustice to individuals, so long as a greater good on the whole and in the long run is thereby produced, would so undermine confidence and cooperation in the social order that the principle must be rejected. The maintenance of social confidence and cooperation is vitally necessary to the good of every member of society. Therefore for the sake of the good of society as a whole, certain rights and obligations must be rigidly upheld, even though, in specific instances, it may be evident that a greater good could be produced if these rights were ignored, the few being made to suffer for the good of the many.

We do not have to consider merely the effect of the actual breaking of the principle in the one particular instance. What is more important is *the effect of recognizing that it is right to break the principle* whenever it appears that a greater good would thereby be done. For the sake of orderly social relations we have to insist upon a certain rigidity of certain rights, such as payment of debts and fulfilment of contracts, as not to be set aside even for the sake of producing some considerably greater good. The point is that, *for the sake of producing the greatest possible good,* society must adopt certain *principles of obligation* (and thus recognize certain rights) which must be maintained rigidly even in cases where a greater good on the whole would result from a breach of the principle—greater, that is, *except for the effect upon society of recognizing that it would be right to break the principle in such cases.*

Are there any such principles which society, for the sake of confidence and cooperation in the social order, needs to make absolute or almost absolute? Probably there are none for which absoluteness can be claimed. Surely no individual could expect any of his rights, even that of his life and good name, to be respected at the cost of the lives, or the social degradation and slavery, of multitudes. But there are many rights which society needs to demand should be respected *on principle,* even where some considerably greater good to a larger number of other persons could be produced if those rights as affecting certain individuals were set aside.

One such case would certainly be the right of the innocent person to his good name and to freedom from the penalties of the law incurred by some other person's crime. If we should recognize it as right for the police, judges, jurors, or other persons to pin a crime on an innocent person and punish him, in any case where they thought the public good would be served by doing so, we would undermine confidence in the law and cooperation in support of it. We must therefore maintain that such action is wrong *in principle* even in a case where the policeman, or other person who might be able to do it, is sure that the public good would thereby be served and that the true facts of the case would never be discovered.

We may know that people sometimes do such things,

but we cannot admit that it would be right to do them unless it should be in some rare case where such breach of principle was necessary to avert a terrible disaster. Public confidence in the social order is not undermined by admission that a vitally important right of one or a few individuals may justifiably be ignored on the rare occasions when that is necessary to avert some great public disaster or produce some very great public good. But confidence would be undermined by admission that anyone may ignore another person's rights whenever he calculates that the end would justify the means.

This same general principle holds with regard to all recognized specific obligations and rights. Wherever there is a recognized principle of human relations on which people rely in their intercourse with one another, either because it is the law, or because it is generally recognized as morally right, honorable, or decent, the keeping of that principle has a value for its own sake. Simply because it is *recognized* as wrong to do otherwise, because the expectations and calculations of others are built upon its general recognition, it has an importance as part of a stable social order. So long as its effect is *in general* wholesome, it should usually be kept even in particular cases where it does not produce the greatest possible good.

There is always a limit to this principle of keeping principles, obeying laws, and not infringing recognized rights. For all the more fundamental human rights, however, the limit is high. We need to be very sure that the greater good served is so great that it will be generally recognized that no one could reasonably expect his rights to be preserved at the cost of the loss of so great a good or the production of such an evil.

We need to be particularly sure, and reluctant to override the rights of others for the sake of some greater good, when that greater good is one that specially suits our own interest. We are all too apt to overestimate the good and underestimate the injury to the rights of others when our own interests are concerned. Other persons, in such cases, are very apt to suspect the purity of our motives.

We are now in a position to see more clearly the rather involved relations between the specific and general obligations. The ground of all obligation is the self's own demand for personal integrity.[4] This requires that we (a) maintain the inner consistency of our own thought and action, (b) in doing so do our best at all times to produce the greatest possible good. In the long run, to do the one, we must, as far as possible, do the other. So, if the implications of the principle of the greatest possible good are fully recognized, it includes adherence to the specific obligations arising from (a), as far as possible. Because the specific obligations arise from specific action, they are, in general, more obvious than the implications of the general obligation, (b); and they are brought into existence quite independently of it. When a specific obligation has been brought into existence, it constitutes a new condition that has to be taken into consideration in any subsequent effort to fulfil the general and ever-present obligation to pursue the greatest possible good. It cannot be ignored without doing harm. And yet it does not override the general obligation, which is permanent and much more fundamental. Sometimes the condition it creates requires that what would have been a fulfilment of the general obligation, had it not been for the creation of the specific obligation, cannot rightly be undertaken, because, in the circumstances created by the specific obligation, the claim that it is right to ignore the specific obligation in those circumstances would be a greater evil than the loss of a certain amount of good involved in the adherence to it.

[4] Cf. Chapter 5, page 158.

But this is not always the case. Sometimes the loss or evil created by adherence to the specific obligation is so great that it overbalances the evil created by the claim that in these circumstances it can rightly be ignored. Thus, in spite of the fact that the specific obligations may be brought into existence independently of it, their fulfilment must always be pursued in association with and subordination to the general obligation. The principle of doing one's best to produce the best remains an ultimate summary of the whole duty of man.

The Principle of Equity

The considerations arising out of the needs of the social order show us that specific recognized rights of individuals must, as a general rule, be upheld even in particular cases where such action does not produce the greatest possible good. We may now ask whether these same facts constitute a sufficient explanation of the cases where the principles of equity (or just distribution) seem to set up a moral demand for some departure from the general principle of seeking to produce the greatest good. Why do we sometimes believe it would be wrong to do something that would increase the total amount of good in a community at the cost of causing a less equitable distribution of goods? By an "equitable" or "just" distribution (as our next section will show) we mean not necessarily an equal distribution but a distribution in which each receives the good that is his due. We may refer again to the example of the tariff presented earlier in this chapter.

Why should a purchase of a greater good on the whole, at the cost of greater inequity of distribution, be regarded as wrong? It can, I think, be taken for granted that there are some cases in which the general consensus would pronounce it wrong. For example, if an already great inequity is greatly increased for the sake of a very slight balance of total good, few, if any, would say it was justified.

Part of the explanation can certainly be derived from an argument that the maintenance of confidence and cooperation in the social order requires a recognition that inequity is always a form of injustice and thus wrong in principle. Society must, if it is to produce the greatest possible good, create conditions wherein each member will be encouraged to cooperate for the common good and will have confidence that his own welfare receives due consideration from his fellows. How can these conditions be fulfilled if it is recognized *in principle* that the majority may inflict any loss or injury on any member, or any minority, at any time that they are convinced that a greater good of the whole would thereby be served? Confidence and cooperation require that each person shall know that it is recognized as his right that his good shall be considered as having the same importance as another's good, that he should never be treated as a mere means to others' good. Confidence and cooperation will be greatly increased if every individual, class, and group knows that society considers it only right to see that, as far as possible, goods are distributed to each according to his due, and that this principle will not be set aside except for some vitally important concern of the common good.

These considerations are perfectly sound, but still it may be questioned whether they really constitute the most important basis of the moral judgment that the intrinsic good of any one person ought to be considered just as important as that of any other person, and that therefore (other things being equal) just as much good is *due* to one person as another, that it is wrong that some should receive much less than their due in order that more fortunate ones should heap up benefits, even if the total good is thereby increased. It seems that we judge *directly* that such disproportion is not right, apart from consideration of the effects of the principle upon the social order in general—though, of course, the direct moral judgment can be reinforced by such considerations.

Since there seems in these cases to be a direct insight as to the rightness of the principle of equity, we must inquire whether this is really possible. It would mean that the obligation to produce the greatest possible good can directly be seen to be an obligation to seek to establish the conditions of full personal development of all, so far as this is possible, and to maintain equality of opportunity for personal development when full opportunity is not possible. This is the form in which the developed moral consciousness of civilized man has come, with a high degree of unanimity, to frame its moral insight. Is it a genuine insight into the nature of obligation or merely a special form imposed upon the concept of obligation by historical conditions, and so likely to change under new historical conditions—to return, for example, to an endorsement of aristocratic preference as advocated by Nietzsche or to race preference as advocated by Hitler? The answer can only be found in a further examination of the relation of obligation as it is manifested in our own consciousness.

As we have already seen, obligation is grounded in the structure of personality as a system of acts of will, each one of which strives after what seems good. In this striving, the act of will is essentially disinterested, except so far as it is given special direction by inherited tendencies or acquired habit. In rational reflection, therefore, this essentially disinterested nature of will manifects itself. If the self is to maintain its rational wholeness, its integrity, it must disinterestedly pursue the greatest possible good. The good, however, is not seen as so many isolated subjective processes. It is systematized into persons; and the goodness of each subjective process is seen as the expression of, and in relation to, a personality as a whole. The goodness of each good process is therefore seen as a part of, and a contribution to, the ongoing, developing life of a person. The goodness of the multiple-conscious life-activity of each person is therefore seen as fused into a whole, the value of an individual, conscious life. Personality is valued for its own sake.

Because the rational will (uninfluenced by specific impulse and habit) is essentially disinterested in pursuit of the good, the development of one personality appeals to it equally with the development of another. There is thus an equal obligation to all; but where development is held back by lack of opportunity, there is a stronger demand, a greater appeal, because the possibilities of further development are greater than in the case of the person who has had much better opportunity and must therefore be expected to be living nearer to his full capacity for good. For this reason the obligation felt by the rational will, as it contemplates the various possibilities for good in the lives of all those persons who might be affected by its actions, takes the form of a demand for equality of opportunity. To do the greatest possible good, and thus to do what is right, one must try to equalize opportunity for the realization of the good.

The problem we have been discussing is therefore only a pseudo problem. It is due to confusion of the good with mere pleasure or with so-called "material goods" which are mere instruments for the realization of intrinsic goods. Only in the most exceptional situations could the true good of any community as a whole be served by measures which decreased the opportunity for personal development of those with lesser opportunities, even though it thereby increased the opportunities of a greater number of those whose opportunities were already greater. There is a law of diminishing returns in connection with the provision of opportunities. Provision for the essential minimum of full bodily and mental health is of the first importance. Further increments may bring forth special talents and further activities positive in form and quality, but the provision of these additional opportunities, comforts, and luxuries produces little real good compared to the loss sustained by those who may thereby be deprived of the means of living a full, normal, healthy life of body and mind.

The fact that we can puzzle ourselves with this pseudo problem is an instance of the way words deceive us. Our actual thought of the good and the right in a concrete instance, such as that of the inequitable tariff proposed in our example, goes straight to the referents. We picture the actual intrinsic goods of human lives involved; we experience the call of the greater good and know what ought to be done. We pronounce the tariff wrong. But the words used in the example deceive us. We are accustomed to think of "prosperity" as a "good"; so too of material "goods" and pleasures. So we concede the possibility of the total good of the community being increased by something that we recognize as inequitable and wrong because our insight into the real referents in the situation has been clearer than the deductions we form from the confusing use of words.

We must recognize, however, that inequality of opportunity is not necessarily wrong. There are special cases where it genuinely ministers to the greatest possible good. For example, society needs a small number of highly trained persons; and this special training and the performance of the special function to which these persons are called constitute opportunities for enjoyment of genuine goods greater than society can possibly give to all its members. Right-minded persons do not complain at such necessary inequalities (so long as they are not stretched beyond what is necessary), for they really serve the common good. Again, in situations of special difficulty it may be necessary in the common interest to create inequalities. Thus a besieged city or a country at war, enduring a shortage of food, may put civilians on a diet that involves serious malnutrition and brings death to some in order to provide the army with a ration that will keep up its fighting strength. Such examples show us that the principle of equity is not an ethical absolute. Like all other ethical principles, it must give way before that of the greatest possible good of all concerned.

EQUALITY AND SPECIAL DESERT

We are considering the ways in which the general obligation to produce the greatest possible good is complicated and qualified by considerations of justice, i.e., by the specific rights of individuals and groups. Among the less specific of these specific rights we have found those that arise from the principle of equity, and this principle, we have seen, rests upon the obligation, so far as possible, to provide each person with equal opportunity for the realization of good in his own life. The principle of equity thus takes the form of the principle of equality of opportunity.

Equality of opportunity, however, cannot take the form of abstract equality of treatment. We should not be giving to two men equality of opportunity to appear well dressed if we gave to each of them a suit of clothes of exactly the same cloth, cut, and size if one of them were very short and the other very tall. Real equality of opportunity requires that the material goods and other factors involved be adapted to meet the special needs of each individual.

For full development of the physical aspect of personality some need more clothes or more food than others, some need more medical care, and so forth. Similarly, for full development of the mental life, some need more special attention than others, some need special training in various arts or sciences, some will attain the full development of their personality on its intellectual side with only a few years of schooling, others only after advanced studies.

Since the principle of the greatest possible good sets us the goal of the greatest possible personal development of all, the principle of equality of opportunity must mean equal opportunity to attain that full development. That means the opportunity for all to attain full development if possible. But what does it mean if it is not possible to grant the opportunities of full development to all? Here we have to use our physiological and psychological knowledge to weigh the amount of good that can be done with limited means. The preservation of life all round comes first; then, so far as possible, the requirements of full physical health. Some attention to intellectual development is necessary, even at the cost of weakening health, because of the great instrumental value, as well as the intrinsic value, of knowledge; but it is not fair to deprive some of the means to a fully healthy body in order to give a select and specially capable few the luxuries of the mind. Fortunately, art, letters, philosophy, and religion can flourish at little physical cost, while science justifies itself as an instrumental value.

In general, the principles that commend themselves as just are the giving of chief attention first to the necessities of life for all and then using whatever surplus is left for proportionately greater attention to those who have special needs. The special needs are of two kinds—those due to special weakness, and those due to special capacities calling for further development. The former have a special appeal in that they are the cause of special suffering, the latter in that they may be useful to the community. We have to try to weigh the total consequences for good, consider the special rights, and provide a due proportion of opportunity for full development where we cannot provide the whole.

On the whole, modern social planning is approaching the problems of just distribution along these lines. We are establishing minimum wages with unemployment insurance, pensions, medical care, free education, and other social services to provide for the minimum needs of a healthy life for all, and we are increasingly providing opportunity for special talent to develop itself. These things we should recognize are not charity or paternalism but simply measures of social justice.

Rights involve obligations. If it is society's obligation to provide equality of opportunity as a right, it is the obligation of every member of society to contribute all he can to make those opportunities possible for all. Thus every member of society is under obligation to contribute as best he can to the social whole. Social obligation is thus two-sided. It can be stated in the excellent slogan which the Communists have preached but never practiced: "From each according to his ability, and to each according to his need." This ethical principle, of course, was not first discovered by the Communists. It is the principle of cooperation upon which the family works. It is implicit in the very nature of human love and is universalized in the Christian concept of the brotherhood of man.

Differences of need, however, are not the only factors that complicate the principle of equity. There are also special deserts arising from special rights. We need not consider here the rights due to special traditional privilege, social status, law, and contract. Nor do we mean the rights claimed on the basis of special ability. Special ability does not constitute a desert. In so far as it requires opportunity for further development, it constitutes a need and we have already considered it as such. For the rest, no one is under special obligation to do anything for another person simply because that person has some special ability; so it confers no rights except those of the due meed of respect so far as it is well used. What possession of special ability does for a man is not to give him special rights over others, but special opportunities of doing and enjoying good, and thus places him under special obligations.

What, then, is meant by special desert? It is usually claimed by those who, by reason of a combination of special effort and special ability (or one or other above) have made a special contribution to the common good. The man with special skill, special knowledge, or special strength, who uses these abilities to do work of special value, considers that he deserves a special share of the social product—that he has a right to greater opportunities to enjoy good. In what way, we may ask, has he put society under obligation? Is he not under obligation, anyway, to use his best talents for the social good? Why should he claim special favor for having fulfilled his obligation?

These questions show that the claim of special desert is much less than it is commonly assumed to be, but they do not nullify it. There is a special obligation to return the benefit, to recognize and reward the special effort. We should note, however, that it is the *special effort* that has a moral claim to reward, not the lucky possession of a special talent. That only creates special obligations. It does, however, require special effort to fulfil special obligations, and society should recognize the fact and make an appropriate return. Society is not under obligation to return to each individual the whole of the benefit received. Each person is under obligation to produce the greatest possible good for all concerned, whether it brings him any return or not. The obligation of the recipient is to acknowledge the benefit received and make such return as will encourage a continuation of the best efforts of those best able to contribute to the common good.

The fact that special effort is required in order to make good social use of special abilities is shown by the fact that when no adequate recognition is made of specially good or specially skilled work there is a strong tendency for it to fall off. The possessors of special ability fall into the temptation to shirk their obligation and produce less than their best if they are not encouraged to use their talents for the common good. To avoid that temptation and turn their talents to the common good (e.g., in extra industrial production), they need the stimulus of special reward; and society has the obligation to recognize their special effort by granting it. This is the moral justification for differences in pay for more and better work, and for learning and skill used in useful work. But, obviously, it does not provide moral justification for any very great differentials.

In addition to the moral justification of reward for special effort, there is, however, a further reason for these differential rates of pay. It is that of society's need of the special efforts of its more talented members. This need is so great that it pays society to offer an extra price for them, usually even more than would be warranted by the moral obligation of rewarding the special effort put forth. In all the more profitable uses of special talent, this factor provides abundant differentials in rates of pay; but society does not always provide adequate differentials for those special services where profits are not involved—as in the labors of many of its teachers, ministers, artists, and other men of science and letters. As an example the following news item speaks for itself. "In Peterborough, England, a school advertised for an experienced cook and an English-Latin-Science teacher with a college degree. Salaries offered: for the teacher, £150 a year; for the cook, £150-180." [5] In many American colleges and universities an equally interesting comparison could be made between the salaries of the professors and the football coaches.

THE PROBLEM OF PUNISHMENT

Thus far we have considered only distributive justice—the right to receive instrumental goods and the obligation to produce them. Now we must turn our attention to punitive justice—the right and the obligation to inflict intrinsic evil and the obligation to accept such infliction. This appears, at first sight, to be a mere expression of anger and the desire for revenge, and to run directly counter to the fundamental ethical principle—that of the obligation to produce the greatest possible good. It is, of course, often mixed with motives of anger and vengeance and thus has led to unjustifiable extremes. But there is, nevertheless, a right to punish that is firmly grounded in the needs of the social order and the duty to produce the greatest possible good.

The existence of orderly society, with social, and especially economic, cooperation, with security and with encouragement to each to put forth his best efforts, depends upon the maintenance of a system of laws, guaranteeing each person in the possession of certain rights. But laws have no effect without powers of enforcement. This means that the law must provide that certain persons shall be given the right, and placed under special obligation by society acting for the common good, to apprehend and

[5] *Time*, April 9, 1945, p. 69.

inflict penalties on those who break the law. This activity of apprehension must be made sufficiently effective, and the penalties must be made sufficiently severe, to deter any prospective lawbreaker from committing a crime if he gives adequate attention to the chances of obtaining advantage or incurring punishment.

Now it is quite clear that the more effective the process of apprehension, and the more certain the infliction of the penalty, the less likely is the prospective criminal to think that the advantage to be gained by crime is worth the risk. Thus the more effective the police and judicial system, the less severe need the penalties be. It is therefore the obligation of society, in seeking to produce the greatest possible good and the least possible evil, to make its police and judiciary as effective as possible and its penalties as small as possible. If detection and punishment could be made nearly certain, then arrest and conviction, with consequent loss of social prestige and trust, would become the greatest part of the punishment necessary for most crimes. But some social and legal penalty there always must be or the law would lose its power to sustain personal rights.

There are, of course, other obligations of society in connection with the prevention of crime besides the apprehension of criminals and the infliction of punishment. The causes of crime lie largely in bad and unfair social conditions, wrong and inadequate education and environmental influences, and preventable diseases of body and mind. It is society's obligation to prevent crime by removing these causes as well as by legal deterrents. It must also be recognized that the criminal is usually not a well-balanced person who coldly reasons that crime would be to his advantage and is worth the risk. Those in danger of temptation to crime therefore need to have its risks clearly and emphatically presented to them, and those who have drifted into criminal habits need not merely be deterred by threat of punishment but restricted in their liberty and opportunity to commit crime and, if possible, given training, discipline, medical and psychological attention, and education such as may result in reform. Indeed, the need and value of methods of reform are coming to overshadow the punitive element in the treatment of crime, especially among youthful offenders where reform has greater possibilities of success.

Thus far we have spoken of the obligations of society, of the state, and of officials to arrest criminals, administer punishment and measures of reform, and adopt all reasonably useful methods to prevent the commission of crime and the development of criminal tendencies. But we have still to ask the question: By what *right* does society, or the state, inflict evil on individuals and call it justifiable punishment? In fulfilling the obligation to produce good by protecting the rights and welfare of the citizens, the state commits infractions of the rights of the criminal—of his liberty, bodily comfort, and many other legitimate interests. It sets out to reform him against his will and even inflicts pain and loss upon him in order to deter *other* persons from committing crimes, thus using him against his will as a means to another's good. If rights are in reciprocal relation to obligations, then the right to inflict punishment must imply an obligation to accept it on the part of the criminal. How has he incurred this obligation?

The answer is that the criminal has injured society and is under special obligation to make reparation for that injury. He has not only caused a loss of material goods, or of life, or the infliction of pain. He has done something that tends to break down society's protective wall of law. If laws could be broken without penalty, then society would lose their protection. If the criminal breaks the law and goes unpunished, then he *encourages* others to break the law. This injures society. So he is under obligation to repair the injury by accepting such punishment as will *discourage* others from following his example. His obligation to accept punishment as reparation for the damage he has done to the law is the ground of society's right to inflict that punishment. Thus society, in punishing him, is not using him as a mere means to the good of others. It is treating him as a rational and morally responsible individual and doing that which enables him to fulfil the moral obligation to society which he has incurred. By accepting punishment as the paying of a debt to society, the criminal does something that is vital to the restoration of his own moral self-respect. Thus punishment must always be a part of the process of reform. It must be recognized as distinct in idea, even though it may well, in fact, form but a small part of the discipline and restriction that reform demands. The important thing, however, to remember, in order to keep our ethical ideas clear, is that punishment is justice. Society has a right to inflict it that is based upon the criminal's obligation to repair the damage he has done to society's protecting wall of law.

Fundamental Human Rights

This chapter on justice should be concluded with a statement on fundamental human rights. Such fundamental rights are those rights of the individual which are so important to the well-being and development of his personality that *they should not be violated in any attempt to produce the greatest possible good except when they enter into unavoidable conflict with one another,* in which case the clash of fundamental rights must be resolved by appeal to the principle of the greatest good of all concerned.

In everyday human relations within our present civilization, there is a very widespread agreement as to the nature of such rights. Yet they are frequently denied in practice in times of difficulty and confusion. One reason for this is that teleological ethical theories, denying any formal absolutes, can conveniently be used to justify violation of individual rights in the name of the common good. Further, such theorists often fail to see that the evil of such action lies, not only in the bad consequences of the violation itself, but in *recognizing that it is right* to violate these rights. They correctly see that no specific right can be absolute, and they fail to see that these fundamental rights are not being made absolute so long as it is recognized that they limit one another, and that where they conflict the issue must be decided by the teleological principle of the greatest good of all concerned.

In constructing a list of such rights, one must be careful not to give such important status to the claims of too many specific rights and yet to give such status to all that are vital to the full development of personality and to the maintenance of the sort of social order in which personality can so develop. These rights will then be concerned with that which is essential to personal development in all its phases. physical, intellectual, social, and moral. They must include not only physical but economic security, not only defense of body and property, but also of character. They must provide for the family life, the political order, and the religious and moral conscience; for personality is stultified if not able to take its part in the civic life, raise a family, make its own adjustment to what it conceives as highest and most worthy, and avoid doing what it regards as wrong. Finally, personality suffers if it is not granted certain fundamental equalities with its fellows.

In the light of these considerations, the following human

rights may well be considered fundamental in the sense defined.

1. Security from unjustified physical violence and imprisonment.
2. Security from false defamation of character.
3. Security of livelihood through adequately remunerated employment.
4. Security of legally acquired property.
5. Freedom to marry and raise a family.
6. Freedom in choice of employment.
7. Freedom of speech and assembly.
8. Freedom of religion and moral conscience.
9. Equality of basic political rights.
10. Equality before the law.
11. Assurance of social care in time of special need.
12. Provision of basic education and cultural opportunity.

These twelve principles will be found to be the basic conceptions which have been given more explicit and expanded formulation in *The Declaration of Human Rights* adopted by the General Assembly of the United Nations at Paris on December 10, 1948.

Chapter 7

FREEDOM, RESPONSIBILITY, AND SIN

Personal Integrity and Moral Effort

Our analysis of the moral nature of man has disclosed the sense of moral obligation as rooted in the need of the self for inner integrity of its purposive life. It has shown that in this connection the fundamental need is to keep that purposive life directed impartially to what seems to the individual to be the greatest possible good of all concerned. It has thus led to the endorsement of that moral ideal which, in an early chapter, we saw to have been the culmination of the ethical insights of the great religions of mankind. And in Chapter 6 we have seen that the specific principles of justice and human rights generally acknowledged in the counsels of nations are derived from and, if rightly interpreted, operate in harmony with that general principle. We also saw that, after properly clarifying our terms, it is possible to point to that in human experience which constitutes the natural human good which it is our duty to seek to produce. We have thus secured a satisfactory answer to all the major problems of ethical theory except one.

The remaining problem is that of *moral* good and evil. We have seen that the moral consciousness recognizes a unique value, not to be confused with natural good, in the voluntary choice of right over wrong, a value which increases with the degree of effort required to make the choice and carry it out. There is a corresponding disvalue attached to the failure to make such effort when needed. It is this value and disvalue that are recognized and asserted in the expression of praise and blame. The question before us now is whether the recognition of this unique value by the moral consciousness is justified by anything unique in the situation involving exercise of moral choice and effort. The question is important for two reasons: first, because a concern for these distinctive moral values plays a large part in the motivation of moral decision in its most crucial phases, and if there is no genuine psychological basis for such distinctions of value, this cannot but affect such motivation; and second, because, if this value distinction is a pseudo distinction based on no real distinction in the volitional life (though it seems to imply one), then our value experience suffers in credibility; it implies something about the nature of the self that is not the case; its significance for an intelligent understanding of the meaning of life is undermined. It is important, therefore, that we should understand precisely what is implied by our sense of moral responsibility and the unique value of moral effort, and that we should know whether there is any good reason for doubting the truth of these implications.

To say that a person is ethically responsible means that he knows what is right in the connection referred to and is able to direct his conduct accordingly. Moral right and wrong, as we have seen, refer to a standard of obligation; and what is obligatory is that which a person is required to do in order to maintain his personal integrity. Now if a person understands the nature of obligation and knows what, in particular, it requires of him, this knowledge may have some causal effect upon his conduct. He will probably desire to maintain his personal integrity for the sake of the mental peace, strength, and comfort it involves; and this desire will have some influence, among other desires, upon his behavior. So knowledge of the nature of the moral demand, in general and in particular, does make a difference; but this causal effect of such knowledge is not what is meant by that capacity for self-direction of conduct that constitutes individual responsibility. It may be that a man knows the nature of obligation and the demands of the moral standard in the particular situation in which he finds himself, and yet he may hesitate, his mind not made up. To say, then, that he is morally responsible is to say that he is still capable of making up his mind to do what is right, and that whether he will do so depends not on any factor outside himself but on something within him.

Right action is action in accord with existing obligations; obligatory action is action required for maintenance of personal integrity; personality is a growing system of activity. Therefore the ideally right action will always be that which contributes most fully to the integrated growth of personality. But personality is a system of will, each part of which is a voluntary attentive process pursuing what seems to it the greatest possibility of good in that to which it gives attention. When that system acts as an integrated whole, therefore, it must pursue the greatest good seen as possible by the personality working as a whole. Further, since the personality working as a whole (and thus using all its faculties to the full) is the personality working at its best, we can state the ideal standard of obligation in very simple terms. It is each person's duty to do his or her best to produce the best possible results for all concerned.

This states the moral standard in subjective terms and it admits that the standard, though absolute in its demands upon each person, is relative to every change and difference in personality and in the relevant situation. Objective standards can only be stated in broad and tentative terms. Every man's obligation is simply to do his best for all. For that and that alone is he responsible. If he does that, he does what is morally right. He may be mistaken. He may be weak in body or mind. He may be weak in will—modern psychiatry has revealed that weakness of will is a disease. If, however, he does his best to produce the best for all, he does what is morally right. This is true, however he may fail as a result of social or individual ignorance, or weakness of body, intellect, or will. His personality, in its demand for integration, can make no other demand of him, and neither God nor man can rightly make any other demand. We can rightly hold one another morally responsible only for the best effort of which each is capable to produce the best for all.

This reveals moral obligation as an obligation to make certain *efforts*. What is the nature of these efforts? There is no particular kind of good after which we ought to strive, nor is there an obligation to be always striving. There is, indeed, no need to tell a person to be always striving. To strive is the essential nature of personality and of life, and all striving, as we have seen, is a striving after what appears as good. So it is not these efforts (efforts to produce particular goods) that present themselves as things we are under obligation to do. The moral demand is the demand that in all these various efforts after various goods we maintain our personal integrity. The unique *moral* effort is the effort to maintain that integrity.

Personal integrity cannot be maintained without this unique moral effort. Every ordinary activity leaves its mark in the structure of personality as a tendency to a habit. The growth of individuality is a process of habit formation. By forming habits, we gain all our special efficiencies and develop our particular drives. These particular drives, however, and those that we inherit as natural appetites and impulses, often run in different directions. Frequently, too, they run counter to the fundamental tendency of all will, which manifests itself in the composite tendency of the self as a whole, to pursue the *greatest* possible good—especially when that is seen as the good of another person. So the drives of habit and impulse often tend to disintegrate personality. When they do so, it requires a distinctive sort of effort to pull ourselves together. Indeed, the price of personal integrity, as of liberty, is eternal vigilance. It requires constant attention and frequent effort to hold habit and impulse in line and *direct* conduct in pursuit of the greatest possible good.

Every normal person is aware that he sometimes makes these efforts. He is also aware that he sometimes does not make them when he believes that he nevertheless could do so. The maintenance of the integrity of his personality as a growing whole requires that he make such effort so far as he can and so far as needed. It does not follow that, if he always made his best effort whenever he could, he would continuously grow toward full development as a perfectly integrated personality. It seems evident that in some personalities and some situations it is much more difficult to maintain anything like perfect and fully integrated personal development than in others. If, however, a person should always make the best effort possible, he would maintain moral perfection. The point is that we have no guarantee that even moral perfection would always produce psychological perfection; and consequently, psychological imperfection is not always due to moral imperfection. Disease, physical fatigue, mental strain, and emotional disturbance may undermine the will and make moral effort much more difficult than at ordinary times, and sometimes impossible. It is well to remember that obligation can never mean more than to do the best one can—and it is not easy to judge when another person is not doing his best.

Though we cannot judge with any certainty when another is making his best effort, we are sometimes clearly conscious not only of making these efforts ourselves, but also of not making them when we believe we could and should. As a result, we let habit and impulse control our behavior. We do the things we believe we ought not and leave undone the things we believe we ought to do. Then we have the sense of guilt, or moral failure; we perceive our action as morally wrong. Here is the source of conscience, praise, and blame, which are powerful factors in their influence upon human behavior. They rest upon the conviction that we sometimes have omitted making an effort that we could have made. This conviction rests upon clear and familiar experience, yet it frequently has been questioned whether the experience is correctly interpreted in saying we could have done what we actually did not do.

Determinism and Indeterminism

Determinism is the theory which maintains that the chain of causation between events is such that the events of the present (including human actions) are absolutely determined by the events of the past, and those of the future by those of the present. Thus it would be quite incorrect to say of any person that he could have done anything different from that which he actually is doing or has done. The two forms in which determinism has been most commonly presented in modern times are those of mechanism and psychological hedonism. Sometimes both forms have been presented together, as by Thomas Hobbes, but they are really inconsistent.

Mechanism maintains that all human behavior is determined by the purely physicochemical interaction of the parts of the body (particularly the molecules of the nervous system) with one another and with outside physical things. Psychological hedonism maintains that all voluntary behavior is determined by the strength of various desires, and that all desires are desires for pleasure.

However, desire for pleasure is a conscious response to felt quality. Mechanism denies that consciousness, in the form of feeling of qualities of pleasure and pain or in any other form, has anything to do with any physical movement, even the smallest change among the molecules of the brain. The mechanist, therefore, can not be a psychological hedonist, nor can the psychological hedonist be a mechanist.

In each of these theories, however, there seems to be an element of truth which is sufficient to refute the other. Pleasure, as we have already seen, cannot be regarded as the only object of desire. There are impulsive urges to pursue specific goals, and many of these certainly seem to be due to habits and physiological tendencies determined by the acquired or inherited structure of the nervous system. On the other hand, it is hardly conceivable that feelings of pleasure and pain play absolutely no part in influencing the course of behavior. If feelings have no function, it is strange that they should have been brought into existence and elaborated in the course of evolution. If physical events can cause pain and pleasure (as they certainly seem to do), then why should not feelings of pain and pleasure have some reaction upon physical events? We do not know the connection between physical and mental events, e.g., between molecular changes in the brain and sensation and desire. But the correlation is so close as to compel belief in *some* connection.[1] There is no good reason to believe that causal connection holds only between physical events.

[1] For a brief statement of my own theory of this connection, see *God in Us* (New York: Harper & Bros., 1945), pp. 50 ff.

Mechanism, therefore, though not disproved, certainly seems implausible.

The surrender of mechanism and psychological hedonism, however, does not imply the surrender of determinism. The determinist can admit psychological and psychophysical causation. All he needs to maintain is that every event, mental and physical, must be completely determined by antecedent events. He can admit that we can, within limits, do what we desire, that we can and do react to pleasure and pain, that we can plan our behavior to achieve our wishes and, in general, carry out our plans. But each of these desires, thoughts, efforts, movements, and feelings, he maintains, is linked in a causal chain in which the later events follow necessarily from the former. We can learn the causes of desire and effort; we can estimate their probable strength, and predict behavior with a good deal of accuracy. We can discover the factors that modify character and learn the ways in which different characters react to certain types of situation. All our dealing with our fellows, all our efforts at education and character training, presuppose the existence of causal relations between experience and behavior. The assumption that behavior is entirely determined by causal factors which we can more or less completely understand is justified, the determinist claims, by the large measure of success we have in influencing and predicting one another's conduct.

This type of determinism, which is neither mechanistic nor hedonistic, is accepted by a great many thinkers today, including (to mention some whose views we have discussed in other connections) Dewey, Mead, Ross, and Moore. The chief reasons advanced for the position are (*a*) the empirical evidence for it such as we have referred to in the previous paragraph; (*b*) a reluctance to admit any exception to the general principle of causation adopted in all scientific inquiry; and (c) an ethical objection to theories of indeterminism.

The empirical evidence, both sides are generally ready to admit, is strong but incomplete. No one denies that the motives to conduct are affected by causal factors of many kinds. The only questions at issue are whether conduct is always determined by the strongest combination of impulses and desires, and whether the strength of desires is *completely* determined by a rigid chain of antecedent events. The indeterminist asserts that there is a volitional factor, the activity of which is not completely determined by antecedent events. This, he believes, either affects the strength of desires or steps in to take control in spite of them.

The determinist has no way of measuring desires to show that it is always the strongest combination that issues in action; he merely assumes that those acted upon must have been strongest. When someone does his duty at great personal sacrifice, the determinist assumes that the desire to adhere to duty was stronger than the opposing desires; but he cannot prove this assumption, nor can he prove that the desire to do one's duty, or any other desire, is determined by a completely rigid chain of antecedents. The empirical argument for determinism must therefore remain inconclusive.

The principle of universal and necessary causal connection, as logicians know, is also incapable of proof. In scientific inquiry it is assumed a priori, and the assumption is abundantly justified by the success of inquiries based upon it. This pragmatic justification is, however, merely an *ethical* justification of our continued use of, and reliance upon, the principle. It does not prove its absolute validity. It means that we are justified in assuming the principle so far as we find that it increases our verifiable knowledge and control of the phenomena thus studied. It does not mean that we are justified in insisting that the principle must still hold good in cases where we cannot verify it and where to assume it implies that certain aspects of our experience are illusory.

It has to be admitted that we cannot verify the assumption that every factor involved in moral decision is so completely determined by its antecedents that it can never be said that a person ever could have done anything different from that which he actually has done. We might well assume complete determination, however, here as elsewhere, if the assumption really helped us to understand and control behavior the better. The assumption does help us so far as the explanation of motives is concerned, but the indeterminist claims that in critical cases it breaks down, and that, in these cases, to assume complete determination by antecedent circumstances belies the sense of freedom at the moment and undermines the subsequent sense of responsibility.

This leads to an examination of the third reason advanced by the determinist for his position. He claims that it is indeterminism rather than determinism that undermines the notion of moral responsibility. This must be admitted as true unless the indeterminist can give some further account of the factor which he claims intervenes to affect or control desire. In saying that this factor is not itself entirely determined by antecedent conditions, he appears to imply that it is a matter of pure chance whether it intervenes or not; but to say that moral decision is a matter of pure chance would undermine the sense of responsibility even more fully and effectively than to say it depends upon factors already present and operative in the character of the self.

If a person is morally responsible for his action, then it must be self-determined; his conduct must, within certain

physical and psychological limits, be self-directed. If the act
of will that overrules his selfish or evil desires is something
that has no causal basis in the self, then the resultant behavior is not something for which the self is responsible.
Responsibility implies self-determination, not absence of
causation. The notion that in moral decision there may
intervene an act of will that has no ground within the self
and no cause without we may call "radical indeterminism."
We must recognize that such a theory is ethically disastrous
and has little logical foundation.

Self-determination and Responsibility

Now the sort of determinism of which we have been
speaking (that maintained, for example, by Dewey and
Mead, by Ross and Moore) does assert a real self-determination of conduct. It can even be said, in an important sense,
to assert moral freedom: freedom is the capacity, within certain limits, to determine one's own conduct. Both determinist and indeterminist, and even the mechanist and
psychological hedonist, agree that every man has a certain
physical and social freedom or self-determination; he can
move about and interact with other persons and things.
The psychological hedonist agrees with the indeterminist
and some other determinists, as against the mechanist, that
the mind has a certain freedom, or power of self-determination, in control of the body. The indeterminist and some
determinists, as against psychological hedonists, recognize
that the will, as an organized set of desires, has a certain
freedom from the influences of mere pleasure and pain; so
that the desire to do one's duty, and so maintain one's self-
respect and that of the community, may determine the
conduct of the self as a whole. This is self-determination in
that the inner core of the self (the rational moral judgment,

formed character, and self-respect) directs conduct against the impulses arising from stimuli that rouse transitory emotion and desires. The feeling of moral responsibility, says the determinist, arises from the recognition that reflective judgment, and the set of desires which the individual recognizes as forming his self or character, play their part in directing conduct. The individual recognizes responsibility because he knows his conduct is, within the relevant limits, self-directed.

Even in this latter case, however, self-determination, says the determinist, does not imply any real indeterminacy. The self plays a part in determining its own conduct. But every factor that enters into the complex constitution of the self is an effect of a chain of causes operating within the self and reaching out into the world beyond it. The self is simply a part of the complete and integrated causal order of the world. It can never be said of any act of the self that it could have been other than it actually is or was.

This review of the case for determinism shows that the question is not one that can be settled on scientific grounds. It concerns the ultimate assumptions of science itself and is therefore beyond scientific proof or disproof. The success of science justifies those assumptions up to the point where the question of moral responsibility arises. There the question becomes a metaphysical one, raising questions of the a priori grounds of the principle of causation, but no sound metaphysical conclusion can be reached without first taking notice of the ethical inquiry. Our question is, therefore: Are we justified, in our metaphysical construction and our ethical conduct, in carrying the scientific assumption of a complete and universal system of causation by antecedent events beyond the point at which it obtains pragmatic justification by its success in interpreting physical and mental phenomena? Should we carry the principle right through all our interpretation of ethical phenomena? Does it help or hinder that interpretation? This narrows down to the question as to whether it enables us to give a more satisfactory account of the ethical sense of responsibility than can be given by any form of indeterminism.

John Dewey defends the deterministic conception of responsibility by arguing that it is independent of the conception that one could have done what one did not actually do. It is a mistake, he says, to suppose that praise and blame have a retrospective instead of a prospective bearing. A person is held liable for what he has done in order that he may take better account of the consequences of his actions in the future. We do not hold a baby, an imbecile, or a falling tree responsible because to do so would not affect their future behavior. On the other hand, a normal person is held accountable in order that he may learn. "The question of whether he might have acted differently from the way in which he did act is irrelevant." [2]

This, however, is a very superficial and one-sided analysis of the problem. It considers the matter only from the standpoint of the person who *administers* praise and blame, reward and punishment. It is true that one reason why we assert that the other person is accountable, and praise or blame him, is in order thereby to influence his future behavior. If we think that reward or punishment may favorably influence a creature's future behavior (whether man or dog), we may administer either without any suggestion of moral responsibility. It is also true that if someone else imputes moral responsibility to us and blames us (whether threatening punishment or not) in some case where we are convinced that *it was not possible to do other than we actually did*, we feel the accusation to be unjustified. No person

[2] John Dewey and James H. Tufts, *Ethics*, (rev. ed.; New York: Henry Holt & Co., 1932), p. 337.

will admit *his own* responsibility in any case where he believes he *could* not have done other than he did.

The sense of guilt, with its resultant resolves and efforts to change an attitude, to attend and learn, undoubtedly depends upon the conviction that the conduct believed to be wrong could have been avoided. When the conscience-stricken or accused person seeks to excuse himself, he seeks for reasons to explain that the acknowledgedly wrong action was beyond his control. He argues that there was a sudden and overwhelming passion, a temporary loss of mental balance, or a failure to grasp the meaning of the situation. If the guilty person can persuade himself he "could not help it," he feels relieved of his guilt, he repudiates blame and claims that punishment is unjustified. It is therefore clear that the efficacy of praise and blame depend upon the assumption of the person concerned that an alternative line of conduct *was* possible. It is a sheer evading of the issue to say that, since the purpose of censure is to change conduct in the future, it therefore is irrelevant whether the action now past could have been different.

Nicolai Hartmann points to the spontaneity of remorse as the clearest possible evidence of man's intuitive awareness of freedom to take alternative courses, and of the fact that, on the occasion for which remorse is felt, the person concerned really could have acted differently. His graphic description is well worth quoting.

The state of guilt is not a thing anticipated, but it is in the highest degree real. It bursts in upon a man like a fate. He makes no mistake about the guilt. It is suddenly there, judging, convicting, overpowering. But nevertheless he feels that this bursting-in is not from the outside. A power rises within himself, which brings evidence against him. No one would load himself with guilt so long as he could avoid it, so long as he could, as it were, say to himself that the matter was not so bad, or that he was not the originator of it. It is against his will that the guilty man takes the load upon himself." [3]

The sense of guilt may well cause shame, but it is not merely the shame of injured pride or self-esteem. A man may be ashamed of shabby clothes, poverty, ignorance, an uncultured accent, or other defect for which he feels himself in no way to blame. In so far as it has not been in his power to prevent these things, he does not regard them as ground of any *moral* censure. Thus at every point we see the decisive distinction. The moral conscience can recognize no blame for evils that the self concerned could not prevent. Yet, though every person abhors the sense of guilt and seeks naturally to avoid it, it impresses itself upon us whenever, in the course of conduct where our ordinary powers of choice seem to us to be unimpaired, we do what we believe to be wrong; the guilt presents itself as logically inescapable so long as we recognize that we could have done right instead of wrong. Concerning the things which we are convinced we could not have done differently, the reflective moral consciousness recognizes it is illogical to entertain any sense of guilt.

In the moral life the praise and blame of others are important, but of very secondary importance compared to the moral judgment a man passes on himself. If a man does not feel himself to blame, then the moral judgment of others appears to him merely an impertinence and an injustice. If he *never* felt himself to blame, then the moral standard would cease to have any meaning beyond that of a convention or law which others, for their own convenience, demand that he should obey. Right and wrong toward others would then become mere matters of personal prudence. Moral values, along with the disvalues (the sense

[3] *Ethics* (London: Geo. Allen & Unwin, 1930), Vol. III, pp. 173-174.

of guilt), would cease to play any part in consciousness. It is for this reason that the assumption of personal responsibility is of such great importance. It is as fundamental as the assumption of our knowledge of the good and the existence of obligations. Fortunately the referent in this case is not obscure. Everyone knows what it means to make an effort to do something he believes he ought to do but would not do from mere spontaneous ("effortless") inclination. The only question is as to the validity of the assumption upon which rests the recognition of guilt—the assumption that in the cases where guilt exists we could have made an effort we did not actually make.

There is another theory of responsibility widely adopted among determinists. It is that represented by G. E. Moore.[4] Though Moore has, for himself, recently acknowledged the inadequacy of the theory[5] it is still widely held and therefore requires to be considered. This theory admits that moral responsibility requires recognition of the fact that it must *in some sense* be true that we sometimes could have done what we actually did not do; but the theory maintains that it is sufficient if this is merely true in the sense that we sometimes *could* have done differently *if we had chosen to do so*. At the same time it is maintained that the occur-

[4] *Ethics* (New York: Henry Holt & Co., 1912), chap. vi.
[5] Cf. *The Philosophy of G. E. Moore*, edited by P. A. Schilpp, published by Northwestern University, Evanston, Illinois, 1942. In reply to my essay in this volume, on "Freedom and Responsibility in Moore's Ethics," Mr. Moore writes, pp. 623-24, "Mr. Garnett has convinced me, by what he says in his essay, that in my *Ethics* I was wrong on two separate points . . . (2) In *Ethics* (pp. 201-2), I said 'It is very difficult to be sure that right and wrong do not really depend on what we *can* do, and not merely on what we can do, *if* we choose,' implying that I was not sure that they don't merely depend on the latter. I now think it was a mistake not to be sure of this. I think it is quite certain, as I gather, Mr. Garnett does, that *ethical* or *moral* right and wrong, or (in Mr. Stevenson's phrase) right and wrong in any 'typically ethical' sense, do *not* depend on what we can do, *if* we choose."

rence or nonoccurrence of a choice is determined rigidly by the chain of antecedent events.

On this view, choice is simply one factor in a causal chain. The only relevant difference between a morally responsible agent and one that is not morally responsible, such as an animal, a fire, or a lunatic, is that the former is the sort of agent sometimes capable of acts of choice. Where an act of choice enters into the chain of causation, the actor is morally responsible because he could have acted differently *if* he had chosen to do so. The act, therefore, is either right or wrong in the ethical sense of those terms. Where no act of choice enters, but the person could have acted differently *if* he had chosen, there is also moral responsibility and the action is ethically either right or wrong.

The plausibility of this statement, however, lies in the fact that when we read "the person could have acted differently *if* he had chosen" we assume that he *could* have chosen differently. We recognize responsibility on the assumption that he had it in his power to make a certain choice or not to make it. But the determinist assumes that no person ever could have made a choice he did not make. The fact that he did not make the choice is taken as indicating that it was not possible for him to make it. Here then is the paradox: he is held to be a responsible moral agent only because sometimes he is able to make choices, but it is recognized that there are some choices he could not have made. Yet he is held morally responsible for not making them! As for the choice he does make, it is held that he could have chosen differently only *if* he had chosen to choose differently; and so ad infinitum. This simply means that since he had not chosen to choose differently he could not choose differently. So we reach the conclusion that, though he could have chosen differently if he had chosen to choose differently, yet, in the existing circumstances, he could not have chosen otherwise than he did.

In the case where there was an alleged act of choice, the absurdity of this position lies in the implication that it was an act the person could not choose not to perform—an act of choice concerning which he had no choice. In the case where the right or wrong act was not deliberately chosen, but for which the person is held responsible because he could have done differently *if* he had chosen, there is another kind of absurdity. It lies in the fact that it attaches the whole significance of moral responsibility—the whole significant difference between moral conduct and nonmoral reaction—to the nonperformance of an act of choice which is recognized to have been impossible. Surely the nonoccurrence of an impossible event has no moral significance. If an action was not caused by an act of choice, and could not have been prevented by any possible act of choice, then choice is irrelevant to it. The mere fact that the agent might, on some other occasion, be able to perform an act of choice, such as would prevent some other action, has no bearing on the action in this particular case.

If the question at issue were merely whether we should scold or punish a person for his action, then the question of his moral responsibility might not arise. We may scold and punish a dog which we do not hold morally responsible. But moral blame involves the assertion that the person should hold *himself* responsible, should blame himself. To tell a person that he should blame himself for a choice that he could not have avoided, or for the nonperformance of an action that he could not have chosen to perform, is to talk nonsense. Yet the fact is that we feel responsible and blame ourselves for not making efforts of choice which we believe we could have made, whether others blame us or not. The peculiar thing is that even the determinist, who believes he never could have made any effort he did not actually make, nevertheless feels himself to blame. The facts of his own inner moral consciousness are not easily made to square with his theory. This is probably the reason why the theory does not do more harm in the way of undermining the sense of responsibility. We always *feel* responsibility in fact even if we deny it in theory.

It must be admitted that it is extremely difficult to frame *any* theory of motivation and choice that does justice to the sense of responsibility. The traditional conception of indeterminacy, which we have called "radical indeterminism," is just as fatal to responsibility as any of the conceptions of determinism we have discussed. Responsibility implies the power of self-determination, and this is denied by any theory that the act of will in its critical moral decisions is uncaused; it is also denied by any theory which places the causal direction of the decisive action entirely in the chain of events that has formed the particular habits and desires of the individual. When I look back on a wrong action for which I can hold myself responsible, I must feel that there was in me, at some moment before the overt action, the power to have made an effort which I did not make but which would have prevented my performance of the wrong action. When I look back on a right action for which I feel I can claim moral responsibility—as depending in some measure on my own choice—I must feel that at some point in the causal chain leading to that action I made an effort to produce or maintain some good, an effort to which I was not compelled by any antecedent circumstances.

MORAL EFFORT AND FREE DECISION

If we are to understand the nature of self-determination, responsibility, and moral freedom, we must examine closely this experience of making efforts and that of omitting to make them. The making of efforts is common, and we can always discover many factors that constitute motives for them. Yet none of these motives, nor any combination of them, appears to be a compelling cause such as we experience when we are pushed hither and thither by physical pressure. The effort is *our response* to the motivating factors with their present stimuli, promises, and threats. It never appears to be completely caused by its antecedents. Nor does it arise spontaneously, of itself, like a desire. We may think we know the cause of a desire; or it may arise without apparent cause. In either case, we do not feel a present responsibility for it as we do for our efforts. Thus the effort differentiates itself both from the activities which appear to us to be clearly subject to causation and from those for which we can discern no cause. The effort is something which we feel ourselves causing. Its cause lies in the self of the present moment when the effort is made.

Now the determinist could admit that the cause of the effort lies in the self of the moment when the effort is made, and he need not be worried by the fact that the self of that moment is not aware of any antecedent conditions from which the effort necessarily follows, for psychological antecedents are often very obscure. He can claim that the self of any present moment is the complex effect of a great multitude of physical and mental antecedents. All these, he says, are part of the same completely interrelated causal system in which there is never anything new that is not merely a new combination of factors already present. So he can admit that the effort is produced by the self of the present moment and still retain his determinism; but he cannot admit that an effort could have been made in any case where no effort actually was made. Yet it is this conviction that is decisive for the sense of responsibility as either moral worth or guilt.

Responsibility as moral worth demands recognition of the claim that one has made an effort that one could have left unmade. Responsibility as guilt admits that one has neglected to make an effort one could have made. Both the moral worth and the guilt are related to the sense of effort, as something demanded by the actual or prospective values and disvalues perceived, but not necessitated by any antecedent event or combination of events. The moral value is felt as attaching to the self by reason of the effort it has thrust into the stream of events that make up experience and its underlying causes. The guilt is felt as attaching to the self by reason of its failure to bring forth the effort upon the occasion when the values present and in prospect demanded it. The moral effort is a mental activity of a unique kind. It is a reasonable object of a favorable attitude and therefore good. It is a unique kind of good thing, a moral good. The guilt is a disvalue attaching to some feeling-striving process that has pursued an end recognized as wrong, a feeling-striving process that is disruptive of personal integrity.

The wrong and guilty act, of course, pursues a good or seeks to avoid an evil. In itself (considered in isolation) it may be positive in form and quality, and therefore a natural good, but it is turned against the more fundamental aim of the self, against the integrated tendency of the self as a whole, against the general tendency to pursue the good that seems greatest. It goes its way under the impulsion of emotion or the drive of established habit or native impulse. Viewed by the self in the light of its own wholeness, it is therefore not a reasonable object of a favorable attitude. In this light it is bad. It has a peculiar kind of negative form—that of being disruptive of personal wholeness or integrity. As the resultant inner strain is felt, it appears negative also in quality; it acquires the peculiar negative quality, as well as the peculiar negative form, of guilt.

The wrong act of will, e.g., the will to utter an angry and stinging remark in revenge for some injury, appears as wrong because it runs counter to the will of the self as a whole to produce the greater good. It is wrong because it divides the will and runs counter to its fundamental intent. It is divisive only when one is actually aware of the alternative goal as right, as the greater good, as the more fundamental intent. An action is therefore morally wrong only where there is conflict. If something bad is done impulsively, without any deliberation or conflict, we should recognize that, if there is any moral fault at all, it lies in earlier choices which created the habits that produced this impulsive action without deliberation; the fault lies deep in the formed character rather than in the immediate action. Where moral fault lies in the immediate action, there is always awareness of the wrongness of the choice. There is a drive towards a certain particular goal that runs counter to the more fundamental intent of the personality; in such cases we cannot escape the conviction that we *could* pursue that more fundamental intent if only we would make a certain effort.

What is the nature of this effort? I think that if we reflectively analyze any case of an effort at self-control, we shall find that it is an effort to retain our vision of the larger and more rational perspective, in which all values are seen together, the near and the distant, the familiar and the unfamiliar, our own and those of other persons. This unity of vision retains unity of action, integrity of personality, but it requires effort; we cannot always make the effort. In conditions of extreme fatigue, under the effect of drugs or of glandular deficiencies, or under the influence of extreme emotion, it may become impossible.

At most of the moments of our waking lives, however, it is possible. It is not always necessary, for at ordinary times we can safely let ourselves go, allowing our normal habits to control, but it becomes morally necessary whenever unusual choices have to be made or strong and one-sided emotions are likely to be aroused. Then we can, and normally do, make the effort to see things whole; and so long as we can maintain proper perspective, we keep our balance and retain our integrity. The particular, impulsive drives of habit and emotion surrender to the demand of the self as a whole.

If this analysis is sound and sufficient, then the power of self-determination *is* this power to gather up our vision of the good into a rational and impartial perspective and to hold it until the particular impulsions of acquired habit and native impulse lose their force and return to their place as subordinate parts of the personality as a whole.

The question of free will is therefore the question of the source of this power. We have recognized that it is not omnipotent. Free will becomes a dangerous doctrine when it suggests that, whatever bad habits we cultivate, we can always set them aside by fiat of will whenever we recognize that it is really important that we should do so. Free will is also a most unfair doctrine if it suggests that any person, no matter how fatigued, however caught unawares and emotionally stirred, however affected by disease, is still morally responsible in full degree. We must therefore recognize that there are factors which may, temporarily or permanently, make the moral effort impossible, and may make it much more difficult on some occasions than others. Our question is not what may oppose it but how it comes into operation. Is it just one of our many particular desires? Is it merely a native impulse that responds on occasion to its appropriate stimuli, or an acquired habit responding automatically to the sort of environmental influences that have framed it?

For the most part, if not entirely, our personality, we know, is a structure composed of these interrelated tendencies, native and acquired. Concerning these, we may well believe, the pattern of causation is complete in terms of antecedent events. The effort at self-control, however, does seem to be something distinct in its nature from all the particular impulsive drives that, together with it, go to form the self. It is a response to perceived value (immediately felt or prospective), as are the particular habits and impulses, but it is not particularized. It possesses no inertia or drive. The particular habits and impulses are specialized tendencies to pursue particular values. Their specialization is due to past experience and consequent effects upon the psychophysical structure; i.e., their specialized operation is part of the general causal pattern of animate nature, but the fundamental will to create the good (the feeling-striving process distinctive of life) thrusts itself creatively and spontaneously amid the operations of inanimate nature. It becomes one more causal factor integrated with the causal whole. It grows and multiplies; it creates more and more individuals with more and more complex feelings. It thus frequently thrusts something new into the total causal situation.

This does not mean that anything happens uncaused. It means that awareness of value, the feeling or anticipation or knowledge of a good, is itself a cause that constantly creates new causal agents of its own kind. These may grow in power. The results are therefore inherently unpredictable. There is no total sum of feeling-striving processes to be variously distributed with calculable results. Feeling-striving may increase, multiply, and decline, and this may occur in the living individual. He may with more or less vigor seek the good. He may more or less persistently strive to see that good as a unified whole, or relax into the pursuits of diverse and conflicting habits.

Every mental activity involves striving, i.e., some modicum of effort, but in the developed human mind the striving has diversified into a multiplicity of efforts that sometimes get at cross-purposes. Intelligence develops the capacity to see the multiple purposes and multiple forms of good at which they aim and see them in the light of the essential aim of all life—the greatest possible good. It then requires the special form of effort we call "moral" to unify these diverse purposes into a harmonious whole; and the only complete unity is attained in the pursuit of what is seen as the greatest possible good.

The distinctive moral effort is therefore the effort to maintain the integrated wholeness of one's volitional activity. Because of the essential nature of will as a positive response to perceived value, it has to take the form of an effort to envision the greatest possible good and to strive to realize it. Because the self is divided in its purposive life of the moment, however, the predominant feature of the effort is that of self-control. Such an effort, of course, is not continuously necessary. It is needed only when division is threatened. The strain of division within the self is the stimulus to which the self, as a system of feeling-striving processes, must respond. The response is a surrender of the individualized, particularized drive. It gives way before the vision of the greater good.

The individualization and particularization are due to the aftereffects of antecedent events. The unique striving characteristic of sentient life is a response to present and prospective form and quality. The act of attention to the greater value constrains but does not compel the surrender of the desire for the less. In that surrender lies the unique turn in the feeling-striving process of the desire, whereby it accepts its subordinate place in the integrated life of the self as a whole. It involves an effort, a striving, and one that is distinct from the particular course of striving to which the habits and impulses framed by antecedent events impelled. The inertia of habit and impulse presses in one direction. The striving after the good turns in another; that striving after the good is the self's own unique contribution to the causal order of the world in which it finds itself. That is why we feel and know it to be free—the distinctive, creative, formative effort of the self, always a fresh, a new, contribution to the causal order of the world, leaving its instrument the body, its structure the mind, and the world around on which body and mind work, essentially different from what they would have been if the effort had never been made.

The effort is a real impact upon the causal order of the world, modifying the causal order that was there before. It is not merely the continuing effect of the mental and physical activities antecedent to it. A world order in which there is life is not a static, block universe. It is a growing universe. Even the feeling-striving processes that are canalized into habits are ever fresh contributions to the world order, predictable because canalized and because their direction and reaction tendencies can be learned. So, too, the effort of the self to maintain its wholeness can to some extent be predicted when its nature is understood. But in every fresh exertion it is creative and gives new direction to the organism in which it operates.

Once we abandon mechanism and admit that the causal order is more than physicochemical (is psychophysical), we are bound to admit that mental causation is of this growing, multiplying kind. To do so, however, is not to abandon the concept of nature as a causal order, or to admit a radical indeterminacy such as would undermine responsibility. When properly understood, it means that we can recognize the self-determination of rational creatures as a process wherein the effort to achieve the good is a real cause, and we can recognize the responsibility of the intelligent individual to make all the effort of which he or she is capable. At the same time we must respect the insight into our own efforts which informs us that sometimes we could have made an effort that we did not actually make. There is nothing in all our knowledge of such a causal order to justify any assertion that this apparent insight is not in accordance with the facts; and since the validity of our sense of moral responsibility depends upon its truth there is the best of reasons for accepting it in our theory of the universe and acting upon it as an assumption of the practical moral life. The sense of moral responsibility is a fact of experience. It is therefore much more reasonable to accept its implications than to declare the experience illusory in order to make the facts fit an unverifiable theory such as that of the absolute determination of every event by antecedent events.

Moral Evil or Sin

Our tragic twentieth century, with its world wars, its poverty in the midst of plenty, its ruthless revolutions of the right and left, its revival of race hatred, and its return to barbarism in the totalitarian states has made the world once more conscious of the reality of human sin. A mood of self-criticism and even of pessimism has overtaken many thoughtful minds, a mood that is in sharp and conscious contrast to the easy conscience and optimism of the nineteenth century, induced by its comparative peace and almost uninterrupted progress. This mood has led, in theological circles, to a new insistence on the positive and inevitable nature of sin. Sin, thus interpreted, is a misuse of man's distinctive capacity for free will; its root is in his pride, which makes him revolt against his finite limitations and seek to assert himself against his fellows and against God.[6]

There is much that is valuable in this revival of the consciousness of sin. Self-criticism is usually wholesome; the persons who consider themselves perfect can be very obnoxious. In particular, the rediscovery of the sinfulness of pride in the lives of persons of generally superior character is a much needed shock to the complacency of those races, classes, nations, and cultural groups which are inclined to take themselves too seriously. Nevertheless, there is an undue pessimism in this movement which might be removed by the correction of a certain fault in its psychological analysis of sin.

If our interpretation is correct, sin does not proceed from man's unique and distinctive freedom, but from a slavery which he shares with the lower animals and from which he can, by his own free effort, escape. An action that is guilty, sinful, or morally evil, as we have already seen, is one that pursues a particular good in circumstances that render this pursuit disruptive of the integrity of personality. Such an action, though in itself positive in form and quality (a natural good), runs counter to the tendency of the self as a whole to pursue the greater good. As such it may be viewed in retrospect as evil on the whole, but it is more than a natural evil. It is seen as morally evil because it flies in the face of knowledge of its tendency to destroy a greater good than it seeks to produce; for it is this flying in the face of the outlook upon the greater good that is disruptive. The self, when it sees where lies the greater good,

[6] Cf. Reinhold Niebuhr, *The Nature and Destiny of Man* (New York: Charles Scribner's Sons, 1943), especially Vol. I, chaps. vii and ix.

normally responds to it. It fails to do so only when some impulsion having the strength imparted by fixed habit, emotion, native appetite, or instinctive tendency overwhelms it. Thus moral wrong, loss of personal integrity, is the effect of the captivity of the self to its own particular drives, rooted in its animal nature and the aftereffects of its own past choices.

What our moral experience tells us is that this captivity is not necessary. By making efforts we can become free. The sense of guilt is the awareness of the unique evil we have done to ourselves in failing to make the effort that would pull the self together, assert its wholeness by maintaining its clear, impartial, and rational vision of the greatest good, and bring the disruptive impulse or desire into line, into subordination to the integrated self. Our moral experience therefore gives ground for hope. By effort of will and rational intelligence we can make ourselves increasingly free.

Freedom, however, is not to be achieved without effort, nor does our experience encourage us to hope for the attainment of perfection. It is here that the realistic and somewhat pessimistic movement in modern theology makes its important contribution to contemporary thought. We can overcome the temptations of the flesh and petty passion, we can develop an interest in social welfare, we can become stable and respectable personalities; but we only do so by the cultivation of habits and, in particular, by the development of habits of self-respect. The good citizen has his proper pride in himself, and it is the source of his stable moral strength against all the petty and sordid temptations into which "sinners" fall. What the good citizen is apt to overlook is that this proper pride can become the root of a new form of sin. It may lead him to scorn the weak. It may create in him class consciousness, race consciousness, and all the prejudices that can make him insensitive to the needs of those who are different from himself. It may make him hard and overweening, uncharitable in his judgments, and oppressive in pursuit of the power which he thinks he knows better than others how to wield.

Thus the typical sin of the better type of man is the sin of pride; the sins of the less well-developed type of personality are more apt to be passion and sensuality. Unfortunately, it is not impossible to become a victim of both, and both involve selfishness; but sin in all its forms is slavery, not the exercise of man's true freedom. Even pride is slavery to a habit; the very habits of thought by which victory over the lower forms of fear and sensuality is achieved become set in forms that inhibit the further reaching out of the spirit to pursue impartially the greatest good. There is a superficial integration which maintains stability of character—but the spiritual life is not allowed to grow. Its more generous outreach is stifled while struggling to be born. In the depth of the personality where pride reigns, there is disintegration still.

The price of liberty is eternal vigilance. This is as true of the freedom of the inner spirit of man from the strangle hold of sin as it is in the life of nations. It is not enough to avoid the follies of youth, become a respectable citizen, and manifest commendable interest in good causes. People with all these virtues can and do uphold social systems that are rotten at the core. They can virtuously cling to the reins of power and order others' lives. They can blindly and proudly ride roughshod over other persons' rights in carrying through a program which their insensitive judgments assure them is for the general good—but the proud architects of these oppressive and dangerous systems are themselves slaves. They do not know the freedom of the spirit which everywhere seeks the greatest good of all, seeing that good impartially from every possible standpoint. They are victims and slaves of that spiritual pride which is the last infirmity of otherwise noble minds. To attain true freedom and true nobility they must practice that self-criticism which will reveal to them the sin within, the sin of pride. They must learn the deepest lesson of the Christian ethic —that charity can live and grow only in company with humility.

Moral Goodness

Our analysis has shown us that moral evil, or guilt, attaches to the action that is disruptive of personal integrity. It is the negative form and quality of an action which turns from the vision of the greater good to pursue the lesser. Such action is always wrong, from the standpoint of the subjective standard, in that it is disintegrative. Right action, according to the objective standard, is that which is really in accord with those principles of action, general and specific, which are required to produce the greatest possible good. From the standpoint of the subjective standard, right action is that which is in accord with the individual's vision of the greatest possible good and his understanding of the means and principles whereby it can be produced. Morally good action must always be right from the subjective standpoint or it could not be positive in form and quality; and action that is subjectively wrong must always be morally evil—negative in form and quality—because it turns from the vision of the greatest good and the recognized standard of right. However, an action may be subjectively right and morally good even though not objectively right; e.g., when one is unavoidably mistaken as to the correct means to the right and good end. Further, an action may be objectively right and yet not be morally good. The action that has a distinctive and purposive moral character is one which involves a purposive and conscious direction toward the right. It involves an envisioning of some approximation to the greatest good which the individual concerned can envision, and a choice of the means and principles that seem to him necessary to attain it.

To be morally good, therefore, an action must have the distinctively moral motive. It must involve an awareness of what is right and a choice of it. The right is chosen, not for bare "right's sake," i.e., for the abstract purpose of fulfilling an obligation, or even for the concrete purpose of maintaining personal integration, but as leading to the greatest possible good. Thus the morally good action sees the ultimate unity of the right and the good. It aims at the right and the greatest possible good as each embodying the other. If it were to aim at a so-called right which was not conceived as truly good, it would hold a nonmoral conception of its goal (e.g., of right as mere convention or enforceable social demand) and so would be a nonmoral action. Further, if an action aims at what is right and the greatest possible good as a mere means to some lower good, then it is not morally good, for it has not really selected the right and the greatest good as its goal; it is a mere accident that it does right in pursuing the lower good. Such an action will be nonmoral or immoral according to the nature of its final aim, i.e., its true motive. Thus an act of philanthropy motivated *entirely* by desire for personal distinction would be nonmoral. An act of bravery motivated predominantly by desire for vengeance and without concern for the rightness of the cause would be immoral, even if the cause were right.

This analysis enables us to see the elements of truth and falsity in Kant's dicta that the only thing that is good in itself is a good will, and that a good will must be one that acts *from* a sense of duty. Kant correctly saw that a morally good action must be one that consciously chooses the right and identifies it with what is most truly good, thus acting from a sense of duty at least in part. But he was incorrectly convinced that moral good is the only intrinsic good, and so thought that no natural goods could be the goal of right action. Moral goods are indeed the highest goods but, as we have already seen, they are not the only intrinsic goods; as we must proceed to show, they are not the direct goal of right action.

Moral good is the highest form of intrinsic good because it calls for the most fully orbed rationality of mental outlook and the most complete integration of every element of will of which the individual is capable. The degree of moral goodness of an action depends on two things. The first is the degree in which the action is subjectively right. The subjective moral standard demands our best efforts (of intellect and will) to obtain the best possible results. When our habits and other natural impulses join in impelling us to the right goal, this is not difficult. We put forth our best efforts with joy and without any special effort of self-control. Intrinsic natural and moral good are united in such activity, and (be it said in opposition to Kant) the presence of natural good does not lessen the moral if the effort is indeed our best. Sometimes, however, our habits and other natural impulses are opposed to the right action and then it is not easy to put forth our best efforts. Here enters the second factor on which the degree of moral goodness depends, and the one that is always most noticeable. This is the special effort of moral self-control whereby we assert our inner freedom, our power to pursue the right and greatest good in spite of habits and native impulses.

The degree of moral goodness in these cases again depends upon the putting forth of our best effort. But here there is need and opportunity for a much greater effort than in the case where natural and habitual inclinations also impel us to do right. It is consequently in these cases of difficulty that the most notable instances of moral goodness occur. When a person does his duty in the face of danger, persecution, pain, financial sacrifice, scorn, hatred, and other forms of opposition, we speak of it as noble, heroic, magnificent. The obvious examples are presented to us in the trials of war and revolution; but "peace hath her victories no less renowned," or at least as deserving of recognition. Further, the person who struggles against an adverse environment, or against glandular disturbances or neurotic tendencies induced in childhood, and in the face of these maintains a considerable measure of self-control and moral decency, may have won battles of greater moral worth than any of the much more honored and respectable members of the community. Jesus seems to have had this in mind in his praise of the widow's mite, in the parable of the Pharisee and the publican, and in the saying that there is more joy in heaven over one sinner that repenteth than over ninety and nine just persons that need no repentance. Finally, we should remember the vigilance required to avoid the higher types of sin that spring from spiritual pride. To have attained stability of character, social success, professional fame, and financial power, and yet to maintain humility in spirit, justice in action, and charity in judgment of one's fellows, probably requires a sustained moral effort as great as any of which human personality is capable.

Moral good, then, is the highest of goods; and the greatest degrees of moral good are those attained in the most difficult of moral tasks; but it is not at the production of moral goods (for example, of great moral efforts) that we should directly aim. The moral goods are actually produced in the effort to produce natural goods—and indeed, not intrinsic but instrumental goods. All moral goods, just in so far as they are moral, are manifestations of the inner freedom, the self-determination, of the personality. We can bring no causal agency to bear upon that. Apart from the stimulating effect of good example we cannot even create conditions which are more favorable than others to the exercise of moral effort. The conditions of the Pharisee are neither more nor less favorable than those of the publican. Moral effort can find need and opportunity everywhere. It does seem that each moral effort we make helps us ourselves to make another; spiritual activity is cumulative and spiritual inertia is deadening. However, each moral effort finds full and sufficient reason in its own goal. We rightly recognize that in making a moral effort we increase our own power to make further moral efforts and we set a stimulating example to others to make moral efforts, but these are only additional and indirect reasons for making the moral effort. The direct and sufficient goal of the moral effort is not these indirect effects upon the inner life of the spirit but the production of the natural human good which we see it as our duty to produce.

This is not making the mistake of setting our sights low. Any other course is a false romanticism that can lead to tragedy. Do we wish to make saints and heroes of ourselves or others? What more can we do than set the example of doing our best with the problems at hand? It is only by actually creating great evils that we can produce the conditions in which there is special need and opportunity for actions of great moral worth, for courage, self-sacrifice, and high devotion to duty. On the other hand, we can and should create the conditions in which right actions will flourish because easy and unopposed by bad habits and selfish impulses. We can and should create the conditions in which every form of natural good will have fullest opportunity. If we do these things, we shall set the sort of example that will call forth moral efforts in others, and we can add the stimulus of honest information and admiration of the great examples of history.

The romanticism that cultivates the desire to be a saint or a hero is harmful and dangerous. In so far as the individual feels he is succeeding in such an aim, he fills himself with spiritual pride. When leaders stimulate their followers to such efforts they not only stimulate pride but add to it hypocrisy. It is wholesome to learn to be ashamed of sin, but it is pernicious to become proud of virtue. We can urge those who will listen to us to do right lest they be put to shame; we can show them that the way of transgressors is hard, that there is joy in service, and satisfaction in duty well done, but the most effective motives for righteousness that we can cultivate in ourselves or others are those of the natural, positive, and direct interests in the welfare and happiness of other human beings. This will include, of course, such training as will cultivate habits of thought and action that will help to keep conduct morally right.

With such interests and training, we can expect the manifestation of that free outreaching of the personality which seeks to envision and create impartially the greatest good. This involves the putting forth of actions that are morally good as well as merely right. When the need arises, a personality so developed may manifest those great and high moral qualities that make it a saint or a hero—but even the actions of the saint and hero are not aimed at being a saint or a hero. They are aimed at preventing suffering, saving lives, encouraging disintegrating personalities to get a new grip on themselves, and bringing laughter to the lips of children. Thus the aim of the moral life is the prosaic one of doing what is right, and what is right is to produce for ourselves and all around us the conditions of sound bodies and sound minds. When we take care of these natural goods, the moral values will flourish of themselves.

Chapter 8

RELIGION IN THE MORAL LIFE

The Moral and the Religious Consciousness

Our analysis of the moral nature of man has shown clearly that the moral consciousness is not necessarily dependent upon any specific religious belief. This is true of it even in its finest form, as a conviction accepting the duty to pursue impartially the good of all. But this fact, that the awareness of moral obligation is independent of religion, does not imply a similar independence on the part of the moral will to fulfil such obligations. Between religious faith and the moral life there is certainly a close connection which needs to be explored. Religion can be a wholesome stimulus to the moral life, or it can produce a serious distortion of it. Morality is a central feature of all religion. Indeed, it can be shown to be the very foundation of it.

Studies in the psychology of religion seem to show clearly that what man believes to be his consciousness of God is rooted in the experience of the moral conscience as it constrains him to concern himself with the welfare of others besides himself.[1] This may be seen both in the relatively gradual growth of the religious interest in normal religious development and in the dramatic changes of life involved in sudden conversion. In the latter there is always present to consciousness a clear distinction between what the individual is apt to call his lower self and his better self. The

[1] For a fuller development of this thesis, cf. A. Campbell Garnett, A Realistic Philosophy of Religion. (New York: Harper & Bros., 1942).

conversion involves a surrender of the former and the triumph of the latter. It is preceded by a period of mental conflict which attains a distressing severity because elements of the "better self" have been psychologically repressed and are struggling to be reborn into the clear light of consciousness and willing acceptance. There is always conviction of sin. This sin may be felt to be directly against God rather than man, but this is due to the fact that the moral consciousness has been fixated in the form of rigid rules conceived as divinely ordained and sanctioned. The duty to God is conceived as including the duty to man. The special sense of sin with which the conversion struggle is concerned may attach to a notion of a duty that seems rather remote from human welfare, but it can always be traced to some connection with the sense of responsibility of man to man.

Sudden conversions are not examples of the first dawning of the conviction of the presence or existence of the divine. They occur in persons in whom an earlier religious development has been repressed and its influence apparently lost for a time, or in persons who have found their earlier religious development unsatisfactory and are having difficulty in adjusting their personal attitudes to newly developing religious convictions. In such cases the essential nature of the moral conflict out of which grows the conviction of the divine is apt to be obscured by theological accretions. It is much more plainly to be seen, however, in the development of religion in the child.

As was found by Starbuck in his early investigations [2] in this field, the idea of God, as accepted by the young child from his early instruction, has no distinctive significance. The line between the natural and the supernatural is not clearly drawn, and God is only one of many persons and

[2] E. D. Starbuck, *The Psychology of Religion*, (New York: Charles Scribner's Sons, 1900).

creatures the child has been told about but has never seen, and one to whom he has learned to attribute various extraordinary powers. He has been taught that God is one of many individuals who reward certain types of behavior and punish others, but the moral issue at first means nothing to him save that behavior is subject to such demands and sanctions by certain persons, particularly parents. Not until the distinction of right and wrong begins to appeal to his reason as something he sees and accepts for himself does the idea of God, as source and sanction of the moral law, acquire any inward meaning for him. Only with the dawn of the distinctively *moral* consciousness do we see the awakening of the distinctively *religious* consciousness.

Moral perception, however, is a plant of slow growth and requires a development of intellectual capacity that rarely comes before middle childhood. It requires, in the first place, a sufficient growth of self-consciousness to be able to distinguish which parts of behavior are a result of responsible decisions and which are not. Secondly, it requires an imaginative capacity to put one's self in the other person's place and see the results of actions from his point of view. Third, and latest and most important, it requires the capacity to distinguish among the social demands to which he is subjected (*a*) those that are expressions of unjustified self-interest, (*b*) those that are the mere expression of custom and convention, like saying "please" and "thank you," and (*c*) those that rest upon a genuine duty or moral obligation. The last of these distinctions is subtle and slow to dawn upon the growing mind, but not until it is clearly made can the moral issue be grasped with rational insight. The point at which this distinction first clarifies itself is, undoubtedly, in connection with those actions which can be seen to injure other persons. The duty of noninjury among friends and companions is the earliest recognized element of the moral code, as it is the most obvious and fundamental.

Long before he becomes capable of making this unique moral distinction, the child has learned the traditional classification of actions as "right" and "wrong." He has also learned some of the reasons given for this classification and perceived the general trend of social endorsement of what is conducive to human welfare and social objection to what is injurious. He has joined with others in saying "This ought to be done" and "That ought not to be done." But this "ought" at first refers only to the demands of authority, custom, and law. These, however, do not become genuine moral demands until by his own acts of moral approval and disapproval he makes them of himself. This is the genuine moral awakening. The moral conscience is now at work giving a new and distinctive meaning to the whole sphere of social relationships.

It is at this point, as Starbuck and other investigators have found, that religion, in the form of the ideas of God and the institutionalized practices of worship, begins to take on a new and "inward" meaning. From being a mere supernatural and unintelligible authority, God becomes the natural and intelligible source of the inner sanctions which now begin to operate. This moral and religious awakening tends to take place at the age of ten or eleven in children who have been brought up in a religious environment with an ethical emphasis, though it varies greatly with the intellectual and emotional development of the child and with the type of religious influence brought to bear upon him. It is gradual. Its growing sense of obligation may be resisted and even repressed. Where the environment encourages such attitudes, however, it tends to issue, in the course of the next few years, in a voluntary and public commitment

to the religious attitude to life and the acceptance of one of
its institutional forms.

Religion is thus, as Immanuel Kant said, the acceptance
of the moral law as divine command; or as Matthew Arnold
said, it is the recognition of a power, not ourselves, that
makes for righteousness. But why, we may ask, should
man be so ready to attribute his moral nature to a myste-
rious power beyond himself? For everywhere we find the
same story. Every primitive tribe attributes its tribal mores
to a supernatural source. Every theology, though it may
identify its God, or gods, with obviously nonmoral forces of
nature, yet regards the divine as source and sanction of the
moral law. Generation after generation accepts the interpretation without question. Only at rare intervals of history
have skeptics arisen in any great numbers to question it.
Why, since the moral law, from the standpoint of the community's needs, is a rational set of demands, should not the
matter be left there and in natural individual interest and
reason?

The explanation lies in the way the moral conscience
impresses itself upon us. It may in general endorse as right
the things we want to do, but it is scarcely noticed then. It
makes its deepest impression when it stands in opposition
to our desires, and this conflict is inevitable. Conscience, as
we have seen in earlier chapters, tends increasingly, as we
think unemotionally on questions of value and obligation,
to demand an impartial concern for the good of all; but the
specific interests and habits that enter into the constitution
of the formed self, or character, and determine its drives,
are never impartial. They are directed upon specific objectives. They have been molded largely by the private needs
of the organism in relation to its environment. They arouse
specific anticipations of personal satisfaction which reinforce the drives with thoughts of prospective pleasure.

They are further energized in specific directions by fears of pain and want. Even the altruistic interests in the welfare of others consist, for the most part, in specific preferences for particular persons and groups, and these social interests are mingled with fears and hatreds of specific individuals and groups resulting from competition and rivalry.

These are the interests that form the familiar self, the interests the individual readily recognizes as his own. Their basic structure was formed before he attained to self-consciousness. The growth of self-consciousness was a growth in explicit awareness of this structure of interests, its relation to the bodily self, and the distinction of self, not-self, and other selves. Conflict within the self between incompatible desires is a familiar enough experience. It presents no theoretical problem, for each of the conflicting desires is readily recognized as his own; but conscience is a different experience. It sits in judgment on the interests of the familiar self and condemns them for their partiality and selfishness, their timidity and pride. It speaks in the inner counsels of the self with an authority that belongs to none of the familiar interests and desires. It is not surprising that thinkers whose minds have dwelled long and deep on this phenomenon concluded that a moral power other than themselves was making itself felt within them. In every culture known to history this is the explanation at which the moral sages have arrived. The masses of the people in every culture, though their experience might not be sufficiently intense nor their thought sufficiently deep to have arrived at such an explanation for themselves, have accepted the interpretation of the moral experience which their sages have offered. Probably only the more deeply-religious individuals in each generation have actually believed that the divine being was present and active in their own experience of conscience, but they have at least been ready to believe that there is a power beyond the human that upholds those demands their conscience tells them are right.

THE TRADITIONAL AND THE CRITICAL CONSCIENCE

When thinkers have become skeptical of religious and moral authority, they have usually adopted the view that conscience is an echo of the demands of the community; but this is an explanation which, as we have seen, though initially plausible in the light of our modern knowledge of human suggestibility, is difficult to sustain. Further, it is never an idea that commends itself to a person directly engaged with a problem of conscience. His conscience claims to sit in judgment upon the demands of others just as clearly as it claims to judge those of his own private interests. The commands of authorities are accepted as right only if they are independently endorsed by conscience, or if conscience has independently decided that such authorities have the right to issue commands and demand obedience. A moral issue can be settled by an appeal to custom or tradition only if conscience has previously endorsed the view that custom or tradition is right. In general, conscience is as clear and definite about the possibility that a social demand may be morally wrong as it is in the conviction that the same may be true of the demands of private self-interest.

Ethical thinking, however, is never done in a social vacuum. Most ethical problems are problems common to a group, and solutions are arrived at in group discussion. Such agreed solutions become a moral tradition, accepted and applied almost without question. Changes in the tradition tend to grow imperceptibly as circumstances call for them. The conscious moral innovator, the prophet possessed of a new and higher moral conviction, is a rare phenomenon. Even he usually looks for support for his demand for change in a new emphasis on some long-recognized principle, and he often claims that he is urging the restoration of the truer moral laws of an earlier age against the decadence of his own times. The tradition in all its specific detail, being endorsed by conscience as right, is regarded as endorsed by divinity itself. When conscience begins to find the tradition wrong, it must either recognize a specific new revelation or appeal to some broad principle, long recognized, and claim that the specific custom which it finds inconsistent with this principle is a false innovation.

The value of religion as a power to uphold the social order is incontestable. The chief complaint made by the critics of religion is not that it fails to uphold the social order, but that it upholds the existing social order too rigidly, standing in the way of necessary reform. On the other hand, we occasionally hear the complaint that religiously motivated individuals and groups are disturbing the social order, clamoring for reconstruction and reform. In the past this reforming zeal of religion has usually been manifested only by individuals with a sense of prophetic mission, standing outside the official circles of religious leadership; and their followers have become small heretical sects, though these sects may later have grown to power and a new orthodoxy. In the present day the prophetic mission of social criticism is being undertaken by many of the outstanding leaders of the great religious bodies, and we hear complaints from the upholders of the existing social order that it is being disturbed by the activities of leaders in such bodies as the World Council of Churches and the Federal Council of Churches of Christ in America.

It is not difficult to see the reason for these conflicting tendencies in the relation of religion to the social order.

Both proceed from the root of religion in the experience of conscience, the experience of a demand which seems like another and higher will within us that seeks in and through us the good of all. This voice of conscience upholds the existing institutions of the social order just in so far as the intellect accepts the tradition which declares those institutions to be wise and good. Even when such institutions produce hardship and injustice in specific cases, their supporters claim, often with good reason, that they work for the greater good of the community as a whole. Often, too, ancient institutions are believed to be directly supported by specific revelations of the deity, establishing and upholding them, so that, even when they have outgrown their usefulness and the need for reform has become urgent, the belief persists that they must serve some wise and good purpose known to the deity if not to man. Thus conscience, supporting what is believed to be good even though it appears to be bad, upholds the existing social order, conserving all social institutions against the attacks of both the enemies of society and the intelligent friends of reform.

This, however, is conscience functioning under guidance of an intellect that is dull and uncritical or blinded by prejudice. When conscience itself, attentive to the inner demand for impartial concern for the good of all, brushes aside prejudice, or the intellect penetrates the errors supporting bad institutions, then the critical and enlightened conscience demands reform; and the individual possessed of a religious commitment finds himself inwardly required to stand for reform. His religion becomes a dynamic that drives him to attack what he is convinced is evil in that established order of society which is upheld both by selfish vested interests and by the conservative traditional conscience of those who still believe it good.

At this point we must refer again to that ambiguity in

the notion of conscience which has been the source of so much difficulty and confusion to religion. Is conscience the voice of God? Religion must answer Yes and No. It cannot maintain that conscience is always right, yet it cannot entirely abandon the conviction expressed by the Apostle Paul when he said that even the Gentiles "show the work of the law written in their hearts, their conscience also bearing witness" (Romans 2:15). In the peculiar authority of the inner voice that accuses and approves, man must recognize that he is confronted by God, or else he must cast from him the whole conception of the divine as a groundless superstition. How then can we reconcile this with the fact of admitted errors in conscientious convictions?

It is strange that Christian theology has never clearly recognized the solution to this problem suggested in the saying of Jesus that all "the law and the prophets" is wrapped up in the single principle known as the "Golden Rule." This rule lays down the principle of impartial concern for the welfare of all. If it be endorsed by conscience as the basic principle of the moral life, then all ethical questions must become purely intellectual questions of its correct application to specific situations. Religion may then, without inconsistency, take the stand that in the ordinary conception of conscience two different elements have been confused. One, which we may call *conscience proper*, is that inner demand which constrains the individual (*a*) to do that which he himself believes to be right, (*b*) to judge the right in the light of an impartial concern for the good of all. It is this element that is predominant in the *critical*, as distinct from the *traditional*, conscience; and it is this constraint that religion must attribute to the divine, because it is the root of the conviction of the existence of a moral power beyond ourselves. The other element in conscience consists of judgments of the human intellect, more or less well grounded, concerning the rules, institutions, and particular actions that would produce the greatest good and distribute it impartially. It is these human judgments that are open to error. Often they consist merely of an uncritical application of traditional standards. To claim divine guidance for them is a dangerous mistake for it may produce fanatical support of laws and institutions that are socially evil in their effects. These are the human, adventitious, and changing elements of conscience; but its fundamental element, which puts the moral "ought" into the whole experience, the constraining influence that authoritatively urges impartial concern for the greatest possible good, may, without inconsistency, be maintained to be, in a very real sense, the voice of God.

The drawing of this distinction within conscience will require a modification of theological conceptions of "natural moral law." There is no law, whether of property, sex, marriage, life, or liberty, that religion should maintain as an absolute. Neither should any individual claim divine support for his conscientious conviction on any specific issue. All laws and all convictions must be admitted to contain the element of human judgment concerning the relative values of different ends and the relative efficacy of different means. Only for the fundamental conviction that it is man's duty to seek impartially the good of all can religion claim, with any show of reason, the authority of the divine.

The claim to divine authority at just this point is of crucial importance. It is religion's great contribution to the moral life. It lifts the fundamental sense of obligation of man to man, the conviction of the fundamentally equal rights of every person, from the plane of a mere postulate to be accepted or rejected at will, or a conviction produced by social conditioning, to that of a cosmic moral law, a demand of the eternal. It leaves man free to change his laws and customs in whatever ways experience shall show to be best; but it demands, with the authority of divinity, that equal consideration be given to all, that there shall be no arbitrary distinction or favoritism of class, race, or creed, that judgment shall not be swayed by pride or selfishness, prejudice or favoritism, but that each shall work impartially for the good of all. It gives to the moral life and the moral law a significance they can acquire in no other way and a dynamic which history shows they sorely need.

Reason and Faith in Religion

Thus far our analysis of the relation of morality and religion has established these three points: (1) The experience of a moral constraint, or sense of obligation, to concern one's self impartially with the good of others arises spontaneously; i.e., it is not a deduction from religious belief, or from long-run self-interest, or merely an effect of social pressures; (2) The belief that this obligation is sustained by a moral power beyond the self and the social group arises from the conflict between it and the interests of the self and the social group; (3) This belief, if true, implies that such a power seeks in and through each the good of all, but it does not imply a divine revelation concerning any specific moral law, institution, or action; i.e., it endorses such principles as the golden rule and love to neighbor, and even to enemy, but nothing more specific than these.

At this point it would seem to be the natural thing to turn to inquire whether this religious belief is true; but here we are doomed to what may at first involve a disappointment. It can neither be proved nor disproved. If held it must be held by faith. At first we seem to be checkmated.

Morality in times of strain sorely needs the sustaining power of a belief that its values are rooted in something beyond the desires of the self, its obligations in something beyond the demands of the social group. It would seem that any moral reality in which such values and obligations were rooted must be morally obligated to reveal itself—or Himself—that we might know beyond a doubt the objective ground of our moral life. Yet there is no such revelation, either in nature or history, that is not open to honest and rational doubt. This very situation seems, in itself, to constitute a refutation of that very belief with which religion supports morality, until a deeper reflection brings to our notice a fourth point. (4) The very uncertainty of the intellect in matters of religion is itself the condition of all that is finest in the moral life.

The things that by common consent mankind has recognized as the noblest and most precious are the love that gives without the assurance of return and the courage that dares to stand for what is believed to be right without the assurance of security or ultimate victory. When we see these virtues maintained by individual or nation, up to the very door of death, we lift our hats in reverence and say, "This was their finest hour." Yet if the promises of eternal reward were shining ever before us, bright and clear and inviting, indubitable in their certainty, such love and courage would have no meaning. They would be reduced to the level of common prudence. They would become invisible in the dazzling light of the personal advantages of righteousness. The gates of heaven would press so close upon us that the human spirit on earth would have no room to stretch its wings. Faith and hope cease to exist when they are turned into certainty, and love loses its crowning glory when it can no longer make a sacrifice.

Does this mean, then, that religious belief is a support

only of the lowly virtue of prudence, while it must blight
and undermine all the finer qualities of the human spirit?
This would be true if religious belief were capable of logical
demonstration or empirical verification, if it could be presented in the forms which the intellect is ready to accept
as practically equivalent to certainty, but this is not the
case. The finer flowers of the moral life are saved because
we cannot find that practical certainty which would stifle
them with the lush growth of prudence. The activity of the
intellect alone, working with the principles of logic and
the evidence of the senses, can neither explain the origin of
the human spirit as a product of the nonspiritual nor dem-
onstrate the necessary existence of a spiritual reality beyond
the human. The belief in such a cosmic spiritual reality
arises primarily out of the experience of value and obligation, not from abstract logic and the senses. It may, I
believe, be reasonably supported by arguments of the latter
kind, but it has been quite as often distorted, confused, and
inhibited by them.

The reason why religious faith cannot stifle the growth
of such finer virtues as sacrificial love and moral courage is
because it is a fruit of these very virtues, not a plant of
independent growth. It grows out of the conflict within
the soul between its egoistic desires and its obligations to
serve the welfare of others. This conflict arises when the
individual becomes aware of the needs of others. It is
tentatively settled as the self is adjusted to serve those
needs, or it stifles the interest in them. It is continuously
revived as the self expands to give wider, stronger, and
more keenly perceptive attention to those needs. Thus the
inner conflict never dies so long as the moral self is growing
and sensitive. The "other and higher will" within the self,
which religion recognizes as its contact with the divine,
stands out as other and higher than the familiar egoistic

self just so long as there is attention to the needs of sacrificial love and moral courage. Thus, that which, to the religious life, is inner evidence of the divine, is produced by the struggle of love with self; and faith is born of the conflict—born out of what religion calls the consciousness of sin, the conflict within between the merely human spirit and the Spirit of God.

The faith that is thus created and sustained becomes a new stimulus to all the virtues. It is obvious, of course, that it becomes a new stimulus to prudence, but if that were all, it would soon die; for prudence consists in thinking of one's self, and in thinking of one's self the conflict within subsides. Faith then loses its inner evidence of the other and higher will opposed to one's own. It becomes a shadow cast by experience of the past, a mere belief about the cosmos, sustained perhaps by rationalistic arguments; or it disappears, and the moral law stands starkly, as a custom or habit supported by human and natural sanctions, but nothing more. Only if the moral life rises above prudence can faith be sustained as something genuinely religious, having its evidence in that within the self which opposes selfishness. Faith then functions by giving a deeper reality to the obligation that confronts us. Our temptation always is to deny the reality of obligation when we do not want to fulfil it. We ask, "Am I my brother's keeper?" To this, without the faith of religion, there is no positive answer, but religion, in all its more highly developed forms, has an answer that is clear, definite, and far-reaching. It gives a rational cosmic setting to the moral life of man that makes the best of which we are capable appear as our reasonable service—instead of as nothing but a strange quixotic impulse.

This analysis of the relation of faith to the moral life discloses two different sources of antagonism between faith and reason. First, there is the familiar one in which reason challenges faith to offer proofs, criticizes the proofs offered, presents its own negative arguments, and even goes so far as to argue that it is impossible to extend human knowledge to the domain in which religion is interested. Second, there is the less obvious difficulty with which we have just been concerned. Certainty in matters of religious belief would undermine the finer phases of the moral life, reducing all virtue to mere prudence. Thus we have the dilemma. If reason cannot prove the convictions of faith, then they are not worthy of belief; but if reason can prove those convictions, then the moral life is mere prudence. To traditional Christianity it was the former horn of the dilemma that was thought the most dangerous, and valiant have been the efforts of Christian philosophers to overcome it. The quest for certainty in matters of religion led to the development of rationalistic philosophy, working on foundations supplied by the Greeks. This led to the doctrine of God as the timeless Eternal Being, the uncaused cause of all that exists. It was a doctrine quite impossible to reconcile with the kind of freedom or self-determination which it is necessary to postulate in order to give responsibility to the moral life. It thus violated in a double way the values it was seeking to support. It cast doubt on the reality of moral freedom and it tended to insinuate a basis of prudence into all the higher virtues. It also put religion into the false position of seeming to be required to prove a certainty in metaphysical doctrine which it is quite impossible to obtain; and as this failure became evident to philosophers, it spread the seeds of skepticism.

In reaction from this position there has been a movement among Protestant theologians to take hold of the dilemma by the other horn—to free theology from metaphysics, recognizing that it is neither possible nor desirable to prove the existence of God. This is a movement in the right direction; from the standpoint of the needs of the moral life, however, it still, as usually presented, contains three defects: (1) It still tends to assert as an article of faith (not knowledge) the doctrine of the timeless, eternal deity from whom all things flow by an absolute necessity. This is incompatible with human responsibility and aspiration and has no justification in any phase of our experience. It is merely an echo in Christian theology of the ancient Greek puzzle concerning time and the infinite regress, a puzzle which most modern philosophers have set aside as arising from confusion of thought. (2) It claims the support of specific revelation, in "the mighty acts of God," both for theological doctrine and for specific moral principles, thus making the mistake of supporting moral absolutes which may conflict with one another. (3) It not only denies that faith needs to prove its convictions by reason, but rejoices in finding paradoxes in the claims of revelation and refuses to admit that faith must at least be reasonable.

If our analysis of the moral life is sound, then these extremes in religion, both rationalist and irrationalist, must be abandoned. The cultivation of the higher values of the moral life does not require that faith shall have no support from reason, but only that there shall be reasonable room for questioning and doubt. On the other hand, responsible moral behavior cannot allow itself to be influenced by the irrational, even when supported by claims of revelation. It must examine such claims and reject what is unreasonable. It can give weight to the claims of faith when it finds them not only "not unreasonable" but positively reasonable. There is therefore need for theology and philosophy to provide a positive defense of the religious view of the universe against its rivals. In such a defense, the facts of the moral life—the experiences of value and obligation—must be given full consideration along with those of the senses. The explanation of these facts is no less important than those of physics and biology, and in relation to questions concerning the range of spirit in the universe it is much more important.

This involves a venture into speculative philosophy—a venture which contemporary empirical philosophers have been very loath to take. Their reluctance has been due to the fact that it is clear from the start that the evidence must be incomplete. No decisive conclusion can be reached, and the venture therefore seems to many a waste of time; but this is to mistake the question at issue. The question is not whether philosophy can provide adequate grounds for religious belief. It cannot do so, and, as we have seen, it is inimical to the moral life, and to religion, to claim that it can do so. The question is whether that interpretation of the moral experience which religious faith has developed, and which stimulates the moral life to its finest endeavor, is reasonable in the light of all our knowledge—at least as reasonable as any other speculative interpretation of the whole of experience. The interpretation in question is the one which sees the source of moral obligation in the connection of our human life with a spiritual reality reaching beyond it, and worthy of our highest devotion. To this question a philosophical skepticism drastically limiting the scope of reasonable speculation is no answer. The question is whether, within the limits of reasonable speculation, whatever they may be, this religious view is as reasonable as any other. If it is, then faith is justified in its commitment to such a view, as defining a way of life. The choice is one rightly determined by the values involved, so long as it is left genuinely open by the inquiries of which reason is capable. If, as I have argued extensively elsewhere, the religious view of the universe is definitely more completely reasonable than any of its alternatives, then faith can rejoice in this further support and meet its trials with greater confidence, but it must never seek to transfer to reason a burden which reason is not fitted to bear. The life of religion, and the moral life even if not religious, must remain a life of faith. The question is not whether we shall live by faith or not, but by what faith we shall endeavor to live.

The Gods of Nontheistic Religion

At this point we should consider the views of those who believe that a finer faith for life—and one that is still genuinely religious—may be found in a philosophy which dispenses with belief in any spiritual reality beyond the human. Among philosophers, the most distinguished American representative of this school of thought is John Dewey. He urges us to be content with knowledge of the sort that science can give and deprecates any attempt at speculative inquiry as to whether one cosmology is more reasonable than another. He believes that there is a "common faith" of mankind, deeper than any of the metaphysical convictions involved in the creeds of religion, which is sufficient as a guide to life, which can become religious in quality, and which would function far better if freed from any reference to a spiritual reality beyond the human.

In the book [3] which is his principal expression of this view, Dewey distinguishes between a "religion," as involving a belief in some unseen higher power, and the "religious," as a quality of experience and attitude bringing about a better, deeper, and most enduring adjustment in life. The distinguishing feature of what he calls the religious "adjustment" is that "it pertains to our being in its entirety. . . .

[3] John Dewey, *A Common Faith* (New Haven: Yale University Press, 1934).

There is a composing and harmonizing of the various elements of our being such that, in spite of changes in the special conditions that surround us, these conditions are also arranged, settled, in relation to us" (p. 16). "The self is always directed [in the religious adjustment] toward something beyond itself and so its own unification depends upon the idea of the integration of the shifting scenes of the world into that imaginative totality we call the Universe" (p. 19). "The inclusiveness of the end in relation to both the self and the 'universe' to which an inclusive self is related is indispensable" (pp. 22-23).

This, for Dewey, however, can be no single, supreme end. The religious faith he seeks is rather "the unification of the self through allegiance to inclusive ideal ends . . . to which the human will responds as worthy of controlling our desires and choices" (p. 33). Such a "unity of all ideal ends arousing us to desire and action," Dewey would call "God" (p. 42) because accepted as worthy to be the supreme object of devotion. This unity is only to be achieved, he believes, through a "devotion, so intense as to be religious, to intelligence as a force in social action" (p. 79). "Were men and women actuated throughout the length and breadth of human relations with the faith and ardor that have at times marked historic religions, the consequences would be incalculable" (p. 81).

Here Dewey correctly analyzes the essential thing that religious faith achieves for the individual. It unifies the self in devotion to something beyond itself that is held to be worthy of supreme devotion. The religious life, or "religion" in a very broad sense of the term, might be defined as such an attitude of devotion. We make a "god" of anything to which we pay supreme devotion. If we choose some unworthy object for such devotion, religion becomes an idolatry. Money, power, and prestige are common objects of such idolatrous religion. Fascism and communism are examples of the idolatries of the state and the party. Every idolatry is dangerous to its devotees, and the devotee dangerous to society. He is dangerous because he has the unity and strength of purpose of a devotee—of a person whose self is unified in devotion to an object beyond himself which he holds to be worthy of the full devotion of the self—and because he gives such devotion to an unworthy object. The unworthy and dangerous objects are those, devotion to which sacrifices one part of the self to some other part or one part of society to some other part. A wholesome religion must be one which maintains the wholeness of both self and society.

Without religion in this broad sense (an attitude of devotion to something beyond the self which is held to be worthy of supreme devotion), life can never be at its best and most effective. Having no supreme goal to give it unity of purpose, it is plagued by shifting and often conflicting aims, and it is in danger of becoming unduly introverted, turned inward upon the self. The wholesome personality must be predominantly extroverted, predominantly interested in the persons and things around and beyond it, rather than in the inwardness of its own feeling processes. We are happiest when we can forget ourselves, lose ourselves, in our interest in something other than ourselves. Indeed, apart from the quickly satiated pleasures of the senses, our only happiness is found in taking an interest in things, becoming actively absorbed in objects, in goals outside ourselves. If we develop a predominant interest in the feelings of the self, we lose our capacity to become absorbed in objects; and in doing so we lose our capacity for happiness. This attitude is the antithesis of religion as we have defined it. It is irreligious. To have a multitude of interests, or objects of devotion, beyond ourselves, without any supreme object to unify them, is simply to be nonreligious. But it is in the religious life, extroverted and unified by devotion to a supreme and worthy object beyond the self, that personality attains its maximum effectiveness and value.

Our problem, therefore, is to select the most worthy object of supreme devotion and cultivate that attitude toward it. To this problem Dewey offers us, not a solution, but a method of solution. For him there is no one ultimate end. He rejects Humanism. "A humanistic religion, if it excludes nature, is pale and thin, as it is presumptuous, when it takes humanity as its object of worship" (p. 54). Unity of the purposive life of the self is to be obtained by an "integration of the shifting scenes of the world into that imaginative totality we call a Universe." We must find "inclusive ideal ends . . . to which the human will responds as worthy," and integrate them into one whole. He sees that this cannot be done by construction of an elaborate vision of an ideal life or ideal society. He is too wise to advocate such Utopianism. Concrete problems have to be solved as we go along, and valid ideals can light us only a little way ahead. It is therefore in loyalty to a *method of inquiry* in solution of this and all our problems that he hopes the self may find unity—loyalty to "intelligence as a force in social action," meaning by intelligence the process of scientific inquiry understood in its broadest sense.

Here speaks the philosopher, expressing his own devotion—a devotion to an activity in which his own soul has found supreme satisfaction. He commends to us the god he has served, a concrete activity and lifework which for him has ramified out into inclusive ideal ends that have absorbed his energies, unified the purposive structure of his life, and integrated him well with the society of which he is a part. It is an object of supreme devotion that has served him well—as he has served it; but *as a concrete activity* it can be an object of supreme devotion only to those whose lifework it is to think and plan. And it must function with decreasing inclusiveness as we pass from the intellectual lifework of the philosopher, which can be made broad and general, to the work of those whose thought and planning must serve more restricted and specialized ends.

Dewey, of course, is aware of this. It is not as a concrete activity for everyone that he invites for it the devotion of the world, but as an ideal of method which may serve to select and integrate other ideal ends into a "universe" of ideal ends to which supreme devotion can worthily be paid. Yet it is as a concrete activity that he has found it satisfactory and developed toward it an attitude of devotion which makes it for him an ideal end that can integrate his universe of ideal ends. To the vast majority of mankind, this ideal of scientific method is a mere abstraction and can never be anything more. He asks the world, through this abstraction, to formulate an imaginative unity of other abstractions and then to cultivate toward this "universe" of abstractions a devotion "so intense as to be religious." It is no wonder that, as he himself observes, this is "one of the few experiments in the attachment of emotion to ideal ends that mankind has not tried" (p. 79). It is an experiment in which some philosophers, like Dewey himself, have succeeded. But for "mankind" in general it is beyond the range of possibility.

It is beyond the range of possibility for the vast majority because it is possible for anyone to develop a devotion that is religious in intensity only to something that is concretely given in experience. The philosopher or scientist may develop an attitude of devotion to the philosophical or scientific activity, and through it he may find a range of ideal objects sufficiently inclusive to integrate his whole life and integrate him with society. If he does thus expand ideally the object of his devotion, it may prove a worthy deity; if he does not so expand it, his devotion may become a minor idolatry, a narrow devotion to an intellectual specialty, of the kind which Dewey himself so often deplores. But no one, except by some pathological process of substitution, can develop an intense devotion to an activity he does not engage in and enjoy, or to any abstraction he does not concretely experience.

The object of religious devotion, therefore, must be something concretely given in experience. In so far as it embodies ideal ends, they must be given concrete form in clearly intelligible and sufficiently impressive symbols. This has its difficulties and dangers because the worshipper's need of the concrete constantly tends to turn his devotion to the symbol itself—the cross, the ikon, the printed word— or to the institution that cherishes the ideals and symbols. In Christianity the historic person of Christ and the gospel story serve marvelously well to give concrete embodiment, very close to direct experience of a personality, to the abstract idea of God and the abstract ideals of conduct that form the ultimate object of Christian devotion. Many a Christian's religion is an attitude of devotion to the person of Jesus and the society and program of what he called "the kingdom of God" rather than to the triune person of the creeds. Many another's, unfortunately, is to the particular human church or sect in which some accident of birth or training has cast his religious life.

Religion, as we have seen, has a name for the selection of a concrete object of supreme devotion which is unworthy of so high a place in human life. It is called "idolatry," and idolatry is a devotion which distorts values and creates narrow fanaticisms. As our last paragraph has shown, it is an evil not confined to paganism, but found also within Christianity and the other ethical religions. It is also an evil which naturalistic and humanistic philosophies are apt to develop. Secularism proves unsatisfactory because it presents no supremely worthy object of devotion to draw forth man's best efforts and give unity to his system of values—the very essence of secularism being the refusal to recognize anything as sacred, i.e., supremely worthy. Humanism suggests that humanity and human values in general should be recognized as supreme, but these are utterly diverse and conflicting; the whole question is, which of these values are of the greater importance, and are all human beings of equal importance? Humanism can reply in one of two ways, one of which is religiously futile and the other idolatrous. The futile reply is to present a system of ethics, with a set of abstract ideals, based merely on an arbitrary "postulate," or, still worse, urged as a means to long-run self-interest. The reply that is idolatrous is the one that presents an articulate program to reform or guide the development of society.

In recent decades humanistic idolatries of this latter sort have manifested their fearful possibilities. Communism, fascism, nazism, and the "Greater East Asia Co-prosperity Sphere" of the Japanese are examples of such articulate programs. They attain concreteness in the party or nation which adopts them, and by their concreteness, definiteness, and adaptation to present and pressing needs they develop zeal and fanaticism in their devotees; but no articulate program and concrete party can have the universality, impartiality, and flexibility needed in a supreme object of devotion which is to draw the best out of human beings without dividing them by party loyalties and stultifying their open-mindedness to every possibility of value. If "Socialism" or "Democracy" or "The American Way of Life" should be given such definite articulation and concrete organization, it would become an idolatry scarcely less dangerous.

The Roots and Fruits of Theistic Belief

Man's choice of a path and goal in life is thus beset with pitfalls and perils. In the outlook of naturalism we seem only to find the choice of a secularism beset with futility because it finds nothing sacred, or a Humanism which either fails to find concreteness and definiteness in its object of devotion or finds them in forms which inevitably become idolatrous. In the outlook of supernaturalistic religion we find the demand for concreteness in the object of devotion all too often leading to similar idolatries. In contemplation of these dangers we are reminded of the warning of the founder of Christianity, "Straight is the gate and narrow is the way that leadeth unto life and few there be that find it." Man needs a "god" of some sort in his life— something that he can look up to as supremely worthy of devotion, something that will call forth his best efforts and give consistent guidance to his choices. And he needs as his God something that is concrete (i.e., something that is in some way given as an element in his immediate experience) yet something too high to betray him into unworthy idolatries. The question for religion and the moral life is this: Where, if anywhere, can man find a God, a supremely worthy object of devotion, that is concrete enough to attract him with sufficient power, yet high enough to impress him with the attributes of universality and impartiality?

The domination of the concrete in the objects of human devotion may well make one wonder how devotion has come to be directed generally to such an intangible object as the God of the great ethical religions. The answer lies in the facts of mystical experience. There is a range of experience which cannot be assimilated to the sensory. The claim of mysticism is that in this experience there is direct awareness of a reality other than that which we are aware of through the senses. The senses are traditionally believed to put us in touch with an independently existing physical world. Mystical experience is traditionally believed to put us in touch with an independently existing spiritual world. So far as philosophy is concerned, neither of these traditional views can be proved or disproved. Metaphysics is too uncertain to pronounce with any confidence concerning the existence of matter or the range of mind. Common sense, however, implicitly believes the materialist interpretation of sensory experience; and it is ready enough to accept the theistic or spiritual interpretation of mystical experience when convinced that such distinctly nonsensory experience exists.

The name "mystical" is often reserved for an experience of a rather rare type involving an element of ecstasy; but if all experience other than the sensory is to be classified as mystical, then this should include the whole range of aesthetic and moral experience. The only question as to the justification for such a classification is whether these experiences put us in touch (as mysticism always claims) with a reality other than that of which we are aware through the senses. Unless the whole of existence, including the self, is material (defining matter as that of which we are aware through the senses), then this must be the case, and few philosophers today endeavor to support a reductionistic materialism that identifies mental events with material. Aesthetic and moral experience must therefore be recognized (by all save complete materialists) as putting us in touch with an immaterial reality beyond the mental activity of the moment, if not beyond the life-history of the self. Both aesthetic and moral experience, as is abundantly evident in the literature in which they are expressed, are capable of conveying strongly the impression that they put us in touch with an immaterial reality, not only beyond the self of the present moment, but also beyond its whole private life history. Ecstatic experience is only one particularly strong, but rare, experience of this kind. The moral experience in which we face an "ought" that we would dearly love to deny, but cannot, is another and much commoner one. It is, as we have already seen, the fundamental basis of the widespread religious conviction that our own desires are confronted within us with a will and a demand that is other and higher than our own.

Here, in this concrete experience of the moral life, is the basis for the conviction of the existence of a moral being beyond ourselves—and equally beyond and higher than all our fellows, and this Being appears as one that in our most immediate experience demands our devotion. The religion that becomes ethically effective in the minds of masses of men is one that responds to this demand. It is a devotion which, by the essential nature of the demanding object to which it responds, tends to unify the purposive life of the individual within and directs his activity in devotion to ends beyond himself, integrating those ends. And, because the moral demand is one which calls upon the individual to concern himself impartially with the welfare of all, it tends, so far as it is clearly and intelligently understood, to integrate the society in which the individual finds himself, and to integrate his society with the social whole.

It is the mystical element, therefore, that gives religion its power to unify and uphold the moral life. This it does by presenting, as an object of devotion beyond the self, a moral and spiritual reality that makes itself felt within the self. Without this element of mysticism, only a few rare souls can maintain a devotion to abstract ideals that is religious in its quality and intensity. It is the recognition, in our experience of values and obligation, of a spiritual reality beyond the human, that gives concreteness to the ideal, and through concreteness gives it power. Thus the moral life of man, though not dependent on the mysticism of religion either for its initiation or direction, is itself the source of that mysticism and finds in it a new dynamic that can stir the flagging spirit and lift it to the heights. Without faith in God, by what William James called "the slow dead heave of the will," a man may stand, against great pressure, for the truth and the right as he sees it; but with that faith, though he still must find the truth and the right by his own intelligence, in the pursuit of it he can "mount up with wings as eagles," he can "run and not be weary," he can "walk and not faint."

What gives power and assurance to the moral life of the religious man is not the distant hope of an eternal reward. That serves merely as a rational answer to the problem of the injustices of life, and as a comfort to those whom life has defeated. Moral vigor requires that one forget the pursuit of private happiness in a deep concern for worthy ends beyond the self. It is still stultified, not reinforced, if the pursuit of private happiness is merely redirected from earth to heaven. The power that religion gives to the moral life comes, therefore, not from turning an eye to a heavenly future, but from a reinforcement and encouragement of the moral will in the living present. The moral will is the will to do what one believes is right and to find, amid perplexities, what is really right. Religion brings to that will the conviction that it is no mere transitory desire, no mere echo of human authority, but that God is with it—indeed, that God is *in* it.

For, with the understanding of the moral nature of man

that has grown out of this study, it is the latter and more inspiring interpretation of the relation of God to the moral will that must be adopted by a religious philosophy. If the life of man has its fountain source in the spiritual life of the universe beyond him, and if the moral will is the most clearly rational expression of a life which is drawn from the eternal source, then the moral will has the form of the divine and is an expression of the divine. The "image of God" in man is not a mere shadow of the infinite felt in his finitude, but the active presence of the Eternal Spirit seeking in and through each of us the good of all. History warns us that the growth of finite free spirits in understanding and harmony with the Eternal is slow and uncertain and sometimes painful; but they do grow. And hope, as well as faith and love, has it place in the mind of the religious man, not only in his vision of another world, but in his outlook upon this world too.

On the other hand, the selfishness and pride, which theology condemns as sin, are introversions of the volitional life, which psychology recognizes as perversions of personality. By introversion is here meant that retroactive direction of will whereby the feeling-states and social status of the self are made final goals of conduct, instead of functioning, as they normally should do, simply to redirect attention upon other objectives beyond the self. The self, therefore, is only wholesome so long as it can, for the most part, forget itself and its feeling-states in interests, in objectives, beyond itself. When the welfare of other human beings becomes the habitual and preferred objective of such a wholesome, predominantly extroverted self, then it manifests the virtue that Christianity calls "brotherly love," the ἀγάπη of the New Testament.

What religion does for the wholesomeness of personality and the cultivation of this finest flower of the moral

life is to draw the self out of itself and direct its attention
to others—and equally to all others—because it presents
those others, even the humblest and least lovely of them, as
souls with a life that is more than earthly, as children of
the Most High. In face of the conviction that the deity
himself is equally concerned with the welfare of all, the
distinctions we base on material and social circumstance
sink into insignificance. Property, prestige, and power cease
to appear as ends and become mere instruments for the
promotion of personality. Impartiality and disinterested-
ness appear as the rule of right reason. A rational respect
for the common good as a kingdom of ends takes on the
added significance and power of a devotion to the kingdom
of God.

INDEX OF NAMES AND TITLES

INDEX OF SUBJECTS

Need, significance of special, 194

Objective and subjective right, 117, 125, 159
Objectivity, 155
Obligation, as basic ethical concept, 108, 112
  as inner constraint, 155, 158, 178, 207
  definition of, 108, 111, 165
  different from emotion, 64
  examples of, 111, 132
  relation to desire, 149
  specific and general, 167, 170, 178, 180, 187
  theory of, 93, 98, 108
Optimism, 4
Original sin, 10
"Ought," meaning of, 73, 109
  source of, 160
"Ought-to-be" and "ought-to-do," 55, 68

Paradox, 46
Personal development, 146, 191, 206, 208
Pessimism, 4, 231
Pleasure theory of natural good, 137, 144
Positivism, 58, 118
Power, desire for, 13
Praise and blame, sanction of, 18, 22, 216, 218, 221
Predestination, 10
Pride, 232, 237, 270
Primitive morality, 16
  defects of, 22
Principles of obligation, 184, 185
Private judgment, the right of, 175
Promises, 167, 171, 178
Prophets, 29, 31, 33, 40, 157
Protestantism, 11, 48, 256
Prudence, 254
Psychology, 14, 95, 241
Punishment, 198
Puritans, 166

Reason, 5, 11, 50
Reasonable attitude, 120, 155

Recognized rights, 176
Religion, definition of, 260
  doctrine of man, 8
  influence on social order, 248
  its interpretation of conscience, 162, 248, 250
  nontheistic, 259
  rationalism and irrationalism in, 257
  relation to morality, 46, 72, 103, 252, 269
Reparation for injury, 168, 171, 178
Responsibility, 205, 213, 216, 221, 224
Reward, justification of special, 197
"Right," Dewey's analysis of, 90
  distinctions and definitions of, 115
  fundamental principle of, 158
  private judgment of, 175
  relation to good, 67, 87
Rights, 36, 166, 173, 175, 177, 179
Romanticism, 238
Rules of conduct, 178

Sanctions, moral, 160
Satisfaction theory of natural good, 142, 147, 153
Secularism, 11, 50, 265
Self-determination, 213, 222, 230
Self-interest, 13, 87, 137, 152
Sin, 3, 5, 154, 209, 217, 230, 242, 270
Skepticism, conclusions regarding, 69
  growth of, 44
  in Logical Positivism, 58
  social consequences, 47
Social conditioning and sense of obligation, 94, 96, 101
Social criticism, 29, 31, 33, 40
Sophists, 32
Stoics, 9, 38, 40
Subjective and objective right, 117, 125, 127, 159, 206

Teleological ethics, 166
Theism, 4, 157, 266